Immigrant Politics and
the Public Library

Recent Titles in
Contributions in Librarianship and Information Science

Immigrant Politics and the Public Library

Edited by Susan Luévano-Molina

Contributions in Librarianship and Information Science, Number 97

GREENWOOD PRESS
Westport, Connecticut • London

Library of Congress Cataloging-in-Publication Data

Immigrant politics and the public library / edited by Susan Luévano-Molina.
     p. cm.—(Contributions in librarianship and information science, ISSN 0084–9243 ;
no. 97)
    Includes bibliographical references and index.
    ISBN 0–313–30524–2 (alk. paper)
    1. Public libraries—Services to immigrants—California.   2. Latin Americans—Services
for—California.   3. Asians—Services for—California.   4. Libraries and state—California.   5.
Immigrants—Government policy—California.   I. Luévano-Molina, Susan.   II. Series.
Z711.8.I46 2001
027.6′3—dc21   2001019987

British Library Cataloguing in Publication Data is available.

Library of Congress Catalog Card Number: 2001019987
ISBN: 0–313–30524–2
ISSN: 0084–9243

First published in 2001

Greenwood Press, 88 Post Road West, Westport, CT 06881
An imprint of Greenwood Publishing Group, Inc.
www.greenwood.com

Printed in the United States of America

The paper used in this book complies with the
Permanent Paper Standard issued by the National
Information Standards Organization (Z39.48–1984).

10 9 8 7 6 5 4 3 2 1

Copyright Acknowledgments

The author and publisher gratefully acknowledge permission for use of the following material:

Chapter 3, "Giving Birth to the Dream: Realizing a Multiethnic, Multiracial Nation" by Rhonda
Rios-Kravitz, originally appeared in the California Library Association's newsletter, *California
Libraries*, in March 1996.

"And Still I Rise" and "Good Morning" in *On the Pulse of Morning* by Maya Angelou, copyright
© 1993 by Maya Angelou. Used by permission of Random House, Inc. and Virago Press.

To scholar, activist, and friend
"Swan" Nign.
This book would not have been possible without you
&
Juan Soldado.

Contents

Acknowledgments

The creation of a book is always a rigorous process. This compilation was no exception. I am grateful to members of the original group of contributors, which included Ninfa Almance Trejo, Evelyn Escatiola, Rhonda Rios-Kravitz, and Ken Knox. They had the commitment and tenacity to see this project through to the publication of this volume. I am especially indebted to Evelyn Escatiola who was my constant booster, sounding board, and friend during the most grueling parts of this effort. Her words of encouragement and support always gave me hope that someday we could finish this project.

I am also deeply obliged to Dr. ChorSwang Nign, Professor of Anthropology at California State University, Los Angeles for her support in my own research endeavors. Without her active interest and guidance I never would have attempted such a complex study project. She gave generously of her time and expertise in all stages of my research. In addition, she continued to offer excellent suggestions during the development of this book. She was always there for me when I needed her advice, direction, and support. Her probing intellect and activism continue to inspire me.

The research team that assisted in my ethnographic study also deserves recognition. Frank Castillo, Anita Varela, and "Pecky" Flores embraced the project with enthusiasm and dedication. I am indebted to all for their professionalism, gift to gab, and extensive knowledge of the immigrant community.

Grants from the California State University, Long Beach and the California Library Association provided monies and release time to complete my research. A much-needed sabbatical leave allowed me to focus on the completion of the book. Dean Roman Kochan and my colleagues at the CSULB, University Library provided the optimal environment for my scholarly endeavors. Travel money, additional time off the reference desk, and a totally supportive work atmosphere all contributed to the success of this effort.

Special thanks goes to all the contributors in this volume for making the very political issues that effect Latino and Asian immigrants come alive in your research and writing. Your contributions are wonderful examples of that all to rare combination of scholarship and activism.

I would also like to acknowledge the indexer of this volume, Ms. Joy Thomas, Librarian at California State University, Long Beach. Your assistance and expertise are greatly appreciated.

Jane Garry, my editor at Greenwood, deserves an award for her patience, encouragement, and advice. Also, Greenwood Senior Production Editor, Nicole Cournoyer was an absolute pleasure to work with. Her pleasant demeanor made the most difficult parts of the production bearable.

Lastly, I thank my family and close friends who continue to sustain and bolster me in all my endeavors including Pita, Linda, Martín, Ráfael, Mark, Julie, "Shanghai" Mike, Diane Ho, Joaquin Macias, Raul Macias, Diego Macias, Maria Luévano, Lilliana Luévano, Paola Luévano Morales, Asha Mei Luévano, Tony Gleaton, Consuelo Campos, Alicia Campos Hankes, Carmen and Angel Alvarez, Tía Nena, Patti and Rich, Richard, Dennis, DeDe, Tía Anita, Paul, Robert, Steve, Beth and the kids, Uncle Bobbie, Maria and Virgie Fletes, Teresa and Lou, Eddie and Sylvia Molina, Bob, Virginia, and Jeanette Amparan, David, Susan and all the kids, Eduarda Díaz-Schwarback, Elena Macias, Marcela Chavez, Pablo Alvarez, Rigo Maldonado, and of course, Reina and Roxie. *Besos y abrazos cariñosos para mi esposo Al y mis hijos Emilio Miguel y Maximiliano Luis.* The joy you bring to my life makes it all worth it.

Introduction:
New Immigrants, Neo-Nativism,
and the Public Library

Susan Luévano-Molina

The divide of race has been America's constant curse. Each new wave of immigrants gives new targets to old prejudices . . . Our rich texture of racial, religious and political diversity will be a godsend in the 21st century. Great re-
wards will come to those who can live together, learn together, work together,
and forge new ties that bind together.
    President William J. Clinton, Inaugural Address (1995, January 21)

The debate over increased immigration has sparked intense political and social
debate over the last half of the twentieth century as the complex movement of
people into this country has intensified. It has transformed not only the United
States but also other countries around the world such as Germany, France, and
Japan. Likewise, large urban centers in the Third World have also experienced
an influx of displaced workers from rural areas. A United Nations study estimates that worldwide there are now over 100 million foreign immigrants in the
world (Meisler, 1993). The primary reason for this surging stream of migrants
is the result of economic factors related to the restructuring of global capital
(Bonilla, Meléndez, Morales, & de los Angeles Torres, 1998; Bonilla &
Morales, 1993; Sassen, 1991, 1994, 1996). In essence, unfettered economic
exchange agreements hammered out in countries around the world have un-
done the barriers to moving capital and goods. A side effect of shaping this
new economic structure has been the major migration of people around the
world.
    Furthermore, many political immigrants have been created by public and
clandestine U.S. military interventions in the nineteenth and twentieth centuries (Chang, 1999; Koelin, 1991). The Philippines, Korea, Vietnam, Iran,
Cambodia, Laos, Chile, Grenada, and Panama have all been arenas of political
conflict. These conflicts along with military coups or civil wars in Latin
America in the last half of the century have created a steady and substantial
quantity of displaced persons from Mexico, Nicaragua, Uruguay, Argentina,
Chile, Guatemala, Honduras, and El Salvador. In addition, other economic

and political refugees have come to the United States from Eastern Europe, China, Cuba, Haiti, and Africa.

In combination with the traditional immigrants that came to the U.S. under the now defunct family reunification principle, a complete picture of the human influx into this country begins to emerge. Currently one out of ten people in the U.S. is an immigrant (Booth, 1998). The Census Bureau estimates that by the year 2000 the United States population will include 9 million immigrants and their offspring who entered the country legally after 1986 (Census Bureau, 1994). By the year 2030 these post–1986 immigrants and their descendants will account for 32 million people (Spencer, 1982, p. 1). As dramatic as these statistics may appear they do not even attempt to provide estimates on undocumented immigrants for whom reliable statistics are subject to great debate. Nevertheless, the Census Bureau estimates that approximately 4 million immigrants reside illegally in the United States (In US, 1995).

Governments in developed countries around the world are calling for restrictions on immigration. In the U.S., this is one issue where political opponents such as President Clinton and Newt Gingrich can agree. Both have called for increased control of the nation's borders (Bornemeier, 1994; Lacey, 1995; Shogren & Healy, 1995).

THE NEW NATIVISM

Sadly, worldwide the mass movement of people has aroused intense hostility against these newcomers (Cornelius, Martin & Hollefield, 1994; Mills, 1994; Reimers, 1992). The new nativism of the late twentieth century has been the cause of fire bombings against Turkish communities in Germany, the deportation of Chinese refugees in Hong Kong, and legislative actions to limit immigration in France (Weiner, 1993).

U.S. citizens have also engaged in a wave of neo-nativism on the local, state, and national basis. This period of immigrant bashing is reminiscent of the 1920s when similar anti-immigrant feelings dominated the country (Calvita, 1996; Rose, 1995; Takaki, 1994). Everything from limiting prenatal care, to controls on language, attacks on multiculturalism, the decline of affirmative action programs, and calls for militarizing the nation's borders have become part of the U.S. phenomenon of ethnic intolerance (Brownstein, 1994). The National Asian Pacific American Legal Consortium (NAPALC), which audits violence against Asian Pacific Americans, found that hate crimes surged in California and New York since the early 1990s (1995). Their annual audit states, "Anti-immigrant sentiment continues to be severe, motivating incidents of violence against Asian Pacific Americans" (1995, p. 1). Even the Sierra Club, the world's largest and most influential environmental organization, tackled the issue when members voted on whether to maintain their neutral stance or speak out against the impact of immigration as the root cause of the world's problems with pollution, and the destruction of natural resources (Cone, 1998). In addition, the recent arrival of boatloads of undocumented Chinese and Haitian immigrants, as well as the increased focus on Middle

Eastern immigrants as a consequence of the bombing of the New York City World Trade Center and conflicts with Iran and Iraq have further fueled anti-immigrant sentiment nationally (Koelin, 1991).

Due in part to vast political fragmentation, intra-group differences, and limited resources, these new diaspora groups were unable to successfully counter the political assaults of anti-immigrant leaders in the 1980s and 1990s (Simon, 1993). As a result, neo-nativists were able to provoke a hysteria which suggested to the majority population that immigrants were responsible for increased unemployment, rising crime, declining educational scores, and a stagnant economy (Bonilla, Meléndez, Morales, & de los Angeles Torres, 1998; Calavita, 1996; Mills, 1994; Perea, 1997). Proposition 187, a 1994 California ballot initiative limiting health, educational, and social services to undocumented immigrants, galvanized national attention on the issue when it was overwhelmingly passed by the electorate.[1] This measure, while not the first attack on the post-1965 immigrants, signified the peak of the extremist anti-immigrant movement on the West coast.

On the national level, there were numerous restrictionist proposals from the halls of Congress during the early 1990s. These new curtailment proposals included calls for denying basic human services to those legal residents who had followed all the rules leading to full citizenship and the elimination of the right of naturalized citizens to call their U.S. born children citizens (Jost, 1995). In addition, Congress's massive overhaul of welfare laws in 1996 imposed broad new restrictions on noncitizens.

Similar to other periods of U.S. nativism, native language retention and the recreation of diverse social and cultural institutions among new immigrants has proved very irritating to longtime U.S. residents and citizens (Suárez-Orozco, Chapter 2 of this volume). Neo-nativist organizations incited a cultural war against immigrants as part of a wider attempt to protest the emergence of new public cultures and immigrant resistance to assimilate to Euro-American cultural norms (Gutierréz, 1996; Mills, 1994). Anti-immigrant activists often cite the struggle to maintain the vestiges of a European centered "common culture" as the justification for actions (Mills, 1994).

However, the most vexing issue among the dominant majority electorate appears to be the presumed use of tax-supported services by immigrant populations. Calavita (1996) provides an excellent analysis of this "immigrants as tax burden" attitude. She notes that it is a historically specific and unique theme of the nativist movement at the end of the twentieth century. Any in-depth analysis of the neo-nativism movement must examine the discontent of voters toward immigrants-as-a-fiscal-burden concept and consider how it might impact libraries as tax-supported institutions.

Who are the neo-nativists? The neo-nativist leaders are dominated by aggressive sectors of the Right including political conservatives, nationalists, and religious fundamentalists (Coniff, 1993; Kanpol & McLaren, 1995). However, the anti-immigrant movement has clearly enjoyed wide popular support across the nation (Hammond, 1994). Plant closures, lower wages, loss of health care, and a declining standard of living for U.S. workers are a few of the concrete conditions that have sparked fear and frustration within the general public. It is imperative to again state that these conditions are the direct consequences of increased competition in the global marketplace (Roberts, 1994). The new nativists leaders have tapped into the deep unease created by the economic downturn and the huge numbers of primarily Latino and Asian immigrants that have reshaped the social fabric of the country (Armbruster, Geron & Bonacich, 1995; Suárez-Orozco, Chapter 2 of this volume). Displaced immigrant workers have become easy targets for blame while the corporations that have restructured the global industrial economy remain distant and relatively unaffected.

WHY CALIFORNIA?

The resurgence of nativism in the United States has become synonymous with immigrant populations in California. Why California? First, diaspora populations are disproportionately concentrated in the Golden State. Since 1965 large scale Asian and Latino migration has contributed to the intensification of existing political, economic, and cultural tensions (Dunn, 1994). Second, the state has faced an extensive and dramatic recession due largely to the dismantling of the defense industry and manufacturing and industrial plant closures. Third, the political climate in California was ripe for the xenophobic ranting of Governor Pete Wilson, a strong and vocal anti-immigrant leader. His political leadership along with an initiative process that made it feasible for anti-immigrant organizations to change the laws of the land has brought embryonic nativist concepts to full bloom in the 1990s. Lastly, the psychological effects of the 1992 Los Angeles riot crystallized the frustration and fear level of voters. These factors all contributed to the desire of the electorate to punish and disenfranchise those populations deemed less deserving of tax-supported social and public services.

CHARACTERISTICS AND SOCIAL CONDITIONS OF THE NEW IMMIGRANTS

From 1971 to 1991, nearly nine million immigrants entered the United States from Asian and Latin American countries. Economics, a higher standard of living, and democratic ideals will continue to attract immigrants of Third World origin to the United States far into the twenty-first century. As mentioned above, nowhere is this more evident than in California, which is identified by the majority of migrants as their primary destination (Dunn, 1994).

Issues of transnationalism or multinationalism suggest a distinct departure from immigrants of past eras.[2] For example, recent immigrants to have a better understanding of what to expect in their region of destination than those that came at the turn of the last century due to advanced telecommunications networks. More often than not, the newcomers will maintain considerable interest, both personal and financial, in their countries of origin. Advanced transportation and telecommunications will also enhance the ease with which diaspora populations are able to travel and communicate with their contacts in the home country. Unlike other historical periods of migration, the National Council for Research on Women (NCRW, 1995) reports that today's immigrants are just as likely to be women as men. The feminization of international migration indicates a strong maintenance of cultural values in the host country, as women are most often the bearers of cultural traditions. Finally, higher birth rates among Asian and Latino females, which comprise the largest proportion of the new immigrant groups, insure that the descendants of these populations will continue to dominate the demographic landscape (Vargas, 1998).

As a consequence of these distinct circumstances, new immigrants will view themselves differently than previous waves of newcomers. They will most likely have multiple identities appropriate to the many social terrains they may encounter in the United States (Bonilla, Meléndez, Morales, & de los Angeles Torres, 1998; Chavez, 1988, 1992, 1994; Smith, 1992). For example, new immigrants may view themselves as U.S. residents, citizens of their country of origin, and most likely members of an oppressed "minority" within the United States. These identities may shift and/or develop with the circumstances of the host and home country.

Like immigrants in other historical periods these populations will continue to be discriminated against by the dominant Euro-American society because of their class, color, and culture. However, the new immigrants circumstances will be further complicated by intra-ethnic conflicts that may sometimes pit native-born ethnic populations against recent arrivals (Gutierréz, 1995; Izumi, 1996). Competition for jobs, language and generational differences, along with historical antagonisms will engender tensions within ethnic communities. Some new immigrants may even find that they are treated as "internal outsiders" within their own cultural group.

Furthermore, new immigrant populations continue to face interethnic/racial conflicts. For example, demographically, Latinos will soon replace African Americans as the largest "minority" majority population in the U.S., while Asian Americans are the fastest growing "minority" group in the nation (Dunn, 1994; Hayes-Bautista, Schink, & Rodríguez, 1994; Nelson & O'Reilly, 2000). These demographic shifts have generated anxieties among minority communities related to resource allocation and political representation.

African American communities, who have long struggled to overcome racism and the resulting economic barriers, have found themselves displaced at the lower end of the employment chain, as cheaper more exploitable Latino and Asian labor has become available (Waldinger, 1996). Employer's preference for cheap immigrant labor, along with plant closures has forced the migration of many African Americans out of Los Angeles County. This has changed housing patterns in the historically African American communities of South Central Los Angeles (Gold, 1999; Rocco, 1997; Smith, 1998). For example, Latino immigrant groups demographically dominate South Central Los Angeles cities such as South Gate, Lynwood, Bell, Cudhay, Maywood, and Vernon. Cities once considered the "quintessential African American ghetto[s]" (Gold, 1999, p. A1) such as Watts, Compton, and Inglewood have only slightly over 50 percent Black populations. A surge of Mexican and Central American residents has transformed the ethnic composition of these areas. While this mix has brought both "tensions and triumphs" Gold notes that "interracial violence has plagued local schools and housing projects" (1999, p. A1).

Dramatic intercultural and economic clashes between African American and Asian Americans in Los Angeles have also created antagonisms and resentments that will not be easily overcome. The 1992 shooting of 15-year-old African American Latasha Harlins by Korean immigrant Du Soon-Ja and the subsequent light sentence given to Du Soon-Ja solidified the cultural and economic distance between these two populations. The targeted destruction of Korean businesses in the Los Angeles uprising, shortly thereafter, has also intensified the volatile relations between these two communities (Gotanda, 1996; Johnson & Farrell, 1996). In addition, Latino and Armenian immigrant youth wage battles of life and death on the streets of Glendale, and Latino and Cambodian gangs shoot it out in low-income neighborhoods of Long Beach.

The political reverberations of the nativist hysteria, while greatly diminished in the new century as the global economy has improved, have profoundly affected all real and imagined immigrants and the governmental institutions which serve them. A significant outcome of the nativist movement has been the forced raising of political consciousness among immigrants, legal and undocumented, as well as those communities of color who could be mistaken for immigrants (Bustillo, 2000; Rosaldo & Flores, 1997). This is especially evident within the state's Latino community where many legal residents have applied for citizenship. The national backlog for naturalization applications has now reached two million. Not surprisingly, most of the two-year backlogs are from California applicants (Stewart, 2000).

In addition, many of the new citizens have begun to participate in the political process as protection against future attacks on immigrant populations (Bustillo, 2000; Flores & Benmayor, 1997; Stewart, 2000.) In California, the increasing immigrant electorate, estimated at two million and rising, was responsible for sweeping in pro-immigrant Democratic Governor Gray Davis in 1998. The Republican party, which strongly backed Proposition 187 and other measures aimed at overturning bilingual education and affirmative action, has witnessed an electorate backlash that is voting Democratic (Bustillo, 2000). The future impact of this voting group is expected to be a huge factor in upcoming national elections. Presidential hopefuls George W. Bush and Al Gore are both courting the Latino community. Bush and Gore have both vocalized opposition to future anti-immigrant legislation mirroring Proposition 187 (Election 2000, 2000). This changing political climate was most visible at the nationally televised 2000 Democratic and Republican national conventions. Both parties lauded the virtues of inclusiveness, featured top-line Latino entertainment, and recited Spanish language one-liners (Bustillo, 2000; Martinez, 2000). Ironically, the latest wave of nativism has created, as George W. Bush put it, *"un nuevo dia"* or a new day (Bustillo, 2000, p. A3) as Latino populations go to the polls in record numbers.

Asian immigrant populations who have also begun to embrace the political process as readily as the Latino community continue to feel the harsh hand of nativism (Sign of the Times, 1999; Wu, 1999). They remain unfairly targeted as the "Other" because of their actual or assumed "foreign born" status. During the late 1990s Chinese Americans have been maligned over links to mainland China, illegal fundraising, and espionage (Wu, 1998).

The Wen Ho Lee espionage case is the perfect example of this type of racial profiling (Cho, 2000; Iritani, 2000). Dr. Lee, a Taiwan-born naturalized citizen and highly respected scientist working on classified research at the Los Alamos Research Lab, was unduly accused of being a spy for the People's Republic of China. The case imploded due to a lack of evidence against Lee. However, in the meantime he was imprisoned in solitary confinement for nine months without ever knowing the charges against him, forced to spend $1.5 million during an 18-month legal battle to clear his name, and finally had to accept a plea-bargained felony to secure his freedom.

The government's actions were widely criticized by the scientific community, President Clinton, and most vociferously by the presiding judge. Yet the damage had been done. As Henry S. Tang, a leader of a group of Chinese Americans called the Committee of 100, stated "No matter how accomplished, no matter how educated, no matter how wealthy, no matter how loyal, one could still be suspected of activities counter to the interests of this country" (Iritani, 2000, p. A11). Alberta Lee, Dr. Lee's daughter and one of the leaders of his legal defense fund stated, "You grow up, and every day in school you say the Pledge of Allegiance, and the last line is 'With liberty and justice for all.' You think 'Yeah, that's how this country works.' You know it's not a perfect world. But you never think it's going to happen to your family" (Cho, 2000, p. 43).

PUBLIC LIBRARIES AND THE POLITICS OF DISCONTENT

The ramifications of this new mosaic of immigrants settling in U.S. communities along with the negative political backlash that has followed are just beginning to be understood and analyzed by librarians. While most library professionals may not fully grasp the intricacies of multinational capitalism or its impact on global migration, as service providers committed to serving the community-at-large, public libraries must deal with the consequences of these circumstances. Library professionals, for the most part, are guided in their practice by the Library Bill of Rights that guarantees library services to all sectors of the community regardless of their background. This document continues to provide the philosophical underpinnings of the profession's service ethic and mission.

The polarizing issues dominating the political and economic landscape make it a certainty that dealing with increasingly diverse communities will continue to be a complicated undertaking for library information specialists.

For example, the economic dilemmas and communities involved are international in scope, America's immigration laws are a cumbersome mess, answers to many service questions remain elusive and in flux, and resources for libraries continue to be limited. Immigrant populations will continue to be blamed for the country's economic and social woes occasionally inflaming acts of aggression and fear. In addition, most new immigrants are not interested in assimilating to Euro-American cultural standards as in past generations. Rather these diaspora communities are more likely to acculturate selective aspects of their new environment while maintaining close ties to their home country, language, and culture. In addition, the new immigrants come from various backgrounds and with vastly different expectations. Finally, class issues will be more clearly defined in the new century with immigrants falling into the lower end of the economic ladder (Morales, 1998). As Bonilla and Morales (1993, p.1) state, "It is now widely understood that one of the economic consequences of the unprecedented expansion of the 1980s in the United States is that the rich got richer while the middle class stagnated and the poor fell farther behind."

All these issues play a significant role in the emerging relations among new immigrants, longtime U.S. residents, and the public library. There are few analytical or practical approaches in the literature that librarians can rely upon to understand and act upon these disparate and often conflicting relationships. The only things that appear evident are that conventional public service models of assimilation will address only part of the issues at hand and that the Library Bill of Rights must continue to serve as the foundational guide to community service.

Librarians across the nation are learning new ways of coping and serving diverse communities. For example, rather than embracing the outdated melting pot paradigm, librarians are developing unique community specific networks and services as a proactive response to the cultural transformations in their local service areas (Zhang, Chapter 10 of this volume).

On the national level, American Library Association (ALA) President Barbara Ford's "Global is Local" theme is one very positive example that recently emphasized the positive aspects of our shrinking global village (Ford, 1997). The passage and implementation of the ALA Spectrum Program designed to recruit and train a more diverse professional cadre is another important program that will serve future generations of Americans (ALA Council, 1997).

Yet within the library literature there is a void of research about this historic period of global migration, immigrant bashing, and public libraries. It seems that the profession has not examined in any detail the demands of this new polity.

It should be noted that most of the research in this volume was completed in the mid-1990s when the anti-immigrant fervor was at its high point in the West. Despite the waning of these contested issues in the new millennium there is no doubt that anti-immigration issues as a result of economic restructuring will resurface. The next time the economy lags or the sense of belonging to a secure tradition of Euro-American culture is shaken, diaspora communities will take the hit (Takaki, 1994). It is not an issue of if, but when.

Consequently, the manuscripts in this volume should resonate for library professionals in the decades to come. *Immigrant Politics and the Public Library* suggests some preliminary working hypotheses based on the most comprehensive research to be conducted on this topic to date. The articles in this collection focus on the fundamental role of public libraries as public tax- supported institutions that serve to deepen and extend the possibilities of democratic public life in an era of popular and widespread immigrant bashing, and increased demographic changes.

The collection is not designed to be an inclusive portrait of any particular group of immigrants. In fact, only the two major immigrant communities, that is, Latinos and Asians, are discussed in any significant detail. The intent of this compilation is rather to offer an in-depth analysis and critique of the anti-immigrant movement and a review, however limited, of the responses of selected public libraries. Finally, the authors propose some solutions to the multifaceted and variable issues related to difference, the American consciousness, and the public library.

RESEARCH TOPICS

The Suárez-Orozco article reviews the foundations of neo-nativism in the United States. Foundational anti-immigrant arguments are laid out and disputed. The unique feature of this article is the psychological analysis of nativism. A close examination of California's Proposition 187 is used to illustrate the author's premise. This article provides the necessary backdrop for all that is to follow.

The next article is a background paper written for the California Library Association by Rios-Kravitz on behalf of the Services to Latinos Round Table in response to the passage of Proposition 187. This eloquently written essay is a plea to the California Library Association to stand up for the rights of immigrant populations. The paper outlines the philosophical and historical basis for the role that libraries should and must play in bridging cultures and affirming diversity. Rios-Kravitz articulates the need to serve immigrant communities in California not only because it is the right thing to do but also because it is critical to the survival of the profession.

It should be noted that the Services to Latinos Roundtable was the only group within the California Library Association, the largest library organization in the state of California, to raise the banner of service as enumerated in the Library Bill of Rights on behalf of immigrant populations after the passage of the "Save our State" initiative. This call was brought forth at the California Library Association conference that ironically was held in Orange County, home of the nativist movement, a week after the 187 victory. The background paper was written to justify a resolution of support that was eventually passed by the California Library Association (CLA) Assembly. The background paper and the CLA Assembly resolution demonstrate the activism of an ethnic caucus and their struggle to bring issues of domination to the forefront. In addition, it demonstrates how professional organizations can be utilized to promote issues that articulate the profession's public service commitment despite a hostile political climate.

The next three articles focus on the large immigrant community of Santa Ana, California. These studies are interesting for many reasons, not least of which is that Santa Ana is the largest immigrant and minority community in Orange County. It is located in the heart of the region that gave birth to the anti-immigrant movement and continues to be their base of operation. The grassroots research conducted in the community and with the Santa Ana Public Library staff members provides a thorough and well articulated appraisal of immigrant attitudes, experiences, and use of the public library.

Luévano-Molina utilizes an ethnographic approach to determine the attitudes and library use patterns of Latino immigrants in Santa Ana, California. She informs us regarding the impact of nativist legislation and pending legislation on the use of the Santa Ana Public Library by Latino immigrants. Luévano-Molina's qualitative research reveals the experiences and impressions of Latino immigrants toward the public library both in the host city and in the home country.

The Knox study centers on a survey of Santa Ana Public Library staff. The survey measures their perceptions of the immigrant community's use of the library and the promotion of library services within the immigrant community. Of special interest were pre- and post-Proposition 187 perceptions of immigrant library usage. This research was conducted in conjunction with the Luévano-Molina study. It offers a confirmation of community attitudes as documented in the ethnographic study.

Aguirre's qualitative studies dovetail nicely with the Luévano-Molina and Knox research. The author examines the role of the public library in developing cultural citizenship and increasing the academic success of Latino immigrant students in Santa Ana, California. Her research details not only the impact of Proposition 187 but also Proposition 227, the anti-immigrant legislation that proposed English-only instruction in California public schools. Together these studies offer a detailed picture of the Santa Ana Latino immigrant community and the public library.

Looking beyond California to Arizona, Almance Trejo reports on survey results measuring Latino immigrant families', nonimmigrant families', teachers', and librarians' reactions to proposed nativist legislation. The author ties cross-sectional survey responses to public library use. Alamance Trejo documents the role of educational institutions in partnership with libraries in deflating the increasingly hostile social reality of immigrants in Tucson, Arizona. The role of immigrant mothers in developing an educational pipeline is also explored.

Zhang examines the anti-affirmative action movement, its impact on public libraries, and on the Asian American community. This article informs readers about the impact of yet another nativist California proposition that banned the use of affirmative action in hiring, education, and contracts.

Zhang's article argues that the affirmative action debate is a part of the neo-nativist agenda. As Asian populations continue to swell due to immigration trends and high birth rates, all efforts to limit or restrict the advancement of these new immigrant communities are interpreted as frontal attacks on equal opportunity in education and the marketplace. In this detailed and meticulously researched article Zhang's data suggests discriminatory consequences against Asian Americans.

Chabrán's article examines the concept of "cyber-segmentation," a theory that he coins in this article. The author is a public policy advocate and technological theorist. He is most interested in combining theory and practice to explore solutions to real world problems. Using his experiences with youth at the Riverside Community-Computing Center, Chabrán considers the cyber-segmentation of the new immigrants within the global digital economy. The author stresses the need for the profession to examine issues of poverty and racism as a basis of analysis before proposing community solutions for people of color, in general, and immigrant populations, in particular. Chabrán further challenges library and information providers to prepare local low-income and immigrant communities for the digital opportunities that will improve their educational and economic attainment.

Zhang contributes a second article that examines public library services to Asian diaspora communities in the Los Angeles area. The author outlines specific best practices as noted by librarians on the front lines. The political nature of securing and providing nontraditional library services is also discussed.

Jeng provides needed baseline definitions of numerous diversity-related terms. The author reminds us that the more we know about each other, the greater respect we will have for each other's humanity and for our distinct manner of being human. Jeng raises the banner of diversity training in library school training. She calls for an accelerated integration of issues of difference into library school curricula. Jeng urges the profession to search for the common ground that binds; even when that means dominant group members must consider changing rather than expecting librarians of color to adapt to the mainstream.

Lastly, Escatiola has created an important review of anti-immigrant legislation literature that focuses on the most hotly contested issues of the 1990s. The bibliography is drawn primarily from social science scholarship. Articles supporting both sides of this issue have been included. The author's essay and list of citations include required readings for librarians serving immigrant populations.

CONCLUSION

Despite the escalation of anti-immigrant measures since the 1980s, a hostile U.S. reception did not and will not stop immigrants from coming. The high demand for cheap labor, the integration of the new workers into regional economies, and the well established immigrant social networks seem to insure the ineffectiveness of state policies in deterring continued immigration (Jonas,

1996; Portes, 1996). Mirroring this trend, the research in this volume suggests that anti-immigrant policies do not necessarily control or limit the actual behavior of immigrants' use of the public library or the integration of the public library in their daily lives. Of course, these nativist measures may temporarily affect library usage but do not necessarily stop the process of creating a community of library users.

While this statement seems to suggest that public libraries will remain a salient public institution among diaspora communities, nothing could be further from the truth. Public libraries must, as the articles here suggest, offer appropriate services, multilingual collections, and employ multilingual staff. Without these unique services community use and integration may not be established or developed.

What makes this challenge different for public libraries from past waves of immigration is the transnational makeup of the new communities, the diversity of immigrants, and the sometimes overt intolerance of the majority population to these newcomers. Some service providers must continue to provide traditional library services while integrating viable services to immigrant populations.

In this era of increased global interconnectedness, economic integration, and transnational linkages, librarians must search for new and different ways to engage and deepen democratic connections among all members of the community. Regardless of the prevailing political rhetoric, the research suggests that the library as a neutral community resource has tremendous social capital that could be exploited to accelerate the integration of new immigrants into local communities. Libraries must remain steadfast in their service vision as outlined in the Library Bill of Rights. They must not abandon diaspora communities when errant political pressures arise.

The public library, like other tax-supported institutions, must review and validate its role and relationship to rapidly expanding immigrant populations. It is hoped that this volume will encourage library service providers to develop a more comprehensive sense of the new immigrant experience in an increasingly borderless world. These conditions have created complex challenges for resistance to bias, as well as constructive opportunities for shaping public service policies of the future. These topics and the bigger issues related to global restructuring and the public library deserve further scholarly analysis. The authors of the volume have taken a step in this effort by providing a forum from which the most recent trends in immigrant politics and the public library can be discussed. Much, much more remains to be done.

NOTES

1.   Proposition 187 passed by a 60 percent to 40 percent margin statewide. Whites constituted 75 percent of the voting electorate, which voted in favor of the initiative. Almost 3 1/2 years later on March 18, 1998, Federal District Judge Mariana R. Pfaelzer ruled that the core provisions of Proposition 187 were unconstitutional. She based much of her decision on Congress' welfare reform bill that placed restrictions on benefits to undocumented and legal residents. The congressional actions supported

Judge Pfaelzer's conclusion that only the federal government can mandate immigration law.

2. Cultural anthropologist, Leo R. Chavez (1997, p. 62) describes transnational immigrants as follows: "The 'new' immigrants are transnational, or people who maintain social linkages back in the home country; they are not bound by national borders and their multiple identities are situated in communities in different nations and in communities that cross nations." This concept is basic to understanding the essence of new immigrant communities. It is a term that every public librarian should add to his or her lexicon.

REFERENCES

American Library Association Council. (1997, August). CDA, Gates, Minority Scholarships, and finding an executive. *American Libraries, 28* (7), 74–78.

Armbruster, R., Geron, K., & Bonacich, E. (1995). The Assault on California's Latino immigrants: The politics of Proposition 187. *International Journal of Urban and Regional Research, 19* (4), 655–63.

Bonilla, F., Meléndez, E., Morales, R., & de los Angeles Torres, M. (1998). *Borderless borders: US Latinos, Latin Americans, and the paradox of interdependence.* Philadelphia, Pa.: Temple University Press.

Bonilla, F. & Morales, R. (Eds.) (1993). *Latinos in a changing economy: Comparative perspectives on growing inequality.* Newbury Park, Calif.: Sage Publications.

Booth, W. (1998, February 22). America's racial and ethnic divides: One nation, indivisible. Is it history? *Washington Post,* p. A1.

Bornemeier, J. (1994, September 15). U.S. study fuels debate on illegal immigrants' impact. *Los Angeles Times,* pp. A1, A26.

Brownstein, R. (1994, November 19). Wilson proposes US version of Prop. 187. *Los Angeles Times,* p. A1.

Bustillo, M. (2000, August 7). State GOP is distancing itself from Prop. 187. *Los Angeles Times,* p. A3.

Calavita, K. (1996, August 1). The new politics of immigration: "Balanced-budget conservatism" and the symbolism of Proposition 187. *Social Problems, 43* (3), 284–305.

Chang, R. S. (1999, November). Asian Pacific Americans and the law: Pain and promise of memory. *American Bar Association Journal, 85,* 68–70.

Chavez, L. R. (1988). Settlers and sojourners: The case of Mexicans in the United States. *Human Organization, 47,* 344–52.

Chavez, L. R. (1992). *Shadowed lives: Undocumented immigrants in American society.* New York: Holt, Rinehart and Winston, Inc.

Chavez, L. R. (1994). The power of imagined community: The settlement of undocumented Mexican and Central Americans in the United States. *American Anthropologist, 96* (1), 52–73.

Chavez, L. R. (1997). Immigration reform and nativism: The nationalist response to the transnationalist challenge. In J. F. Perea (Ed.) *Immigrants out!: The new nativism and the anti-immigrant impulse in the United States* (pp. 61–77). New York: New York University Press.

Cho, J. (2000, March 31). After the fire: The lingering aftershocks of the Wen Ho Lee investigation. *A. Magazine, 10,* 43.

Clinton, W. J. (1997, January 21). Clinton text: A new sense of responsibility. *Los Angeles Times,* p. A11.

Cone, M. (1998, April 26). Sierra Club to remain neutral on immigration. *Los Angeles Times,* pp. A1, A34.

Coniff, R. (1993, October). The war on aliens: The right calls the shots. *Progressive, 5* (10), 22–29.

Cornelius, W. A., Martin, P. L., & Hoffefield, J. F. (1994). *Controlling immigration: A global perspective.* Stanford, Calif.: Stanford University Press.

Dunn, A. (1994, October 30). In California, the numbers add up to anxiety. *New York Times*, p. D3.

Edmonston, B. & Passel, J. S. (Eds.) (1994). *Immigration and ethnicity: The integration of America's newest arrivals.* Washington, D.C.: Urban Institute Press.

Election 2000/Presidential race: Immigration challenges. (2000, September 10). *Los Angeles Times*, p. M4.

Flores, W. V. & Benmayor, R. (Eds.) (1997). *Latino cultural citizenship.* Boston: Beacon.

Ford, B. J. (1997, October). How to go global. *American Libraries, 29* (9), 35.

Gold, M. (1999, July 7). A new Watts awaits visit by President. *Los Angeles Times*, p. A1.

Gotanda, N. (1996). Multiculturalism and racial stratification. In A. F. Gordon & C. Newfield (Eds.) *Mapping multi-culturalism* (pp. 238–52). Minneapolis, Minn.: University of Minnesota Press.

Gutierréz, D. G. (1995). *Walls and mirrors: Mexican Americans, Mexican immigrants, and the politics of ethnicity.* Berkeley, Calif.: University of California Press.

Gutierréz, D. G. (Ed.) (1996). *Between two worlds: Mexican immigrants in the United States.* Wilmington, D.E.: Scholarly Resources.

Hammond, B. (1994, June 15). Grass-roots movement pushes SOS initiative. *San Francisco Chronicle,* p. A21.

Hayes-Bautista, D. E., Schink, W. O., & Rodríguez, G. (1994). *Latino immigrants in Los Angeles: A portrait from the 1990 census.* Los Angeles: Alta California Policy Research Center.

Hing, B. O. & Lee, R. (Eds.) (1996). *The state of Asian Pacific America: Reframing the immigration debate, a public policy report.* Los Angeles, CA: Leadership Education for Asian Pacifics, Inc.

Hondagneu-Sotelo, P. (1994). *Gendered transitions: Mexican experiences of immigration.* Berkeley, Calif.: University of California Press.

In US, 1 in 11 foreign-born, census finds. (1995, August 29). *Los Angeles Times*, p. A20.

Iritani, E. (2000, September 25). Lee case proved to be an awakening. *Los Angeles Times*, p. A11.

Izumi, L. (1996, July 1). There are Asians, and Asians. *National Review, 48* (12), 25–27.

Johnson, J. H. & Farrell, W. C. (1996). The fire this time: The genesis of the Los Angeles rebellion of 1992. In J. C. Boger & J. W. Wegner (Eds.) *Race, poverty and American cities* (pp. 166–85). Chapel Hill: University of North Carolina Press.

Jonas, S. (1996). Rethinking immigration policy and citizenship in the Americas. *Social Justice: A Journal of Crime, Conflict and World Order, 23* (3), 68–85.

Jost, K. (1995, February 3). Cracking down on immigration. *CQ Researcher, 5* (5), 97–115.

Kanpol, B. & McLaren, P. (Eds.) (1995). *Critical multiculturalism: Uncommon voices in a common struggle.* Westport, Conn.: Bergin & Garvey.

Koelin, P. H. (1991). *Refugees from revolution: U.S. policy and third world migra-*

tion. Boulder, Colo.: Westview.

Lacey, M. (1995, March 16). New task force targets illegal immigration. *Los Angeles Times*, p. A3.

Lamphere, L., Stepick, A., & Grenier, G. (Eds.) (1994). *Newcomers in the workplace: Immigrants and restructuring of the U.S. economy*. Philadelphia, Pa.: Temple University Press.

Martinez, R. (2000, August 20). The new political plotline; The day ravers and immigrants almost danced. *Los Angeles Times*, p. M1.

Meisler, S. (1993, July 7). Migration viewed as "human crisis." *Los Angeles Times,* p. A4.

Mills, N. (Ed.) (1994). *Arguing immigration: The debate over the changing face of America*. New York: Simon & Schuster.

National Asian Pacific American Legal Consortium. (1995). *Audit of violence against Asian Pacific Americans: The consequences of intolerance in America, 1995*. Washington, D.C.: Author.

National Council for Research on Women. (1995). The feminization of immigration. *Issues Quarterly, 1* (3), 1–7.

Nelson, S. S. & O'Reilly, R. (2000, August 20). Minorities become majority in State, Census officials say. *Los Angeles Times*, pp. A1, A16.

Perea, J. F. (Ed.) (1997). *Immigrants out!: The new nativism and the anti-immigrant impulse in the United States*. New York: New York University Press.

Portes, A. (1996). Transnational communities: Their emergence and significance in the contemporary world system. In R. P. Korzeniewicz and W. C. Smith (Eds.) *Latin American in the world economy* (pp. 151–68.) Westport, Conn.: Greenwood Publishing Group.

Reimers, D. M. (1992). *Still the golden door: The third world comes to America*. New York: Columbia University Press.

Roberts, S. V. (1994, October 3). Shutting the golden door: Economic fears, ethnic prejudice and politics as usual make the melting pot a pressure cooker. *U.S. News & World Report, 117* (13), 36–40.

Rocco, R. (1997). Citizenship, culture, and community: Restructuring in Southeast Los Angeles. In W. V. Flores & R. Benmayor (Eds.) *Latino cultural citizenship* (pp. 97–123). Boston: Beacon.

Rosaldo, R. & Flores, W. V. (1997). Identity, conflict, and evolving Latino communities: Cultural citizenship in San Jose, California. In W. V. Flores & R. Benmayor (Eds.) *Latino cultural citizenship* (pp. 57–96). Boston: Beacon.

Rose, F. (1995, April 26). Anti-immigrant measures of the past bear striking resemblance to today. *Wall Street Journal*, p. A6.

Sassen, S. (1991). *The global city: New York, London, Tokyo*. Princeton, N.J.: Princeton University Press.

Sassen, S. (1994). *The mobility of labor and capital*. New York: Cambridge University Press.

Sassen, S. (1996). *Losing controls: Sovereignty in the age of globalization*. New York: Columbia University Press.

Shogren, E. & Healy, M. (1995, February 9). Gingrich backs Wilson on illegal immigrant costs. *Los Angeles Times*, p. A1.

Sign of the times: Major events in recent Asian American history–at a glance. (1999, November 30). *A. Magazine, 9*, 68.

Simon, R. J. (1993). *The ambivalent welcome: Print media, public opinion and immigration*. Westport, Conn.: Greenwood Publishing Group.

Smith, D. (1998, October 28). School test scores missing parts of the equation. *Los*

Angeles Times, p. A1.

Smith, M. P. (1992). Postmodernism, urban ethnography, and the new social space of ethnic identity. *Theory and Society, 21*, 493–531.

Spencer, G. (1982). *Projections of the Population of the United States by Age, Sex and Race: 1988 to 2080.* (U.S. Census Bureau, Current Population Reports. Series P-25, no. 1018). Washington, D.C.: Government Printing Office.

Stewart, J. Y. (2000, August 29). INS sued over delays in processing applications. *Los Angeles Times*, p. A3.

Takaki, R. (1994). *A different mirror: A history of multicultural America.* New York: Little, Brown & Co.

The Need for Strangers: Proposition 187 and the Immigration Malaise

Marcelo M. Suárez-Orozco

On November 8, 1994, California voters overwhelmingly approved Proposition 187, known as the "Save our State" initiative. The Proposition read as follows:

[The People of California] have suffered and are suffering economic hardship caused by the presence of illegal aliens in this state.

That they have suffered and are suffering personal injury and damage caused by the criminal conduct of illegal aliens in this state.

That they have a right to protection of their government from any person or persons entering this country unlawfully.

Therefore, the people of California declare their intention to provide for cooperation between their agencies of state and local government with the federal government, and to establish a system of required notification by and between such agencies to prevent illegal aliens in the United States from receiving benefits or public services in the State of California. (Proposition 187: Text of Proposed Law)

Proposition 187 will, *inter alia,* exclude an estimated 400,000 undocumented immigrant children from public elementary and secondary educational institutions. The Proposition's incendiary language, and the unsettling debate around it (for example, see Ayres, 1994a; Noble, 1994), is revealing of the anxieties produced by immigration today.

Sigmund Freud claimed that hysteria was the malaise of his civilization. As we approach the end of our century, hysteria over immigration has become one of the great discontents of our civilization. And as was the case in Freud's time, before we can cure this hysteria, we must carefully consider the relative importance of fact and fantasy in its making. Slogans that new immigrants are driven into the wealthy postindustrial democracies by the magnet of the welfare state or to commit crimes may be catchy in political campaigns but are empirically dubious and intellectually dishonest.

TRANSNATIONAL MALAISE AND THE IMMIGRATION UPHEAVAL

What *are* some of the relevant facts? First, immigration is not a California problem, a Southwest problem, or even an American problem. With well over 100 million immigrants worldwide, immigration today is a global problem. In November 1994, voters in Flanders, Belgium, elected a member of the neo-Nazi Vlaams Blok party mayor of the elegant city of Antwerp. The Vlaams Blok's narrow political platform is well captured in their slogan, "Our people first, seal our borders, send the immigrants home." Just a few months earlier in neighboring France, the outspoken Minister of Interior Charles Pasqua, announced that his office would begin plans to send "boatloads and trainloads" of new immigrants and asylum seekers back home to North Africa. Paraphrasing Tolstoy's famous diagnosis, when it comes to immigration, all the families of the postindustrial democratic world are unhappy in the same way.

A second fact is that a big part of today's immigration crisis is of our own making. Policies to recruit foreign workers to feed the industrial nations' voracious appetite for inexpensive labor has ignited—via transnational labor-recruiting networks, wage differentials, and family reunification—much of the recent undocumented population movement. When he was a U.S. Senator, California's Governor Pete Wilson promoted policies to bring in temporary farm workers in response to the needs of California's big agribusinesses.

A third fact is that even in the context of severe anti-immigrant sentiment, the need for cheap foreign workers remains constant. In post-Proposition 187 California, agricultural enterprises fear labor shortages. Conservative analyst Martin Anderson—former domestic policy advisor to President Reagan and now a Fellow at the Hoover Institute—has recently advocated new "guest worker programs, under which foreign nationals who wish to work in the United States could do so lawfully with dignity, with no threat of being hunted down and deported" (del Olmo, 1995, p. 2). In the past, many such "guest workers" have overstayed their permits. Furthermore, labor-recruiting networks—in certain sectors of the economy employers often prefer to hire the relatives and friends of immigrant workers they trust (Waldinger, 1994)—generate new cycles of undocumented migration.

A fourth fact is that recent immigration has been a by-product of global economic and political transformations. Liberalization of Third World economies—in much of Latin America engineered largely by Harvard trained economists—has stimulated migratory patterns. In Mexico and Central Mexico a fierce pattern of competitive allocation of land between land-poor peasants and powerful transnational interests will continue to be a major factor in immigration. Over the next two decades the North American Free Trade Agreement (NAFTA)-related economic transformations will "push" perhaps two to three million Mexican farmers off the land.

Other transnational economic developments go hand-in-hand with immigration—be it legal or undocumented. The United States Treasury estimated that the January 1995 currency devaluation in Mexico would likely increase undocumented immigration to the United States by as much as 30 percent.

In Europe very similar dynamics exist. Even in the face of strong and growing anti-immigrant attitudes, foreign workers will be vital to the economies of Belgium, France, and Germany. In the European case, political upheaval—including the end of the Cold War and the spread of ethno nationalistic conflicts such as those in the former Yugoslavia—has accelerated population movements.

PROPOSITION 187: POLITICS AS CATHARSIS

Catharsis is defined as a discharge of emotions but not necessarily a cure of an underlying pathology. Proposition 187 may have served the voter of California as a discharge for emotions—anger and frustration with a severe economic recession that hit California particularly hard over the last four years; anger and anxieties about the declining expectations, crowded schools, and stunning demographic changes (political minorities are fast becoming California's demographic majority); dislocations and apprehension brought about by seemingly unending cycles of deadly and costly disasters including earthquakes, urban wildfires, and most recently floods; and finally, rage and terror in the wake of the Rodney King beating, trials, and the urban upheaval they generated. In short, Californians have had plenty of frustration, endangerment, and injury as often leading to aggression. Whereas the underlying frustrations are varied and complex, lashing out at immigrants concentrates much anger and frustration into a single focus. Yet, it is very unlikely that this discharge of anger will "cure" California's malaise.

Proposition 187 is both a beginning and an end. It is the beginning of a new kind of marginality in California. It is also the beginning of a long and costly legal battle over whether it is constitutional to keep undocumented immigrant children out of school and ineligible to receive publicly funded health care. Hours after it was voted into law, Proposition 187 was challenged in the courts. Most of Proposition 187 will not be enforced, pending the outcome of the current litigation.

Proposition 187 can be seen as the end or climax of a series of developments. In the months leading to the November 1994 election, several polls suggested that many Americans felt "that immigration was now harmful" (Mills, 1994b, p. 18).

Broadly speaking, the California referendum reflects six distinct but related areas of concern in the debate over the new immigrants. First, many Americans feel there are now too many immigrants coming into the United States. With over 700,000 new documented immigrants and an estimated 300,000 new unauthorized immigrants arriving each year, a historic high, many feel that immigration must be stopped.

A second fear relates to the fact that immigration control—including employer sanctions—have largely failed to contain waves of new undocumented immigrants. As Demetrios Papademetriou, head of the Carnegie Endowment's Immigration Policy Program, put it, there is a feeling in the public that "immigration is out of control; our borders have fallen" (Weiner, 1993, p. 1).

The third concern relates to fears about the fact that the great majority of today's immigrants are culturally and ethnically different from the great bulk of the European-born immigrants of previous decades and centuries. Today 81 percent of all new arrivals are from Latin America, the Caribbean, and Asia. In contrast, in 1940, 70 percent of all immigrants came from Europe.

Fourth, there is a related fear that the new immigrants and their children are not "assimilating" to the institutions of mainstream society in the way previous waves of European migrants assimilated. There is concern that new arrivals, particularly those from Latin America, do not seek citizenship, as did previous waves of immigrants. Some have referred to Immigration and Naturalization Service figures suggesting that applications for naturalization (citizenship) from immigrants have dropped from 67 percent of all eligible immigrants in 1943 to only 37 percent in 1992 (Sontag, 1993, p. 1).

Fifth, there is the explosive charge that the new arrivals are disproportionately contributing to the problem of crime in America. This is an empirically unfounded charge and an issue that cannot be addressed in detail in this article. Nonetheless, it contains powerful psychological overtones that I will explore.

It is not an accident that Proposition 187 is a California product. California has the highest number of new immigrants: since the early 1990s, California has been receiving annually some 200,000 documented and an estimated 100,000 undocumented new immigrants. Furthermore, the new arrivals tend to be highly concentrated in certain areas. Los Angeles is today one of the largest cities of Spanish speakers in the world. Indeed, of the "estimated five million immigrants who moved to California since 1970, two-thirds moved to the vast sprawl of the Los Angeles basin" (Dunn, 1994, p. 3).

In the last few years California has been facing serious socioeconomic upheavals, including huge loses in its military-industrial base and other key industries. To make matters worse, California suffered a number of devastating—and costly—natural disasters including urban wildfires and earthquakes. The economic crisis led to severe budget cuts at the same time as many Californians were forced to rebuild their homes and their lives after the disasters. Surveys suggest that voters are particularly anxious about their socioeconomic losses and lack of security. This unhappy combination has ignited a furious debate about the "costs" and "benefits" associated with the problem of undocumented immigrants—the data are simply not good enough.

An admittedly crass—but currently popular—index of economic "costs" is how much the new immigrants use in social services—welfare benefits (for which undocumented immigrants are not eligible), health care, costs associated with the criminal justice system, and costs associated with educating immigrant children in public schools. These "costs," some economists argue, can be evaluated against what immigrants "pay" in terms of taxes—local, state, and federal.

Yet, even in making such rough estimates, economists have failed to arrive at a satisfactory consensus. Broadly speaking there are two schools of thought: those who see the new immigration as an economic burden and those who see the new immigration as an economic benefit. Those who see immigration as a burden maintain that the new immigrants simply cannot resist the seductive entitlements of the welfare state (Borjas, 1994, pp. 76–80). According to this school of thought, the new immigrants end up "costing" more in terms of the services they use than they contribute through tax payments. In a highly publicized report, Rice University economist Donald Huddle concluded that immigrants—both legal and undocumented—"present in the United States in 1992 cost all levels of government that year more than $45 billion above and beyond the taxes that they paid" (Huddle, 1993, p. 1).

Those who see the new immigration as an economic plus disagree. Indeed, they seem to speak another language altogether. Some experts have argued that the new arrivals—documented and undocumented—contribute far more to the economy than they use in services (Fierman, 1994, pp. 67–75; Francese, 1994, pp. 85–89; Passel, 1994). Passel re-examined Huddle's figures and concluded that far from "costing" more than $45 billion, immigrants—legal and undocumented—contributed a new surplus of $28.7 billion nationwide and a new surplus to the California economy of $12 billion (Passel, 1994, p. 1).

Other experts emphasize that beyond their fair share of the tax bill, immigrants generate a wealth of positive economic activity (Meissner, 1992). Some argue that recent arrivals have been critical in keeping within the United States low-paying industries that would have likely migrated overseas without an immigrant labor force (Miles, 1994, p. 132; Rothstein, 1994, p. 48–63). Other observers have noted that although there are regional differences, new arrivals do not on aggregate depress the wages of native workers (Fierman, 1994, p. 70).

Other researchers have noted that the new immigrants played a critical role by reinvigorating abandoned urban zones, opening ethnic businesses, and via the "multiplier effect," creating job opportunities for the native born. Fierman writes, "Compelling evidence even shows that immigrants boost overall employment on balance . . . [F]or every one-hundred person increase in the population of adult immigrants, the number of new jobs rose by forty-six. By contrast for every one-hundred native born Americans, the number of new jobs rose by just twenty-five" (Fierman, 1994, p. 70). Yet, others argue that immigrant workers will be increasingly critical when large numbers of baby-boomers begin to retire in large numbers and become consumers of social security and Medicare (Francese, 1994, p. 89; Rothstein, 1994, pp. 55–57).

In short, there is ample evidence to reject the assertion that immigrants—both documented and undocumented—are the cause of economic hardship as the proponents of Proposition 187 have claimed. Even George Borjas, a controversial voice in the immigrant debate, concludes his somewhat sensationalist essay entitled "Tired, Poor, on Welfare" with a thoroughly uncontroversial assessment, "At the national level, therefore, it would not be farfetched to conclude that immigration is near a washout" (Borjas, 1994, p. 78). Not farfetched at all! Likewise, Linda Chavez, hardly an advocate of open borders, writes "Studies in the 1980s estimated that both legal and illegal immigrants were net contributors to the California economy paying more in taxes than they received in services and creating jobs rather than displacing American workers" (Chavez, 1994a, p. 33).

There is enough evidence, therefore, to suggest that the current hysteria over immigration has little to do with objective measures of economic costs and benefits. Indeed, we concur with Nathan Glazer's observation that "economics in general can give no large answer as to what the immigration policy of the nation should be (Glazer, 1994, p. 42).

Proposition 187 is based on another empirically dubious assertion: that Californians "have suffered and are suffering personal injury and damage caused by the criminal conduct of illegal aliens in this state" (Proposition 187). These psychologically charged indictments—drawn from powerful paranoid images of the "Other" as persecutorial criminal—are simply not based on any serious empirical evidence. The idea that undocumented immigrants, professional border bandits aside, are a major cause of serious crime in California today is empirically unfounded. If anything, the only serious empirical study of undocumented immigrants and crime suggests that they are far more likely to be the targets of violent crime than its perpetrators (Wolf, 1998).

In addition to its dubious assumptions about migrants and the economy and crime, Proposition 187 is based on the equally problematic assertion that "California's bounty of social services is the magnet drawing illegal immigrants across the border" (Noble, 1994, p. 11). Systematic studies suggest that it is simply not true that immigrants—documented or undocumented—are drawn by the "magnet" of the welfare state. Indeed, studies suggest that most new arrivals come to reunite with family members already in the United States, or in search of better employment opportunities (Cornelius, 1993, p. 31). Undocumented immigrants are already banned from receiving most social services. Some of the anxiety generated by the new immigration has to do with the fact that the federal government keeps the great bulk of the taxes generated by immigrants, whereas the local governments are responsible for providing most services—including health and education.

From our theoretical point of view, these constructs—Other as parasite, Other as criminal—are largely projective fantasies serving archaic psychological needs in times of great upheaval and social anxiety. California has recently endured major upheavals—natural, social, economic, and cultural. The Rodney King affair was a social earthquake that many are still mourning. Political minorities are fast becoming the numerical majority of the state. The state has endured four years of severe economic stagnation, and its prospects for recovery are not bright.

In a climate of frustration over nature, the economy, the budget crisis, and rapid demographic changes, those who are least like the dominant population have been singled out as the cause of much badness. Psychological theorists of such varied perspectives as Freud (1930), Dollard, Miller, Mower & Sears (1939), Kohut (1972), Fromm (1973), and Mitchell (1993) have argued that frustration, injury, endangerment, and upheaval often lead to malignant aggression.

My contention is that Californians are dealing with the unsettling problems of the recent past by using the immigrant Other to contain overwhelming anxieties. I concur with Julia Kristeva when she writes, "the strange [Freud's uncanny] appears as a defense put up by the distraught self: it protects itself...[by] the image of a malevolent double into which it expels the share of destruction it cannot contain" (Kristeva, 1991, pp. 183–84). Yet, there is a price to pay in the economy of hatred. The uncanny, "malevolent double," constructed to contain badness, cannot fail but to activate powerful persecutorial fantasies. Hence, we come psychoculturally to close the circle of fear and hatred. The Other, which is charged with "badness," is now also experienced as persecutorial criminal or parasite, draining precious resources.

Powerful envy fantasies are critical ingredients in the organization of irrational fears and Other-hating. Consider the ferocity of the language presented to California voters: "Proposition 187 will be the first giant stride in ultimately ending the ILLEGAL ALIEN invasion. It has been estimated that ILLEGAL ALIENS are costing taxpayers in excess of 5 billion dollars a year. While our own citizens and legal residents go wanting, those who choose to enter our country ILLEGALLY get royal treatment at the expense of the California taxpayer" (Proposition 187; Argument in Favor of Proposition 187, p. 54; emphasis in the original).

In a world of limited goods where somebody's (undocumented immigrants') gain is framed as occurring at somebody else's (citizens' and legal residents') loss, envy becomes a dominant interpersonal concern. Framing immigration as a zero-sum issue (their gain is our loss) can only fuel righteous anger. It is far from settled that undocumented immigrants cost the taxpayers of California "in excess of 5 billion dollars a year" (Passel, 1994). But invoking the parasitic Other is of strategic importance to gather up fury in the next announcement, "while our own . . . go wanting . . . [they] get royal treatment." Constructing the debate as a simple—and simplistic—they-win-we-lose proposition becomes a building block in the construction of hatred and anger lashing out.

Heuristic models are only relevant when they can elucidate the devil in the details. Why, we may ask, is this terror and hatred of migrants and refugees emerging as a worldwide epidemic now? Beyond psychodynamic insight we are in urgent need of a theory of new social formations. Some facts suggest themselves as important new theoretical understandings. First, the old demarcations of the world are being rapidly unsettled. The new formations seem to be engendering important contradictions and paradoxes.

We are in the era of post-nationalist projects, or what might be called the era of supra-nation building—from the European Union to NAFTA—just when regressive forms of ethnicity are making a fatal comeback as the dominant idiom of belonging. In the new Europe, there are no Belgians, only Walloons and Flemish. In post-Communist, post-border, post-wall Europe, new *psycho-cultural* borders are being furiously constructed.

Other contradictory formations abound. For example, there is evidence to suggest that some sectors of economies of all postindustrial societies are developing an enduring addiction to "plastic," disposable, cheap, *foreign* workers at a time of relative high, and lasting, unemployment among native workers. This has been a particularly severe problem in California and in parts of Europe, fueling xenophobic anger among working-class natives in diverse settings.

There is evidence that—the histrionic fits of right wing politicians aside—countries dealing with severe anxieties about the "immigrant problem" (including France, Belgium, and Germany), because of low birthrates and other sociological factors, will have to continue to import "designer" migrant laborers—laborers targeted to specific sectors of the economy—in the near future.

COMING ATTRACTIONS: THE FUTURE PROPOSITION 187

Proposition 187 is currently facing several legal challenges. There is evidence that Proposition 187 may be unconstitutional. It may be in violation of several laws, including the 1982 Supreme Court ruling in *Plyer v. Doe*. In the majority opinion, which struck down a Texas statute denying school enrollment to undocumented immigrant children, the Supreme Court noted, "that these children can neither affect their parents' conduct nor their own undocumented status" (*Plyer v. Doe*, 1981, p. 203). Acting against children for any transgressions their parents may have committed, a common tactic in totalitarian regimes, is immoral and in the opinion of the Court, against "fundamental conceptions of justice" (*Plyer v. Doe*, 1981, p. 220). In the majority opinion, the Supreme Court noted,

[P]ersuasive arguments support the view that a State may withhold its beneficence from those whose very presence within the United States is the product of their own unlawful conduct. These arguments do not apply with the same force to classifications imposing disabilities on the minor children of such illegal entrants. At the least, those who elect to enter our territory by stealth and in violation of our law should be prepared to bear the consequences, including, but not limited to, deportation. But the children of those illegal entrants are not comparably situated . . .Even if the State found it expedient to control the conduct of adults by acting against their children, legislation directing the onus of a parent's misconduct against his children does not comport with fundamental conceptions of justice . . .But [the Texas statute] is directed against children, and imposes its discriminatory burden on the basis of a legal characteristic over which children can have little control. It is thus difficult to conceive of a rational justification for penalizing these children for their presence within the United States. Yet that appears to be precisely the effect of [the Texas statute]. (*Plyer v. Doe*, 1981, pp. 219–20)

In the Texas case, the Supreme Court noted that even if public education is not a "right" granted to individuals by the Constitution, it is neither "merely some governmental 'benefit' indistinguishable from other forms of social welfare" (*Plyer v. Doe*, 1981, p. 221). Rather, "public education has a pivotal role in maintaining the fabric of our society and in sustaining our political and cultural heritage; the deprivation of education takes an inestimable toll on the social, economic, intellectual, and psychological well-being of the individual, and poses an obstacle to individual achievement" (*Plyer v. Doe*, 1981, p. 203). Furthermore, given that—due to amnesty and other legal factors—the "illegal alien of today may well be the legal alien of tomorrow" (*Plyer v. Doe*, 1981, p. 207), denying access to public education to undocumented immigrant children will have negative long-term social consequences: "already disadvantaged as a result of poverty, lack of English-speaking ability, and undeniable racial prejudices, [the children] will become permanently locked into the lowest socio-economic class (*Plyer v. Doe*, 1981, p. 207).

Many of the issues considered in the Supreme Court's *Plyer v. Doe* opinion seem pertinent to central aspects of Proposition 187. Indeed, Chief Judge Matthew Byrne, Jr., of the Federal District Court in Los Angeles issued a temporary restraining order prohibiting the State of California from implementing Proposition 187. One of the suits filed claims that "Proposition 187 violates the Supremacy Clause of the United States Constitution, which grants the federal government the exclusive power to regulate immigration. The suit also asserts that the measure violates the 14th Amendment's due process guarantees by denying benefits without equal protection by encouraging discrimination against persons who appear or sound 'foreign,' and by denying education to children, in blatant violation of the Supreme Court's binding ruling in *Plyer v. Doe* (1982)" (MALDEF, 1994, pp. 1-2).

Even as Proposition 187 faces a long legal battle, it is likely that other states, including Arizona, Florida, and Texas, will follow the California example and enact similar laws in the near future.

What are the likely consequences of Proposition 187?

Proposition 187 will not add any resources to control the United States' international borders. Control of U.S. borders is a responsibility of the Federal Government. Therefore, the State of California cannot have its own border control agenda independent of federal policy. Proposition 187 will not add any new equipment or border patrol agents along the Southern border.

Although Proposition 187 bills itself as the "Save Our State" initiative, there is some evidence to suggest that it may end up drowning the state. According to data provided by the independent office of California's Legislative Analyst, Proposition 187 may have devastating fiscal effects. The Legislative Analyst states,

The most significant fiscal effects of the initiative fall into the following three categories,

-Program Savings. The state and local governments (primarily countries) would realize savings from denying certain benefits and services to persons who cannot document their citizenship or legal immigration status. These savings could be in the range of $200 million annually, based on the current estimated use of these benefits and services by illegal immigrants.

-Verification Costs. The state, local governments and schools would incur significant costs to verify citizenship or immigration status of students, parents, persons seeking health care or social services, and persons who are arrested. Ongoing annual costs could be in the tens of millions of dollars, with first-year costs considerably higher (potentially in excess of $100 million).

-Potential Losses of Federal Funds. The measure places at risk up to $15 billion annually in federal funding for education, health and welfare programs due to conflicts with federal requirements. (Proposition 187; Analysis by the Legislative Analyst, p. 52)

In the words of Pat Dingsdale, President of the California State PTA, Proposition 187 "took a bad situation and made it much worse—$10 billion worse! Meanwhile, Proposition 187 does absolutely nothing to beef up enforcement at the border or crack down on employers who hire undocumented workers" (Proposition 187; Rebuttal to Argument in Favor of Proposition 187). It is possible that the economic effects of Proposition 187 may be highly counterproductive—surely erasing any short-term savings. There will also be costs associated with prosecuting those who refuse to report undocumented immigrants.

Given that there are no studies to support the assertion that immigrants come to California to plug into the welfare system, it is doubtful that, as its proponents predict, most new undocumented immigrants settled in the United States will return home as a result of Proposition 187. Furthermore, since many families are "mixed" in having both legal and undocumented members—a U.S.-born child is a "legal" while there may be a Mexican-born undocumented child—it is very unlikely that a significant number of such "mixed" families will pick up and return to Mexico. Furthermore, the recent devaluation of the Mexican peso by 40 percent and the economic crisis in that country make it very unlikely that families will return *en masse*.

Proposition 187 requires school districts to verify the legal status of students in California. By January 1, 1996, the legal status of parents or guardians must also be verified by the schools. It is estimated that over 400,000 students could be expelled from California's public schools under the new law. Undocumented migrants will also be barred from attending community colleges, the California State University System, and the University of California System.

Under Proposition 187, undocumented immigrants are ineligible for all public health services, except for emergency medical care. (Undocumented immigrants are already ineligible for welfare programs.) State officers responsible for providing health, welfare, and public education services are required under the new law to report, "suspected" undocumented immigrants to the United States Immigration and Naturalization Service (INS). The costs associated with implementing these programs could be very high.

There may be additional costs associated with medical problems. There are preliminary reports that undocumented immigrants are now even more hesitant to obtain medical aid for fear of being reported to the INS. Some fatalities that could have been prevented have already been reported. As people fail to receive proper medical attention, serious—and, incidentally, much more costly—medical problems are likely to develop. Germs, unlike laws, do not discriminate: unvaccinated undocumented children will be equally contagious to citizens and immigrants alike.

Other costs, which cannot be easily measured in dollars and cents, will surely be paid. Given its vagueness, it is likely that the law would turn every immigrant (legal and undocumented), every person with an accent, every "foreign looking" person into a "suspect." This is likely to engender suspicion and mistrust, especially in a state with a large foreign-born population.

There is also the troubling issue of turning teachers, school personnel, health practitioners, and administrators into agents of the INS. If fully implemented, it is not clear whether these professionals—bound by their own professional code of ethics—will comply with their new responsibilities to report suspected undocumented immigrants to the INS. If non-compliance becomes a serious issue, there could be substantial costs associated with prosecuting and punishing professionals who refuse to obey the law. Furthermore, non-compliance would undermine the argument that undocumented immigration is undesirable—regardless of whether undocumented immigrants are a plus to the economy and to society at large—if for no other reason than by the fact that their very presence in the United States engenders contempt for the law.

There are reports that Proposition 187 has worsened the terror of "being caught" among undocumented immigrants. Proposition 187, if fully implemented, will surely engender a much wider circle of fear, from the ever-feared INS or *migra*, to teachers, school personnel, doctors, and nurses. It will reactivate and accentuate issues of marginality and shame, particularly among vulnerable undocumented immigrant children.

Immigration in the Western world today has all the features of a full-blown hysteria: fact and fantasy have become hopelessly intertwined, generating a great deal of anxiety and rage. As in all hysterias, the current concern is out of proportion to the actual threat. The terror that every growing "wave" of undocumented migrants and refugees are rushing to "flood" the shores of the more developed world is out of proportion to what is happening in reality. The United States today attracts only a small portion of the worldwide population of immigrants and refugees. Doris Meissner, the current INS Commissioner, wrote in 1992, "Whether motivated by economic or political reasons, or a mixture of both, the vast majority of migrants remain within their own countries. The next largest share move across national boundaries within the less-developed world, and a relatively small share cross the borders to industrially advanced states" (Meissner, 1992, p. 66).

Melanie Klein elaborated the theory that we need others to contain our anxieties and focus our destructiveness (the "bad object"). Likewise, throughout much of history the Western world has had its need for "Others." At various times the Muslim world has been Europe's "outer Other," and Jews have been its "inner Other." More recently, following the great atrocities of the Holocaust, the Western world saw the Soviet Union assume the place of the "Evil Empire." The Soviets, of course, played the role of the "bad guys" quite well. Indeed, during the Cold War the Soviet Union became a container of our anxieties and hatred. With the collapse of the Soviet system, the most recent container that kept our anxieties and sense of purpose in focus was broken. We are now looking for another container. We are, once again, in need of strangers: immigrants, mothers-on-welfare, gays—be aware.

REFERENCES

Ayres, B. D. (1994a, November 11). Curb on aliens dims dreams in Hollywood. *New York Times*, p. A28.

Ayres, B. D. (1994b, November 17). Court block new rule on immigration. *New York Times*, p. A16.

Borjas, G. (1994). Tired, poor, on welfare. In N. Mills (Ed.) *Arguing immigration: The debate over the changing face of America* (pp. 76–80). New York: Simon & Schuster.

Brimelow, P. (1992, June 22). Time to rethink immigration? *National Review, 44,* 30–42.

Brinkley, J. (1994, October 15). California's woes on aliens appear largely self-inflicted. *New York Times*, p. A1.

Brownstein, R. (1994, November 19). Wilson proposes US version of Prop. 187. *Los Angeles Times*, p. A1.

Chavez, L. (1994a). Immigration politics. In N. Mills (Ed.) *Arguing immigration: The debate over the changing face of America* (pp. 31–36). New York: Simon & Schuster.

Chavez, L. (1994b, December 9). More Mexicans, more profits. *New York Times*, p. A33.

Cleeland, N. (1994, November 17). Judge puts hold on most of Prop. 187. *San Diego Union-Tribune*, p. A1.

Clinton, W. J. (1995, January 15). State of the union address. *Boston Globe*, p. A1.

Cornelius, W. (1993, July 12). Neo-nativist feed on myopic fears. *Los Angeles Times*, p. B7.

Cowley, G., Murr, A., & Miller, S. (1994, December 5). Good politics, bad medicine. *Newsweek, 124* (23), 31–34.

del Olmo, F. (1995, January 31). Open the door to Mexican workers. *Los Angeles Times*, p. B7.

Dollard, J., Miller, N. E., Mower, O. H., & Sears, R. R. (1939). *Frustration and Aggression*. New Haven, Conn.: Yale University Press.

Dunn, A. (1994, October 30). In California, the numbers add up to anxiety. *New York Times*, p. D3.

Feldman, P. & McDonnell, R. (1994, November 14). Prop. 187 sponsors swept up in national whirlwind. *Los Angeles Times*, p. A1.

Feldman, P. & Rainey, J. (1994, November 17). Parts of Prop. 187 blocked by judge. *Los Angeles Times*, p. A1.

Fierman, J. (1994). Is immigration hurting the US? In N. Mills (Ed.) *Arguing immigration: The debate over the changing face of America* (pp. 67–75). New York: Simon & Schuster.

Francese, P. (1994). Aging America needs foreign blood. In N. Mills (Ed.) *Arguing immigration: The debate over the changing face of America* (pp. 85–89). New York: Simon & Schuster.

Freud, S. (1930). *Civilization and its discontents*. (Ed. and trans. by J. Strachey). New York: W. W. Norton.

Fromm, E. (1973). *The anatomy of human destructiveness*. New York: Henry Holt.

Glazer, N. (1994). The closing door. In N. Mills (Ed.) *Arguing immigration: The debate over the changing face of America* (pp. 37–47). New York: Simon & Schuster.

Huddle, D. L. (1993, July). *The costs of immigration.* Washington, D.C.: Carrying Capacity Network.

Klein, M. & Riviere, J. (1954). *Love, hate, and preparation.* New York: W. W. Norton.

Kohut, H. (1972). Thoughts on narcissism and narcissistic rage. *Psychoanalytic Study of the Child, 27,* 360-400.

Kristeva, J. (1991). *Strangers to ourselves.* New York: Columbia University Press.

MALDEF (Mexican American Legal Defense and Educational Fund) (1994, November 16). *Temporary restraining order granted against Proposition 187.* News Release.

McCarthy, C. (1994). *The crossing.* New York: Knopf.

McDonnell, P. (1994, November 20). Complex family ties tangle simple premise of Prop.187. *Los Angeles Times,* p. A1.

McDonnell, P. (1994, November 26). Health clinics report declines after Prop. 187. *Los Angeles Times,* p. A1.

Meissner, D. (1992). Managing migrations. *Foreign Policy, 86,* 66-83.

Mills, J. (1994a). Blacks vs. browns. In N. Mills (Ed.) *Arguing immigration: The debate over the changing face of America* (pp. 101–42). New York: Simon & Schuster.

Mills, J. (Ed.) (1994b). *Arguing immigration: The debate over the changing face of America.* New York: Simon & Schuster.

Mitchell, S. A. (1993). Aggression and the endangered self. *Psychoanalytic Quarterly, 62,* 351–82.

Noble, K. (1994, November 11). California immigration measure faces rocky legal path. *New York Times,* p. B20.

Passel, J. (1994). Immigration and taxes: A reappraisal of Huddle's "The cost of immigrants." Washington, D.C.: The Urban Institute Press.

Pear, R. (1994, November 27). Deciding who gets what in America. *New York Times,* p. D5.

Plyer v. Doe: Appeal from the US Court of Appeals for the fifth circuit. (1981). October Terms of the United States Supreme Court.

Proposition 187 (1994). *Illegal aliens. Ineligibility for public services. Verification and reporting. Initiative statute.* Sacramento, Calif.: State of California.

Rodriguez, L. (1994, December 3). View of reaction to Proposition 187. *Houston Chronicle,* p. A33.

Rothstein, R. (1994). Immigration dilemmas. In N. Mills (Ed.) *Arguing immigration: The debate over the changing face of America* (pp. 48–66). New York: Simon & Schuster.

Sanger, D. (1995, January 18). Mexico crisis seen spurring flow of aliens. *New York Times,* p. A3.

Sherwood, B. (1994, November 27). California leads the way, alas. *New York Times,* p. D11.

Sontag, D. (1993, July 25). Immigrants forgoing citizenship while pursuing American dream. *New York Times,* p. A1.

Suárez-Orozco, C. & Suárez-Orozco, M. M. (1994). The cultural psychology of Hispanic immigrants. In T. Weaver (Ed.), *The handbook of Hispanic cultures in the United States: Anthropology* (pp. 130–67). Houston, Tex.: Arte Publico.

Waldinger, R. (1994). *Black/immigrant competition reassessed: New evidence from Los Angeles.* Unpublished doctoral dissertation, University of California, Los Angeles, Los Angeles., CA.

Weiner, T. (1993, June 13). On these shores immigrants find a new wave of hostility. *New York Times*, p. D1.

Western Europe's nationalists: The rise of the outside right. (1994, October 15). *Economist, 333* (7885), 68–70.

Wolf, D. H. (1994, December 9). "The Rae and Parker study of undocumented alien fiscal impact: How accurate?" *Testimony to the Immigrant Hearing and Public Forum of Bill Morrow*, Assemblyman, Seventy-Third District. Oceanside City Hall, Oceanside, Calif.

Wolf, D. H. (1998). Undocumented aliens and crime: The case of San Diego County. La Jolla, Calif.: Center for U.S.-Mexican Studies, University of California, San Diego.

Wood, D. (1994, November 22). California's Prop. 187 puts illegal immigrants on edge. *Christian Science Monitor*, p. B2.

Giving Birth to the Dream: Realizing a Multiethnic, Multiracial Nation

Rhonda Rios-Kravitz

You may write me down in history
With your bitter twisted lies,
You may trod me in the very dirt
But still, like dust I'll rise.

Out of the huts of history's shame
I rise
Up from a past that's rotted in pain
I rise

Bringing gifts that my ancestors gave,
I am the dream and the hope of the slave.
I rise
I rise
I rise.

Maya Angelou, from the poem "And Still I Rise"

United States history, as it relates to immigration, is "rooted in pain" a pain that today sears the lives of our newcomers who come predominantly from the Caribbean Basin, Central America, Mexico, and Southeast Asia. The faces of our newcomers are no longer predominantly white European as they were at the turn of the century. And sadly today, many newcomers find out very quickly that race matters. As our past mirrors, immigration and race are still very contentious topics, especially now that the numbers of newcomers approximates the large numbers that came to the United States at the turn of the century.

This chapter will examine the anti-immigration legislation in California and the key role librarians play in bridging cultures and affirming diversity. Librarians, through leadership and institutional will, can work to assure that all people, regardless of immigrant status, have a right to information in our local, state, and national public libraries.

In California, the anti-immigrant, anti-ethnic sentiment has reared its head through state initiative/propositions, such as Proposition 187 (November 1994), which would have denied public services to undocumented immigrants but was for the most part struck down in the courts; Proposition 209 (November 1996), which passed and eliminated preferences for women and minorities in the assignment of state government contracts and admission to state universities; and Proposition 227 (June 1998), which will ask voters to end bilingual education as we know it today.

It is ironic, that although we define ourselves as a nation of immigrants and pride ourselves on our ethnic identities, we do not critically look back at our history. This history shows a nation of immigrants victimized by a backlash of opposition and anti-immigrant legislation.

In California, the issue of immigration is not new, nor is the animosity experienced by immigrants. In fact, that animosity is as old as the state and when one examines the state's history one can argue that the anti-immigrant rhetoric of the past was an outgrowth of economics and race.

California's history began auspiciously in 1849 when delegates at the California Constitutional Convention unanimously approved a provision guaranteeing the bilingual publication of the state's laws in English and Spanish. They also adopted an amendment that stated "neither slavery nor involuntary servitude, unless for punishment of crimes, shall ever be tolerated in the state" (Garcia, 1997). However, that "positive" attitude would soon end.

In 1850–1851, the U.S. government negotiated eighteen treaties with the California Indians. Under these treaties the Native Californian Indians relinquished all rights and claims in exchange for 8.5 million acres. However, the California U.S. senators objected and eventually only 624,000 acres of largely worthless land was reserved for the Native Californians.

In 1879, a statewide referendum asking Californians to oppose continued Chinese immigration passed with 94 percent of the vote. The motto of the Workingman's Party of California at the time was "The Chinese Must Go." The Party also called the Chinese "the most debased order of humanity known to the civilized world" (Amott & Matthaei, 1991). In 1882 the Chinese Exclusion Act was passed. This federal law terminated and prohibited the Chinese from becoming citizens. The only purpose of this act was for racial exclusion. In 1907, the United States and Japan signed the "Gentlemen's Agreement" barring unskilled Japanese from entering the United States. Several years later in 1913, California passed the Alien Land Law. This act prohibited land ownership by immigrants ineligible for naturalized citizenship and thus effectively excluded the Japanese immigrants. In 1942, 120,000 people of Japanese ancestry, two-thirds born in the United States, were interned in camps as the result of Executive Order 9066 signed by Franklin Roosevelt.

Persons of Mexican ancestry, too, have long suffered the effects of racism and immigrant scapegoating. During the 1910s, as a result of the labor shortages created by World War I, between 11,000 and 22,000 migrant workers came each year from Mexico to work in the United States. By the 1920s that number had risen to 50,000 each year. However, when the Great Depression hit, Mexican and Chicano workers were faced with joblessness and racism as the White population blamed them for their continued unemployment. In 1929, the United States established the Border Patrol, making it a felony to enter the United States illegally. Between 1925 and 1929 more than 400,000 people of Mexican ancestry, including U.S. citizens and their children were repatriated back to Mexico. In Los Angeles County alone, over 12,000 people were "repatriated" to Mexico in fifteen "repatriation trains." During World War II, labor shortages again opened the border and Mexican workers were admitted into the United States under the Bracero Program. This program continued through 1964, way beyond the end of the war. Growers and other employers were able to keep the program renewed for decades after the war ended, hiring Mexican laborers to work in the fields for low wages and under poor working conditions. In the early 1950s the country experienced another economic downturn and the federal government mounted "Operation Wetback." One million undocumented immigrants were sent back to Mexico in 1954, which included "suspected" immigrants who were citizens of the United States. Thus, the border opened and closed as the need for labor rose or declined.

In 1965, rioting broke out in the city of Watts, California. Thirty-four people were killed and residents, mainly African Americans decried the poor economic conditions and mistreatment by Whites. The same year, César Chávez and the Filipino grape pickers went on strike for higher wages.

In 1974, Allan Bakke filed a reverse discrimination suit after being denied admission to the University of California Medical School in Davis. In 1978, on a 5–4 vote, the U.S. Supreme Court ruled that quotas were illegal but said that race could still be used as factor when evaluating applicants for admission.

In 1986, Californians approved Proposition 63, the "English Only" initiative that preserved "the role of English as the common language." In 1995, the University of California Board of Regents voted to end affirmative action based on race or gender in admissions, hiring, and contracting. Governor Pete Wilson issued a legislative order dismantling affirmative action programs in state government.

In January 1998, a state appellate court gave Governor Wilson the authority to cut off prenatal care for more than 70,000 undocumented immigrants.

Given this history, what is the responsibility of libraries and librarians? The Services to Latinos Round Table (SLRT) of the California Library Association (CLA) decided to respond to Proposition 187, which could have had a horrendous impact on school libraries, and wrote a resolution that was passed by CLA, with editorial changes, on November 15, 1994. The resolution "resolved that the California Library Association supports in principle, legal challenges to the implementation of Proposition 187 in California" (CLA Assembly, 1994). In taking this position, SLRT and CLA reaffirmed that every person, regardless of immigration status, should be assured access to librar-ies—public, academic, special, school—without fear of reprisals.

Proposition 187 denied undocumented immigrants their rights to public schooling, nonemergency health care, and welfare and would have required all service providers to report "suspected illegal aliens" to California's Attorney General and to the Immigration and Naturalization Service. Personnel in school libraries and academic libraries, as service providers, could have been called on and/or required to report "suspected illegal aliens." This philosophy flew in the face of California's libraries attempts to respond positively to the state's increasing ethnic and racial diversity.

Californian librarians working with the various ethnic library caucuses have long argued that people of color are likely to approach or see a library with a great deal of suspicion. Proposition 187, had it not been fought in the courts, very likely would have enhanced even more strongly the fears of peo-ple of color, and new immigrants, legal or illegal, and made it more difficult for any library to play a key role in helping to bridge different cultures and languages.

Sadly, on November 8, 1994, 59 percent of California's voters approved the passage of Proposition 187. Of those voting, 75–80 percent were White, 10 percent were African American, 8–10 percent Latino, and 4–5 percent Asian American. California is 57 percent White, 25 percent Latino, 9 percent Asian American and 7 percent African American. The median age of the voter was fifty. The White aging population that voted was not representative of people of color, of legal immigrants, or of youth.

In 1994, the defenders of Proposition 187 argued that economic worries were, once again, reasons to deny immigrants service. Jane McCammon, a Contra Costa volunteer, in qualifying the proposition for the ballot, stated: "We have a massive unemployment rate. We have people with no benefits. We have college graduates who can't find a job. We've got too many prob-lems to continue to allow a large number of illegal and legal immigrants into this country" (Chance, 1994).

Immigrants, particularly Latino immigrants, are being scapegoated for California's economic woes. If deportations, such as those that occurred in the 1930s and the 1950s of Mexican immigrants, are to be avoided, it is impera-tive that we as librarians speak with others against unjust immigration policies.

McCammon's statement included one of the most politically charged myths that continues to surround the issue of immigration today; namely that the fiscal impact of immigrants is negative. However, the prestigious, non-profit Washington, D.C. Urban Institute reported in May 1994 that immigrants pay $30 billion more in taxes every year than they receive in benefits and ser-vices. This study also found that 2 percent of immigrants reported receiving welfare as compared to 3.7 percent of the native-born U. S. population. In ad-dition, the number of jobs that immigrants take from native-born Americans was trivial (Study, 1996).

The study by the Urban Institute validated an earlier study by the Tomas Rivera Center (TRC) entitled "How Much Do Immigrants Really Cost?" The

TRC study found that immigrants actually generated $12 billion to the state and $28 billion to the nation as a whole. The TRC also released a report in March 1994, which showed that the report most often used to support the theory that immigrants drain the economy, Donald Huddle's "The Net Cost of Immigrants to California," was flawed, methodologically unsound, and misleading. The Huddle study reported that in the year 1992, 11.8 million legal immigrants cost the government $45 billion above the taxes they paid. However, Jeffrey Passel and Rebecca Clark of the Urban Institute, who were commissioned by the TRC, stated in the TRC report:

1. The study assumed that immigrants who enter the United States after 1994 pay absolutely no taxes.

2. Huddle's projections of the future immigrant population assumed that no immigrants would die or leave the country after 1992.

3. Huddle consistently overestimated the number of immigrants by 27 percent, 2.7 million people—estimating that the United States is home to 4 million undocumented immigrants.

4. Huddle ignored the positive economic impact of immigrants, including benefits from consumer spending and immigrant-owned businesses.

5. Huddle misinterpreted previous research and claimed an extremely large displacement of native workers by immigrants that is not supported by the data.

6. Huddle failed to consider tax revenues generated by immigrants, particularly in the form of FICA taxes, property taxes, and revenues generated from licenses and fees.

7. In calculating the cost of immigrants to the state, Huddle used a ratio formula. That is, if 10 percent of the population is immigrants, then immigrants account for 10 percent of the costs of entitlement or benefit programs. Huddle applied this proportionate cost model regardless of age or eligibility characteristics of immigrants for the various programs, which affects their program utilization. (Passell & Clark, 1994)

Sadly, Proposition 187 reminds us that racism is more serious than many would like to admit. The continuing acrimonious public debate over anti-discrimination policies and the ongoing incidents of racially motivated violence all belie the notion that racism is declining. Jeff Lustig and Dick Walker wrote: "Proposition 187 draws on the state's worst traditions of racism and nativism to scapegoat illegal immigrants for California's current economic and social ills" (Lustig & Walker, 1995).

However, it is too simplistic to attribute the current debate about immigrants to economics alone. This analysis prevents us from looking critically at the historic inequalities, long-standing stereotypes, and scapegoating that have been part of California's and the nation's history. The economic arguments mask the need for serious discussion on race in America. It is important to note that concerns about the ethnic composition of California are also at work.

For at the same time that defense cutbacks and a recession have produced a massive economic upheaval, so too has California undergone a rapid demographic change. In 1998, when California is experiencing a robust economy, anti-immigrant propositions such as Proposition 227, the anti-bilingual initiative, still continue to surface and suggest that race does matter!

The story of California, like other states, is one of change. California has become increasingly diverse, culturally and linguistically. By the turn of the century there will be no single majority ethnic or racial group. From 1970 to 2000, California's White population will have gone from an 80 percent majority to a less than 50 percent plurality. In California today, White pupils are already a minority. Latinos account for 31.4 percent of public school enrollment, African Americans 8.9 percent, and Asians approximately 11 percent. In San Jose, bearers of the Vietnamese surname Nguyen outnumber the Jones'.

California was built by a very diverse group of people. Many urban cities can point to neighborhood communities populated with ethnic/racial populations that have lived in California for generations. In the twenty-first century, Latino and nonwhite racial and ethnic groups in the United States will outnumber nonLatino Whites for the first time. The idea that the typical U.S. citizen, as someone who traces her/his descent in a direct line to Europe, will be out-of-date and inaccurate. Today, the United States is a microcosm of the world and that is good news.

Yet during hard economic times, it seems people are always eager to blame others and to see the growth of the immigrant population as a clear and present danger. Mario Cuomo, in an article entitled "Why Have Immigrants Become Scapegoats" (Cuomo, 1993) speaks to the experiences of immigrants and the need to keep "open the golden door" and the need to "help the immigrants and in turn be helped by them." He wrote:

I was born in South Jamaica, Queens, of immigrant parents. Everyone in that neighborhood came from somewhere else. I thank God this country didn't say to them, 'We can't afford you. You might take someone's job, or cost us too much.' I'm glad they didn't ask my father if he could speak English, because he couldn't. I'm glad they didn't ask my mother if she could count, because she couldn't. They didn't go to school a day in Italy. I'm glad they didn't ask my father what special skills he bought to this great and dynamic nation; because there was no special expertise to the way he handled a shovel when he dug trenches for sewer pipe. I'm glad they let him in anyway.

What is to be done? How do we rise and keep open that golden door despite a past rooted in pain? The year 2000 is fast approaching, and as a country and a state, we are still faced with the question of how we become a nation that values and acknowledges the contributions of all ethnic and racial groups and how we become a nation that does not scapegoat immigrants.

Henry Cisneros has spoken of the raw energy that immigrants have brought to his country. In a stirring speech to librarians he stated:

I think that these numbers (population diversity) say something very powerful, and what they say is that to me; the issue of how we treat minorities has now transcended a civil rights question. It's no longer a question of living up to our national ideals, it's no longer a question of doing our duty of compassion and charity, it's no longer a question of following civil rights laws, it's become much more basic than that. I think it really is, at some point, a question of survival for our country. (Cisneros, 1988)

Fortunately, Proposition 187 was not enacted into law. Immediately after its passage immigrant rights groups, including the American Civil Liberties Union (ACLU) and the Mexican American Legal Defense and Education Fund (MALDEF), sued in the courts. A preliminary injunction was issued in December 1995 and barred the enforcement of most of the provisions in the Proposition. In granting the injunction, U.S. District Court Justice Mariana Pfaelzer said California could not deny federally funded service though it could refuse to spend its own money on undocumented immigrants (for example, prenatal and long-term care for the elderly). In November 1997, Judge Pfaelzer again ruled that most of Proposition 187 was unconstitutional. The only sections that were left intact were sections 2, 3, and 10, which dealt with the criminal aspects of illegal immigration. In her decision, she once again concluded that federal welfare law preempted the implementation of the provisions of Proposition 187.

However, the spirit of Proposition 187 was not dead. Governor Wilson invoked the new welfare reform law in his effort to deny prenatal care to undocumented women. Although immigrant rights groups filed suit, a state appellate court gave Governor Wilson the authority to cut off prenatal care for more than 70,000 undocumented immigrants in January 1998.

The welfare reform act, P.L. 104–193, the "Personal Responsibility and Work Opportunity Reconciliation Act of 1996" was signed into law by President Clinton on August 22, 1996. It too had devastating provisions for immigrants. For current legal immigrants, there is a ban on their receipt of Social Security Insurance and food stamps. States have the option to provide or bar state funded programs for current and new immigrants. New immigrants are barred from federal means-tested benefits for five years. After the five-year bar, new immigrants that have sponsors must include their sponsors' income when applying for federal means-tested benefits, until the immigrant attains citizenship or ten years of work. States also have the option to determine current immigrants' eligibility for Temporary Assistance for Needy Families (TANF), Medicaid, and Social Services Block Grants (SSBG) for new immigrants after the five-year bar. Undocumented immigrants are ineligible for federal, state, and local public benefits.

In March 1998 a survey was conducted by the Boston-based Physicians for Human Rights among Latino and Asian American legal immigrants at inner-city clinics and community centers in California, Illinois, and Texas. They found "an alarmingly high prevalence of food insecurity and hunger." This human rights group urged the restoration of food stamp benefits to legal immigrants (Branigin, 1998).

The assault on immigrants continues. Thus, it is critical that librarians continue to raise their voices and be a strong force advocating for the rights of all people.

Local, state, and national library organizations must model values that uphold multiculturalism. People living in the United States should be able to point to our libraries as one way of showing how we as a nation can acknowledge the contributions of all people.

Libraries play an important role in providing information to enable immigrants to function effectively in society. As institutions, libraries have worked hard to ensure that immigrants, regardless of national origin or language fluency, have equitable access to all services and programs.

California, through its State Library, Legislative Declaration, Education Code, Section 19300 (1977), reflects the efforts of libraries to value diversity. The Code states that the mission of California's public libraries is to serve as:

a supplement to the formal system of free public education, and a source of information and inspiration to persons all ages, and a resource for continuing education and reeducation beyond the years of formal education.

The State law also states:

It is in the interest of the people of the state that all people have free and convenient access to all library resources that might enrich their lives, regardless of where they live. The public library is a primary source of information, recreation, and education to persons of all ages, any location or any economic circumstance. (California Library Services Act, 1997)

This mission statement, although specifically addressing public libraries, is also valued by academic, school, and special libraries. As library professionals we need to provide leadership on a state level and ensure that the policies that govern our state library organization proactively affirm the goals of multiculturalism and clearly affirm the rights of individual users to use libraries regardless of race, ethnicity, or immigrant status. Without clear leadership from librarians individually, and collectively as a professional organization, the needs of immigrants and their use of library facilities and services, will become lost in highly politicized battles over immigration and affirmative action.

Libraries need to be able to distribute information to immigrant families about their legal rights, including enrolling children in schools regardless of immigration status. As librarians, we need to assure that every immigrant child is guaranteed a comprehensive education, including access to public, school, and academic libraries without fear of reprisals. Libraries must also continue to:

1. build and network resource materials for immigrants, including resources in the native languages of our immigrant;

2. initiate links with schools to provide tutoring services;

3. offer ESL and literacy instruction programming;

4. offer space for job training programs for adults;

5. provide an environment that is supportive of diversity and free from prejudice and harassment;

6. intensify efforts to provide a more adequate understanding of the information needs of the state's ethnic and racial populations;

7. adopt effective planning and evaluation techniques for library services to the state's ethnic and racial populations;

8. build collections that reflect the cultural backgrounds and histories of our immigrant populations;

9. proactively recruit, retain, and advance people of color into the profession;

10. provide life long learning opportunities for all people; and

11. show an institutional will and leadership that supports a democratic sensibility and warns against the politics of exclusion.

Our survival as a profession is rooted in our success and commitment to diversity. It is also rooted in how successful we are at becoming a vital institution for all people, regardless of race or ethnicity. We must speak with a clear and loud voice against the cynicism and scapegoating that prompts initiatives like Proposition 187, Proposition 209 (the anti-affirmative action initiative), and the upcoming Proposition 227 (the anti-bilingual initiative). We as professionals have a responsibility to "Save Our State" in antithesis to Proposition 187, and stand for a vision that embraces hope and maintains "The Dream." In the words of Maya Angelou:

> History, despite its wrenching pain,
> Cannot be unlived, but if faced
> With courage, need not be lived again.
>
> Lift up your eyes
> Upon this day breaking for you.
> Give birth again
> To the dream....
>
> Here on the pulse of this new day
> You may have the grace to look up and out
> And into your sister's eyes,
> And into your brother's face,
> Your country,
> And say simply
> Very simply
> With hope—

"Good morning" (Angelou, 1993)

Now is the time to demonstrate our institutional will with hope and affirmation, and join the public debate supporting multiculturalism and diversity.

Our libraries need to be places that promote critical exchange and broad reflection. It is time, not only to say "Good Morning," but also "Good Afternoon" and "Good Evening" to all with dignity and respect.

APPENDIX: CALIFORNIA LIBRARY ASSOCIATION ASSEMBLY RESOLUTIONS ON PROPOSITION 187 AND AFFIRMATIVE ACTION

WHEREAS, the California Library Association (CLA) and Services to Latinos Round Table (SLRT) support the principles enumerated in the Library Bill of Rights; and

WHEREAS, CLA and SLRT support literacy and lifelong learning; and

WHEREAS, CLA and SLRT support the delivery of library services to all individuals in California's diverse communities; and

WHEREAS, CLA and SLRT provide leadership in the promotion improvement of library services and librarianship;

THEREFORE BE IT RESOLVED, that the California Library Association supports in principle, legal challenges to the implementation of Proposition 187 in California.

WHEREAS, The California Library Association (CLA) has valued diversity in its mission statement; and

WHEREAS, CLA has recognized the research which shows that while the United States workforce is increasingly diverse and progress has been made toward the elimination of discrimination and exclusion in the workplace, research has also showed that the rate of change has been discouragingly slow and that barriers to the advancement of people of color continue to exist on three levels: societal, internal, an governmental; and

WHEREAS, CLA has affirmed the recruitment, hire, and advancement of people of color into the profession; and

WHEREAS, CLA has targeted scholarships and mentorships to assist this process; and

WHEREAS, CLA has affirmed the advancement of people of color into management and decision-making positions;

THEREFORE BE IT RESOLVED that as we approach the year 2000, CLA values and acknowledges the benefits, resources, and contributions of all ethnicities and racial groups; and

RESOLVED that we represent a diverse and dynamic constituency and through our library institutions (public, school, academic, and special), we shall facilitate our users ability to interact effectively and work productively with multicultural populations; and

RESOLVED that the workforce diversity is a high priority and that aggressive steps still need to be taken in the recruitment, hiring, and advancement of people of color in the library profession; and

RESOLVED that affirmative action programs are essential to correcting the past and improving the future; and

RESOLVED that CLA remains committed to affirmative action programs and scholarships to assist people of color and remains committed to enhancing such programs; and

RESOLVED that CLA strongly opposes anti-affirmative action legislation and initiatives and reaffirms its commitment to affirmative action; and be it further

RESOLVED that there is a need to address the issues that underlie the causes of inequality and discrimination and that libraries can assist users, educators, institutions, businesses, and governmental organizations in finding information about the issues that underlie the causes of inequality and discrimination.

REFERENCES

Amott, T. L., & Matthaei, J. A. (1991). *Race, gender & work*. Boston: South End Press, p. 203.

Angelou, M. (1993). *"And still I rise."* *On the pulse of the morning*. New York: Random House.

Angelou, M. (1993). "Good Morning." *On the pulse of the morning*. New York: Random House.

Branigin, W. (1998, May 11). Food stamps for legal immigrants urged. *Sacramento Bee*, p. A4.

California Library Association Assembly. Resolutions on Proposition 187 (1994, November 15). Anaheim, Calif.

California Library Services Act (1997). *California Education Code*, Section 18701.

California State Library. Legislative Declaration (1997*). California Education Code*, Section 19300.

Chance, A. (1994, March 20). Long history of economic, racial fears. *Sacramento Bee*, p. A23.

Cisneros, H. G. (1988). Keynote address by Mayor Henry Cisneros. In N. Jaco (Ed.) *A state of change: California's ethnic future and libraries. Conference and awareness forum proceedings*. Stanford, Calif., pp. 27–45.

Cuomo, M. (1993, October 24). Why have immigrants become scapegoats? *Sacramento Bee*, p. F3.

Garcia, P. (1997, October 26). Race, ethnicity and conflict in California's history. *Sacramento Bee*, p. A13.

Lustig, J. & Walker, D. (1995). *No way out: Immigrants and the new California*. Berkeley, Calif.: Coalition for Human Rights and Social Justice.

Passell, J., & Clark, R. (1994, March). *Faulty immigration studies mislead policymakers and inflame anti-immigrant sentiment*. Washington, D.C.: Urban Institute; Pomona, Calif.: Tomas Rivera Center.

Study: Immigrants help U.S. economy. (1996, May 25). *Sacramento Bee*, p. A6.

4

Mexican/Latino Immigrants and the Santa Ana Public Library: An Urban Ethnography

Susan Luévano-Molina

A review of the literature reveals an absence of research conducted by library professionals within Mexican/Latino immigrant communities to determine their perceptions of the public library and how, if at all, current or proposed anti-immigration legislation has impacted library usage. This information is important not only because it makes clear the role that libraries play as mediating sites of learning and cultural acquisition, but because it presses the notion that the United States is an open and democratic society. Moreover, the issue provides librarians an opportunity to address societal conditions central to the lives of immigrant communities that will dominate the demographic landscape in California within the next twenty years.

This article summarizes the findings of an ethnographic study conducted in Santa Ana, California, a highly immigrant predominantly Mexican community in central Orange County, during a period of high anti-immigrant sentiment and nativist legislation. This research provides an examination of the immigrant Mexican/Latino communities' perceptions and experiences with the Santa Ana Public Library. The results of this work and the Knox (Chapter 5 of this volume) study provide public libraries with recent data, gathered and analyzed from a distinctly public library perspective.

BACKGROUND

Santa Ana is a low-income and primarily working-class city located thirty miles south of Los Angeles, California. This city occupies 27.1 square miles right in the center of Orange County. It is home to one of the largest concentrations of Mexicans living in the United States with a population over 100,000 and is noted for having the highest concentration of Spanish speakers in the state (Baxter, 1998). In the Santa Ana Unified School District, the county's largest, three-fourths of the students speak limited English. This densely populated urban community accommodates 10,839.2 persons per square mile or approximately 4.28 persons per family.

Santa Ana has long served as the county seat. Federal and county offices provide employment to a daily influx of workers and county residents who then leave the city shortly after working hours. These federal and county facilities are the only reason most non-city residents would consider entering Orange County's inner city. The very Latinized city of Santa Ana provides a sharp demographic and cultural contrast to the more affluent and more ethnically balanced surrounding cities of Irvine, Orange, Anaheim, and Tustin.

Santa Ana, like many other California cities, was transformed by the post-1965 wave of primarily Mexican immigrants.[1] Following kinship patterns, entire families and in some cases entire communities from particular regions of Mexico have settled in the city. In 1990, Santa Ana had an official population that was 65 percent Hispanic. This estimate is considered low given the high numbers of undocumented residents that were not enumerated in the last census.[2]

White flight accompanied the rapid increase of Mexican immigrants to the city starting in the early 1970s. By the late 1970s the city had adopted some clear policies of accommodation to the newcomers. Starting in the late 1970s the city required bilingual skills of all newly hired public services personnel. More interestingly, the city embraced a policy of ignoring the immigration status of its residents except when specific federal or state program regulations mandated restricted access. Philosophically the city has embraced the need to serve all residents irrespective of immigration related concerns. This position is maintained to this day.

Within the last fifteen years the debate over immigration has increasingly occupied the center of political, cultural, educational, and social debate in California. Santa Ana, despite its enlightened municipal policies, was not immune to the backlash against immigrants created by the dramatic population increases of the last twenty-five years, the politically conservative Reagan and Bush years, and the deep recessionary period of the early 1990s.

Seemingly unrestrained immigrant bashing calling for the rejection and ejection of Latino immigrants, both legal and undocumented, and the fortification/militarization of the southern borders with Mexico have been the wedge issues of the last several electoral campaigns (Cornelius, 1996). English Language Only, the "Save Our State Initiative," known as Proposition 187,[3] Proposition 209, the so-called "Civil Rights Initiative," which eliminated affirmative action considerations from state contracting and educational admission programs, along with allegations of "non-citizen" (read "naturalized immigrant") voter fraud, have been loudly and viciously voiced, and in most cases, voted upon in the Golden State.

An important sociopolitical aspect of this research is the fact that Orange County is home to the creators of the highly nativist legislation passed by California voters in 1994, commonly known as Proposition 187. The county remains the national center of this controversial but popular xenophobic movement (Chavez, 1997). Orange County is also prominent nationwide for its past colorful and conservative legislators such as Rep. Robert Dornan, Rep. Dana Rohrbacher, and Rep. William Dannameyer. In addition, a conservative voting bloc has historically made Orange County a safe haven for support and implementation of Republican policies.

The study discussed here was conducted in 1996, two years after the passage of Proposition 187. It was designed to explore perceptions about the public library and library use patterns among Spanish-speaking adult immigrants. More specifically, the study was focused on gathering the opinions, attitudes, and experiences of community participants since November of 1994 when California voters approved Proposition 187. This state legislation and other federal legislation targeting immigrant populations, both undocumented and legal, did not directly mention public libraries. However, it was of interest to the principal investigator to understand and document any unforeseen effects on Latino immigrants' perceptions or use of public library services during this potent anti-immigrant period and in the heartland of the nativist movement.

RESEARCH OBJECTIVES

The research objectives included but were not limited to the disclosure and description of the following:

1. Mexican/Latino immigrants' perceptions of the public library.

2. Mexican/Latino immigrants' public library usage.

3. How perceptions of the public library may be similar or dissimilar to the dominant culture.

4. How library usage may be similar or dissimilar to the dominant culture.

5. The Mexican/Latino communities' awareness of recent and proposed anti-immigrant legislation, for example, Proposition 187.

6. Whether or not the participants had been deterred from using the public library because of growing anti-immigrant sentiments or recent legislation.

7. Level of concern regarding possible future anti-immigrant legislation that might someday prevent Mexican/Latino immigrants from using public libraries.

8. The refinement and expansion of ethnographic methods in conducting library research.

METHODOLOGY

This study was based on ethnographic interviews conducted with Mexican/Latino immigrants residing in the City of Santa Ana. The interviews were composed of open-ended questions, targeting 50 Spanish-speaking Mexican/Latino immigrants, including 25 men and 25 women. The fieldwork was conducted between January 1996 and November 1996 at local elementary schools, neighborhood markets, on street corners where men wait for work, in public plazas, and private homes.

Study participants were selected using a snowball sample technique[4] and from on the spot contact with strangers. All interviews were conducted within a three-mile range of a library facility or bookmobile stop to ensure that access to a public library was not a factor in the informant's potential lack of use or exposure to a public library facility. All participants were required to be residents of the city and at least eighteen years old.

The full scope of the project was explained to the informants before beginning the interview process. Confidentiality of the discourse was stressed. Potential interviewees were instructed that there were no right or wrong responses. They were also made aware that declining to answer a question(s) was always an option. All respondents were provided contact information so that they could ask follow-up questions or concerns. Participation in the study was contingent on the verbal consent of the informant.

Ethnographic research requires constant feedback from one stage to another. Preliminary findings were shared with members of Reforma[5] beginning in August 1996. The study findings have continued to be examined and challenged by other librarians specializing in library services to Latinos. Revisions and further analysis have followed these sessions.

Ethnography

An ethnographic approach was selected in an effort to gather reliable in-depth data. This unique methodology offered a format in which complex cultural and social factors could be equated into an assessment that gave shape and meaning to library attitudes and use factors. Ethnographic research attempts to map or construct meaning through cultural description and analysis. Thus, in explaining or constructing meaning from field notes, one can extract a shared framework of a community to formulate theories about what is happening and then translate these ideas to a larger audience, in this case, the library community.

Ethnography acknowledges the connecting of a distinct set of social practices with a certain place, (for example, using the local public library) because it has been given or has acquired a social profile or identity. The institution under scrutiny then becomes a representation for a distinct culture or way of life. To connect the public library with anti-immigrant legislation brings new dimensions of meaning to bear on our understanding of what these two variables represent for Mexican/Latino immigrants. This method of community study allowed the investigators to map a full range of feelings, tensions, and lived experiences that describe the social reality.

Ethnographic research required that the primary investigator physically enter the Mexican/Latino immigrants' world. All interviews were conducted on community turf, in public areas, or in home visits. This close range approach added tremendously to the rich cultural context in which the queries took place. This investigative approach was also preferred for its populist selection of informants. Common ordinary people were provided the opportunity to express their viewpoints and experiences. The gatekeeper approach (Metoyer-Duran, 1993), valuable in other settings, was deemed inappropriate for this study given that the clandestine immigration status of many respondents' would have made it difficult to gather representative members of this community in a more formal setting.

Ethnography also allowed for comments to be gathered and analyzed in the language of the informants. Language structured field notes and entered into every analysis and insight. The use of the Spanish language, the predominant language of Santa Ana, greatly enhanced rapport and confidence during encounters with informants.

Lastly and most importantly, this research method provided for an understanding of the interconnecting relationships between ideology, power, culture, and social practice. Culture could be analyzed using the lived experiences and behaviors that are the result of the unequal distribution of power and resources along lines such as ethnicity, class, and gender. Ethnography allowed the investigator to study the imposition of anti-immigrant legislation, which reflects the dominant societies' values in this locale, as well as the subsequent antagonistic relations and the resistance that has emerged as a response to this domination.

Open-Ended Interviews

The respondent interview format was designed to create a profile of the informant along with extended open-ended questions about the various study topics. The format was designed by the principal investigator with assistance from cultural anthropologist, Dr. ChorSwang Nign.[6] The University Research Office, California State University, Long Beach, provided oversight in the development of the open-ended questions. Special effort was made to protect the identity of the human subjects involved in the study given that many of the informants were undocumented immigrants or what is commonly called *sin papeles*. Consequently, they were not asked to sign a formal consent form nor required to have their interview taped, if they felt uncomfortable.

The interview questions were created in English and translated into Spanish by professional translators. The six part instrument included a:

1. Detailed introduction to the research process and consent of the participant;

2. Personal background information;

3. Awareness of the public library;

4. Awareness of anti-immigrant legislation;

5. Correlation between anti-immigrant legislation and public library use/perceptions; and

6. Statement of closure.

The investigator filled out a post-evaluation for each completed session.

The interviews were administered in Spanish, unless the respondent preferred to speak in English. Bilingual/bicultural librarians, and selected community members using appropriate anthropological data gathering techniques of observation, engagement, and dialogue conducted the interviews.

Data gathering was incredibly labor intensive and could not have been achieved without the assistance of a highly skilled research team.[7]

A taxonomic analysis followed the data gathering stage. That is, a set of categories were determined and organized on the basis of a single articulated relationship. The taxonomy revealed subsets and the way in which these subsets were related to the overall project. This form of evaluation enabled the primary investigator to determine thought, value, and action patterns.

Fieldwork

Capturing the many voices of Santa Ana's Mexican/Latino immigrants was a challenge. The summary qualitative and quantitative data provided here are reflective of the informants who trusted us with their stories, experiences, and opinions. While a few residents declined the request to participate, most generously gave their time.

The primary investigator had extensive previous knowledge and involvement within the Santa Ana Latino community. Luévano-Molina, was born and raised in Santa Ana, worked at the Santa Ana Campus of the Rancho Santiago Community College, Nealley Library, for fourteen years, and had also conducted a community analysis study for the Santa Ana Public Library in the early 1980s. Nevertheless, the fieldwork required a great deal of time in the community. The research team hung out at bookmobile stops, elementary schools, community centers, shopping centers, donut shops, and corners where men wait to work.

The population that was least receptive to participation was undocumented Latina homemakers with children. We discovered that some women were uncomfortable discussing matters that they perceived as potentially injurious to the well being of their families and their residency in the United States. This was despite the fact that snowballing was used to identify potential interviewees.

While we did encounter other Latina homemakers who agreed to participate and whose immigration status happened to be undocumented, this example illustrates the element of fear that is pervasive in communities of out-of-status persons living in the United States. This apprehension has been heightened by the anti-immigration rhetoric of this period that specifically targets children and spouses (Chavez, 1997, pp. 70–72). The fact that women and children enhance the chances of settlement and cultural reproduction in the United States makes them increasingly vulnerable to nativist attacks.

The research team also encountered numerous surreal situations during the process of conducting interviews in public locations filled with people. For example, once someone ran frantically through the crowd shouting *Migra!*[8] Everyone momentarily froze knowing that if such a raid occurred Immigration and Naturalization Service (INS) agents might arrest anyone who looked "foreign," often times disregarding the stated immigration status of the suspect. When it was clear that the alarm was false everyone nonchalantly returned to whatever they were doing.

At our most successful research site, a donut shop where immigrant men gathered daily to network and socialize before going to work, participants related that police harassment was a constant threat. One of the study participants was recently beaten for no apparent reason by local police officers right next to the donut shop where our interviews regularly occurred. This group of men provided a blow-by-blow description of the altercation as a police patrol car parked within ten feet of the donut shop observing our conversations and the dramatization of the attack.

These experiences provided the backdrop or context in which we conducted our fieldwork. They were both real and symbolic of the everyday stress that Latino immigrants, regardless of their immigration status, are subjected to. They represent the typical experiences that connect the individual immigrant to the wider social reality of the immigrant community.

FINDINGS

The participants were typically young, primarily low-income, and working class. Although one respondent had arrived as recently as the day previous to the interview, others had resided in Santa Ana for over forty years. The participants averaged 8.8 years of residency in Santa Ana. The majority of participants were of Mexican origin (88 percent) while the remaining respondents (12 percent) were from Central and South America.

Spanish was the predominant language of the informants. Many noted excellent verbal skills in Spanish but limited writing and reading skills. Only a handful of respondents indicated complete biliteracy in Spanish and English. Among those informants who were bilingual there was a definite preference for communicating in Spanish. Only two of these bilingual participants preferred to be interviewed in English even though they were fluent Spanish language speakers. In all but a few cases there was a direct correlation between complete language fluency and years of education attainment.

The informants reflected a young population. The 18–29 cohort was the largest at 32 percent, followed by the 30–39 group at 30 percent. Consequently, the under forty cohorts represented 62 percent of the total sample. The over forty respondents comprised 32 percent of those interviewed; the 40–49 age-group at 18 percent; 50–59 age-group at 14 percent; and the over 60 age-group at 4 percent. A small number of participants, 2 percent, declined to divulge this information.

As noted earlier, Mexicans are the predominant ethnic migrant population in Santa Ana. States of Mexico that were widely represented included Michoacan (21 percent), Guerrero (17 percent), and Jalisco (15 percent). Participants from other Central and Latin American countries cited El Salvador, Guatemala, and Ecuador as their native home.

Income was low for all respondents regardless of educational attainment, gender, immigration status, fluency in English, or length of residency in Santa

Ana. Most respondents could be categorized as working poor. Only 32 percent made more than $10,000 per year. This finding is consistent with other
social science studies that indicate Latinos in urban and suburban areas experience disproportionately high poverty rates and that these rates are evident even
in the third generation after settlement in the United States (Hayes-Bautista,
1994, p. 4). Informants were more likely not to answer this question than any
other inquiry raised in the interview process. Twenty-six percent of interviewees stated that they did not know their income or declined to answer (20 percent).

The educational characteristics of the informants are intriguing as they
serve as the pivotal indicators of potential library use (Berelson, 1949; Marchant, 1991; Scheppke, 1994). The participants' educational attainment was
low by mainstream standards. However, they reflect the educational norms of
Mexico where the average length of schooling is 6.6 years (Monsivais, 1997).
Some 12 percent had less than three years of education; 36 percent had completed elementary (in Mexico this includes 6 years of formal education known
as *primaria*) 26 percent had completed *secundaria* or high school; 20 percent
were college graduates, and 10 percent had attended professional schools.

Slightly over half of the participants were citizens or legal residents, 12
percent and 42 percent respectively. Almost half (46 percent) of the participants were undocumented residents. Another 2 percent of the informants identified themselves as having the unique status known as political asylum.

All respondents were asked why they came to the United States. Only a
handful came to this country as infants or children. The majority, male and
female, responded similarly to José, a two-year resident of the city who works
for a landscape company:

I am here to seek the improvement of my children and the security of my own future.
Here I can work and make more money than in Mexico. In Mexico there is no opportunity for a better tomorrow.

High awareness of the Santa Ana Public Library was documented. The
majority of the participants had very positive impressions of the city library
system even though half of the participants had never entered a public library
or bookmobile in Santa Ana. Perceptions of the library as a sacrosanct, almost
utopian institution were similar for all participants regardless of generational,
class, gender, or ethnic lines. Marisela, a young woman who worked in a gro-
cery store and dreams of someday attending college, stated:

The public library allows anyone who wants to move forward, to take out books and
study. It makes me happy that children have the library to use for their studies. The
library is like gold. This service makes us all (the community) feel closer.

Arturo, a three-year resident of Santa Ana from Michoacan who works in
a tire repair shop and has little formal education stated simply and eloquently
that, "A library in the community always improves people's humanity." This
type of awareness and regard for the public library is similar to findings in

more mainstream populations (D'Elia & Rodger, 1995, 1996; Estabrook, 1997; Institute for the Future, 1996).

A fascinating revelation was the high use of public libraries in the home country among current Santa Ana Public Library users.[9] This finding was completely unexpected as the library literature reveals little about the development of the Mexican public library system. Mexican library users were primarily from urban areas but even participants from less developed regions had some exposure to a public library.

Nearly half (48 percent) of the participants had personally visited a library or bookmobile in Santa Ana. Of those using the library over half felt that neither the passage of Proposition 187, or more recent nativist legislation or pending legislation had deterred them in any way from using the public library. Library use among those who identified themselves, as undocumented was 33 percent. All but one of these out-of-status library users self-identified as Mexican. An impressive 36 percent of all respondents had Santa Ana Public Library user cards as compared to an estimated 10 percent to 28 percent for the general population (Berelson, 1949; D'Elia & Rodger, 1995, 1996; Estabrook, 1991).

Conversely, this finding supports the California study conducted by the Institute for the Future (1996) that indicates that Hispanics and Asians are the heaviest public library users in the state. Among library cardholders 16 percent noted that the entire family had valid library cards. Households with school age children were most likely to use the public library. Hüero, a ten-year resident of Santa Ana, whose entire family has library cards, noted that:

It makes me so happy that my children are anxious to go to the library. We go once a week. They can't wait! The kids have an opportunity to study and to enjoy learning. It is a time when the whole family can be together and relax in a pleasant environment.

Only two residents noted great displeasure with the public library. One was a highly educated naturalized citizen with a law degree who had lived in the United States for thirty-one years. He found the public library a cold and uninviting institution. Furthermore, he stated that the public library was lacking in materials of interest to him. The second disgruntled library user was a female head of household who until recently was a regular library user. She was upset about overdue book charges. This informant indicated that she would not use the library again for fear of accruing further debt.

Virtually all study participants were knowledgeable about the fall 1994 passage of Proposition 187. There was high awareness of related anti-immigrant legislation and current events regarding Latino immigrants. For example, numerous respondents cited the highly televised car chase and beatings of non-resisting undocumented immigrants by San Bernardino police in April 1996 and the pending vote on Proposition 209, a California ballot initiative designed to outlaw state affirmative action programs. This high level of political awareness was consistent among all informants regardless of their length of residency in the United States, age, gender, income, or immigration status. Most noted the excellent coverage of these issues on Spanish language radio and television along with their own increasing apprehension about the immigrant backlash as reasons for their attention to these issues.

The overwhelming majority of respondents (88 percent) felt that if Proposition 187 were implemented, it would negatively affect them and their families, regardless of their immigration status. Participants stated that they would continue to be stigmatized by their obvious physical and/or cultural characteristics. The dehumanization and criminalization of Mexican/Latinos, whether legal or "illegal," by the majority population was an acknowledged fact among the participants. An 18-year-old gardener named Carlos who has lived in the United States for eleven years, said:

I understand how racism works. They discriminate against us simply because we are Latinos. They think we are all criminals. Yet, we are the ones who clean their houses, work in the fields, or clean floors. No White person would do that. It all comes down to racism, again and again, racism against Latinos.

The informants considered this discriminatory behavior irrational, unjustifiable, and hypocritical. Long hours, low wages, and the completion of menial or low-skilled labor allow the interviewees to feel a sense of worth, accomplishment, and pride in their daily lives. They noted that their sense of entitlement to community services such as the public library was due to what they felt they had contributed to the community as a whole by their personal labor and through their taxes. Rebecca, a nanny for a family in Irvine, put it this way:

We are the same as everybody else! We have the right to use the library, the parks, and the schools. I work hard taking care of other people's children, day in and day out, so that my children will have a better future. Besides I pay my taxes. I think that public information should be made available on an impartial basis to help the community.

The strongest emotional reactions were displayed when informants were asked to comment on the possibility of future restricted access to the public library based on immigration status. Half the respondents indicated that they would never stop using the Santa Ana Public Library. Even informants who had never used a public library before indicated that, if need be, they would find some way to use the facilities. As Efren, a middle-aged father and twenty-year resident of Santa Ana, who had never personally used the library, phrased it,

I will never stop using the public library. It is the only way I have to provide affordable entertainment and distractions for my children. I would be very mad if anyone in this community were denied entrance. It would be un-American! Here in the United States citizens and residents of this community have the same rights. But what do I know? I believe that if this happened it would be due to prejudice against Latinos. We have to fight against these kinds of restrictions! It would not be just to let this happen.

Over half the participants did not feel that their immigration status had anything to do with their use or lack of use of the SAPL. Most respondents noted strong sentiments regarding the library as a neutral, tax-supported space that should be available to all city residents regardless of immigration status. As a college educated Salvadorean nurse named María who presently works as a domestic and is raising a son born in the United States told me:

Knowledge belongs to everyone. It is a human right to study in a library without restrictions. I have paid taxes and worked hard in this country. I am very proud of the little that I have. I really think that everyone in the community would and does benefit from having the public library. I would never stop using it unless they permanently closed it.

Many immigrants cited how they use the public library. The primary responses were either for their own life-long learning, to assist their children in completing school assignments, or for recreational purposes. The presence of school age children in the household was the indicative characteristic of potential library use. Respondents with dependent youths increased their library use to supplement educational and recreational materials in the household. A similar finding was noted in New Jersey (Riskind, 1992). In this study low-income communities with large numbers of dependent children had higher rates of library use than higher income communities with lower rates of dependent youth.

Despite the fact that many participants expressed increased anxiety when using the public library, given the prevailing anti-immigrant mood in Orange County, 95 percent of the library users stated that they had not noticed any difference in treatment at any permanent library facility or bookmobile stop since the 1994 passage of the "Save Our State Initiative." Isabel, a forty-year resident and longtime library user said,

The library staff is always helpful and courteous. I have not noticed any differences at all in the way I am treated. I have to admit that I was nervous about using the library after Prop. 187. Many people think that all Mexicans are illegals. So you never know how people will treat you.

SIGNIFICANCE OF THE STUDY

Findings of the Santa Ana case study challenge many existing research conclusions about Hispanics as a whole and Mexican immigrant populations, in particular. First, Mexican immigrants are very much aware of the public library and hold it in the same high esteem, if not higher, than as the normative population. The library as an institution is a signifier of hope in the Mexican community. It symbolizes the proverbial "equal playing field" so often discussed in other diversity debates. The public library is perceived as creating the preconditions for social mobility and equal opportunity. Informants feel comfortable stating that they can go to their local public library, for self or family improvement and low-cost entertainment. As one 25-year-old male informant from Michoacan who had arrived in Santa Ana the day previous to our interview and was returning to the city for the second time stated, *la bib-*

lioteca es una fuente de oportunidad (the library is a center for opportunity). While the studies of the Institute for the Future, Estabrook, and D'Elia and Rodger do not query participants about their immigration status, their research suggests that minorities, particularly low-income users, appreciate the library more than the mainstream population (D'Elia & Rodger, 1996; Estabrook, 1997; Institute for the Future, 1996).

Immigrants lack of exposure and access to public library systems in their home countries is considered "common knowledge" in the library field (Institute for the Future, 1996; Padilla, 1991). However, among the informants who had used the public library there was a high number (50 percent) who had been library users in Mexico.

It should be noted that the Mexican public library system has experienced tremendous growth in the last decade and a half. Between 1982 and 1992 over 4,000 new public libraries have been established (Magaloni, 1993). These figures represent a 1,000 percent expansion of libraries in approximately ten years. These libraries serve over 71 million Mexican readers in urban and rural areas of Mexico. Their rapid development has depended on the help and support of local communities. Mexican public libraries, which are highly centralized, have been integrated in the cultural fabric of many communities that twenty years ago had no facility.

Many of the younger respondents who had resided in the United States less than fifteen years and regularly return to their home country had benefited from Mexico's budding national library system. This finding suggests the emergence of transnational migrant library users. As immigrants continue to relocate to the United States, public libraries should expect that the number of transnational migrant library users who reside in Mexican immigrant communities will continue to increase.

The ramifications of Mexican immigrants' appreciation of libraries and exposure to libraries in their home countries cannot be overstated. Further analysis of these findings are critical to understanding how immigrants may become connected to a new home country and how they may begin to feel comfortable and accountable to their adopted place of residency. As newcomers arrive from Mexico will they seek out the library in greater numbers assuming their past positive experiences in the home country? Can transnational migrant's library use patterns be sustained if appropriate staff and materials are not provided? How might transnational migrants who are also library users be persuaded to openly demonstrate their support for public libraries? Additional research is needed to document the development of this emerging trend.

The profile of the Mexican immigrant library user is very different from the dominant society (Luévano-Molina, 2000). The results of this case study indicate that educational achievement is not a key factor in determining library use. Participants using the library had an average of six years of education. This finding runs contrary to other recent adult user studies (D'Elia & Rodger, 1995, 1996; Estabrook, 1997; Institute for the Future, 1996).

Also notable is the low-income status of the participants. Income is another key factor used in determining potential library usage and is closely linked to educational achievement (Scheppke, 1994). If anything, the low-income status of the participants appears to have contributed to increased public library use in Santa Ana. Many respondents noted a lack of discretionary money was the main reason that they used the library. Reading and watching videos provide low-cost enjoyment for many residents in Santa Ana who have few other entertainment options.

Virtually every respondent possessed detailed knowledge of Proposition 187 and awareness about other current pending nativist legislation. Terms such as "racist" and "discriminatory" were often used to describe the motivation behind these political actions. Undoubtedly, a side effect of the anti-immigrant movement has been the rising political consciousness of Mexican/Latino immigrants. Study findings suggest that this politicalization process has occurred irrespective of gender, class, educational attainment, age, immigration status, or ethnicity. Whether this awareness will lead to constructive social agency among the immigrant community remains to be demonstrated and analyzed.

However, recent indications are encouraging. Latinos voted en masse against Proposition 187 in 1994 and Proposition 209 in 1996. More recently Latino parents have rallied against Proposition 227, which would effectively eliminate bilingual education in the state of California. Their vocal demonstration of support for bilingual education encouraged a vote of the Santa Ana Unified School Board district against the initiative that will be decided on June 2, 1998. From a community perspective, all of these initiatives are viewed as anti-immigrant and anti-Latino.

In the highly contested 1996 election of Rep. Loretta Sanchez over long-time incumbent Rep. Bob Dornan in the 38th Congressional district, which includes Santa Ana, Latino voters tipped the scales in favor of the Latina candidate. In addition, the number of immigrants who are currently applying for citizenship has risen dramatically in Santa Ana and the state. Hermandad Mexicana Nacional, a Santa Ana-based immigrants rights group, helped thousands of legal residents become citizens and registered about 1,300 voters before the November 1996 election.[10] Analysts attribute this surge to the current anti-immigrant rhetoric and legislation that has limited or eliminated entitlements for legal immigrants. Another interesting development that may also contribute to U.S. citizenry is the newly approved nationality clause of the Mexican constitution. This amendment will allow millions of Mexican-born citizens to maintain their nationality rights even if they choose to become naturalized U.S. citizens. As the law is retrospective, even naturalized U.S. citizens and their children are now eligible to reclaim their Mexican nationality. Mexican nationals enjoy the right to own property, work, and/or invest in the country; voting is not permitted. Besides easing the facilitation of business ventures and the transnational movement of people, observers predict that the law will encourage the number of Mexican citizens who choose to become U.S. citizens.

According to Raul Hinojosa, a UCLA political scientist,

The U.S.-Mexican immigration situation is huge and unique in the world. Never has there been such an influx of people with so many remaining ambiguous about losing their old nationality. This resulted in part from reasons of identity, in part from a feeling that they were not really welcome (in the U.S.) and that their votes didn't matter and to a certain extent, that they would feel like traitors to Mexico. All of these have been swept away in recent years. People here are realizing a resurgence of identity. (Smith, 1998, p. A8)

Hinojosa also noted that, "the Mexican government has become more open and accepting of the importance of the Mexican people living in the United States and has been treating them with more respect" (Smith, 1998, p. A8).

The Mexican nationality issue may play itself out in two areas. The possible increase of U.S. citizenship has already been discussed. The second vast area of consequence is the increasing number of transnational communities that will root themselves in two countries and continue to have large stakes in both.

Most respondents felt that anti-immigrant legislation would negatively impact the Latino community as a whole by limiting employment, health services, and future opportunities for children, regardless of their immigration status. This sentiment was expressed across ethnic, gender, class, immigration, and generational lines. This perception implies one distinct community rather than multiple groups.

This notion of community identity irrespective of immigration status or national origin is a relatively new development. While outsiders may view Latinos as a monolithic group there are actually distinct cultural groups within the Mexican community that are based on acculturation patterns, generational, regional, and class differences. Undocumented immigrants are often at the bottom of this ethnic stratification.

The racialized position of Latino immigrants in Orange County and specifically in Santa Ana has forged a vision of *la comunidad* that is inclusive of all Latinos, regardless of immigration status. The notion of difference or an "Other" among informants was practically nonexistent. Results of the Santa Ana study manifest a remarkably consistent sense of unity between Latino citizens, legal residents, and undocumented persons. This notion of a unified community has been forged more from the shared oppression of the anti-immigrant movement, than from cultural commonalities.

Participants who currently use the public library expressed some anxiety about using the facility and particularly about asking for assistance. This attitude was documented among informants regardless of their immigration status. This apprehension indicates that Mexican/Latino immigrants are apprehensive about contact with any public institution, even those such as the public library that has served them well in the past. The staff survey conducted by Knox (Chapter 5 of this volume) verifies Santa Ana Public Library staffs' impression that immigrants, in general, seem more hesitant to ask for assistance since the passage of Proposition 187. This wariness is the only negative impact on

Latino immigrant library users that was documented in both the ethnographic analysis and the staff survey.

A strong sense of communal rejection and erasure by the dominant society exists in the neighborhoods of Santa Ana. Despite this sense of alienation from the mainstream society the participants expressed a strong consensus regarding their ownership of the public library system in the community. Concerns about possible denial of library services to undocumented residents of the city brought expressions of indignation from both legal and undocumented respondents. Informants clearly desired that the public library remain a communal resource available to those who live, work, and contribute to the community. Many informants eloquently articulated the collective good that comes from an educated and well-informed community.

These attitudes provide further evidence that the public library fulfills a need for the positive reinforcement of the communities' cultural and educational activities. The library setting is perceived as an important social space for cultural reproduction and economic integration. These factors were important to all interviewees including those who had never used the library. This data must be correlated with the motivational factors that play a major role in the psyche of the respondents. The interviewed Mexican/Latino immigrants were most driven to achieve for themselves and their families but also constantly mentioned the forming of a positive social identity for the Latino community as a whole. Latino immigrants are inclusive in their vision of the "community" and focused on the positive effects of the public library on the community as a whole.

The participants in the study felt that as long as residents pay taxes they have a right to expect public services. The egalitarian position of the city of Santa Ana regarding the equal treatment of residents has clearly reinforced this belief among Latino residents even though it is not always consistently played out, for example police harassment. These sentiments are in sharp contrast to opinions of the dominant society. The 1990s anti-immigrant discourse on the local and statewide levels were rift with anger and resentment toward the newcomers who were credited with overloading and freeloading off an already overburdened system. Immigrants have been deemed less worthy of public services than other community members. To be an immigrant today is to be a burden or cost to society rather than an asset (Calavita, 1996; Perea, 1997; Urciuoli, 1996).

Respondents continually referred to the library as a neutral space, open to the entire community. This sense of neutrality is similar to the mainstream population and to other California library users as noted in the Institute for the Future study (1996). However, it must be stressed that the actual inclusion and incorporation of immigrant communities during this anti-immigrant period vary widely from municipality to municipality and state to state.

The Santa Ana Public Library collection, staff, and services received high marks from respondents who had used them. The quality and quantity of services, collections, and bilingual staff were mentioned constantly as the drawing card for community residents. Appreciation of the excellent facilities was also noted. Bookmobile services also received much praise from regular users.

It is very likely that the results of this case study would have been quite different if not for the dynamic multicultural nature of the library services, collection, and staff. The Santa Ana Public Library has done an outstanding job in reaching its majority population that is Mexican, highly immigrant, low income, and working class. The library provides appropriate services including large Spanish language collections, bilingual staff, after-school study centers, and continual outreach activities (Gonzalez, 1997). Children's services have the highest service priority given the large youth population of Santa Ana. The Santa Ana Public Library staff survey conducted by Knox (Chapter 5 of this volume) indicates a high level of commitment to and understanding of the community.

Library administration in Santa Ana is clearly focused on the foremost population it serves. The staff's high public services standards and regard for the community have been clearly transmitted to their users. Remarkably, the public services staff at the Santa Ana Public Library have made their substantially immigrant users feel accepted and well-served during a period of unprecedented immigrant bashing. The fact that this has occurred in the center of Orange County where these sentiments abound is quite astonishing.

The Santa Ana case study appears to contradict the findings of the Institute for the Future (1996), which documents a 50 percent decline in library use among predominate Spanish-speakers. In the case study described here Spanish monolingualism was never mentioned as a deterrent to using the public library. On the contrary, the local public library received commendation for its excellent Spanish language resources and bilingual staff. One must wonder if the Spanish-speakers involved in the Institute for the Future study had access to public libraries that provided similarly appropriate Spanish language collections and bilingual staff?

CONCLUSION

This study provides insight into a community that is highly visible throughout California, yet often not present in the public library. The study results offer the profession insight into the lived experiences of Mexican/Latino immigrants and how these immigrants regard the public library in an increasingly stratified and hierarchical political, economic, and social climate. The study reveals that the politics of inclusion can and will work for public libraries who are willing to affirm their commitment to providing appropriate services and staff to attract targeted users. Other public libraries should consider examining the many successful programs and services offered by the Santa Ana Public Library system.

The Santa Ana Public Library is one institution where Latino immigrants view themselves as interconnected to the existing social order and perceive themselves as equal members of the larger community. Their involvement with the public library contributes to their transition from sojourners to settlers in the United States.

The selected research methodology has provided an excellent tool for assessing the complex and multifaceted pulse of the Santa Ana immigrant community. The depth and breadth of the data collection and the ability to easily include common everyday people, particularly clandestine populations, made this methodology a wonderful choice for the study. However, the requirements for conducting ethnographic research are many. It demands a group of trained researchers, an extended study period, and many, many hours of fieldwork. Financial and institutional support are also necessary to complete this type of study within a reasonable time frame.[11]

The major implication of the study concerns the possibility of cultivating a new type of library user. These new and future library users will increasingly be Latino immigrants and their children, particularly in California. While they will maintain linguistically diverse capabilities in English and Spanish, the Spanish language will continue to dominate the everyday interactions of Latino migrants. These potential users will have a high regard for their community library, increased exposure to public libraries in their home country, and will use the library regardless of low educational achievement, low income, or immigration status, if needed services, bilingual staff, and Spanish language resources are provided and promoted. These users could be developed into loyal library supporters as the desire for positive cultural spaces that are distinctly Latino continues to grow. A transnational migrant library user prototype is emerging. These binational library users reflect the new global order that has become international in its economic and demographic structure (de la Pena Cook & Geist, 1995; Sommerville, 1995). The transnational features of migrating Mexican populations and the continuing maturation of the Mexican public library system will make this type of user more common in the decades ahead. Library and information science programs should develop research programs that emphasize the study of globalization on libraries. More immediately, a cross-cultural study comparing Asian immigrants in the United States with Latino immigrants would greatly inform the profession about the lived experiences of the two largest migrant groups.

The transnational nature of migrant communities, of any ethnic background, implies that these populations will not limit their sense of community to just one locale or one group. Rather, they will become adept at maintaining multiple identities that allow them to develop feelings of belonging to their local community without losing connection to their home country. This trend will continue as global restructuring continues to diminish the importance of nation-states.

The evidence gathered in this ethnographic research confirms that we must transform our understanding of Mexican immigrant library users as more, not less, likely to become avid library users and supporters. This assertion supports other recent opinion surveys in which minorities indicated a greater interest and support for the public library than their majority counterparts. Consider that despite the widely supported immigrant bashing and the draconian legislation of the last fifteen years, the Mexican/Latino population in Santa Ana remains adamant about their entitlement to and ownership of library services.

Other ethnographic studies conducted by Rocco (1997) and Rosaldo and Flores (1997) document similar findings in Los Angeles and San Jose, California. Although their research deals with Latino communities in a much broader social context they both documented

> a strong sense of membership in a larger Latino community that has the right to have access to major institutions, to being given a fair and equal opportunity for social and economic mobility, and to practice and maintain a strong continuity with the culture of their country of origin. (Flores & Benmayor, 1997, p. 19)

This well-defined sense of agency is a necessary factor in the future development of Latino community identity and solidarity.

The enigmatic issues surrounding the immigration debate show no signs of dissipating, nor does a drop in transnational migration appear eminent. Library policy makers must resist entering into the debate about the value or costs associated with immigrants in their communities. This discussion will only essentialize ethnic representation in the community. Rather, library decision makers should attempt to serve immigrants as an integral part of the general community. Library administrators must determine under what conditions they can provide appropriate services and negotiate shared concerns. They must find common ground for immigrant inclusion, community building, democratic decision-making, and empowerment.

NOTES

1. The most obvious cause of the increased number of immigrants to the United States was the 1965 Immigration Act amendments which abolished the country by country quotas and instead focused on family reunification. Political refugees from Vietnam and other Southeast Asian countries were admitted to the United States following the end of the Vietnam War. In addition, global restructuring made the United States a logical destination for displaced workers worldwide. Lastly, many immigrants have arrived "illegally," most of them over the U.S.-Mexican border.

2. The terms "undocumented," "out-of-status," or "*sin papeles*" refer to people who are in the United States without the proper immigration papers. These are the preferred terms used in this study, as they are not judgmental but descriptive and neutral. This is untrue of more value laden terms such as "illegal" or "wetback" which imply criminality, as well as other negative connotations (Kanellos, 1994, p. 180).

3. Proposition 187 passed by a 59 percent to 41 percent margin statewide. Whites constituted 75 percent of the voting electorate that voted in favor of the initiative. Almost 3 1/2 years later on March 18, 1998, Federal District Judge Mariana R. Pfaelzer ruled that the core provisions of Proposition 187 were unconstitutional. She based much of her decision on Congress' welfare reform bill, which placed restrictions on benefits to undocumented and legal residents. The congressional actions supported Judge Pfaelzer's conclusion that only the federal government can mandate immigration law.

4. Snowballing is a sampling technique used by ethnographers. It involves using the informants' own kinship and friendship networks as a basis for drawing a sample. For example, half of the participants were approached by a respondent who lived in the targeted neighborhood, was related or acquainted with the potential respondents, and whose undocumented status was known to them.

5. Reforma, the National Association to Promote Library and Information Services to the Spanish Speaking represents the interests of Latino communities across the United States within the library community. An affiliate organization of the American Library Association, Reforma's members are primarily librarians and library staff who serve Latino constituencies.

6. Dr. ChorSwang Nign is an Associate Professor of Anthropology at California State University, Los Angeles. She has conducted numerous ethnographic studies in the United States and Asia. Dr. Nign has published extensively in the field of cultural studies, anthropology, Asian, Asian American, and Chicano/Latino studies.

7. The research team was a highly trained group of bilingual and bicultural professionals. In addition, one undocumented community member was employed in the project.

8. *Migra* is the Spanish vernacular for the Immigration and Naturalization Service (INS) agents who make sweeps in neighborhoods where they suspect a high percentage of undocumented persons work or reside.

9. Participants were carefully queried at two points during the interview to be sure that they understood the difference between a library (*biblioteca*) and a bookstore (*libreria*), as these terms are often confused.

10. The success of Loretta Sanchez who won the election over Dornan by 984 votes was tied to alleged voter fraud by Hermandad Mexicana Nacional. A yearlong investigation by the Orange County Grand Jury in which the organization's image was badly damaged by charges that it orchestrated felonious voting among noncitizens vindicated both Hermandad Mexicana Nacional and Nativo L. Lopez, Executive Director of the Santa Ana-based organization.

11. Funding and release time for this study was provided by a California Library Association, Research and Publications Committee Grant and a California State University, Long Beach, Affirmative Action Faculty Development Award.

REFERENCES

Anderson, B. L. (1994). The library as community center. *Library Trends, 42,* 395–403.

Baxter, K. (1998, May 3). Angels making play for Latinos' business. *Los Angeles Times*, p . A1, A26–A27.

Berelson, B. (1949). *The Library's Public*. Westport, Conn.: Greenwood.

Calavita, K. (1996, August 1). The new politics of immigration: "Balanced-budget conservatism" and the symbolism of Proposition 187. *Social Problems, 43* (3), 284–305.

Chavez, L. R. (1988). Settlers and sojourners: The case of Mexicans in the United States. *Human Organization, 47,* 344–52.

Chavez, L. R. (1992). *Shadowed lives: Undocumented immigrants in American society.* New York: Holt, Rinehart and Winston, Inc.

Chavez, L. R. (1994). The power of imagined community: The settlement of undocumented Mexican and Central Americans in the United States. *American Anthropologist, 96* (1), 52 –73.

Chavez, L. R. (1997). Immigration reform and nativism: The nationalist response to the transnationalist challenge. In J. F. Perea, (Ed.) *Immigrants out!: The new nativism and the anti-immigrant impulse in the United States* (pp. 61–77). New York: New York University Press.

Cornelius, W. A. (1996, November 15). Economics, culture and the politics of cutting immigration. *The Chronicle of Higher Education,* p. B4.

Cornelius, W. A. & Hollifield, J. (1995). *Controlling immigration: A global perspective.* Palo Alto, Calif.: Stanford University Press.

County of Orange. CAO/Forecast & Analysis Center. (1992). City of Santa Ana. *U.S. Census Bureau. Summary Tape File 1, City & Community Profiles.* Santa Ana, Calif.: Author, 181–86.

County of Orange. CAO/Forecast & Analysis Center. (1992). City of Santa Ana *U.S. Census Bureau. Summary Tape File 1, Selected Housing and Household Characteristics.* Santa Ana, Calif.: Author, 153–250.

D'Elia, G. & Rodger, E. J. (1995). The roles of the public library in the community. *Public Libraries, 34,* 94–98.

D'Elia, G. & Rodger, E. J. (1996). Customer satisfaction with public libraries. *Public Libraries, 35,* 292–97.

de la Pena Cook, K. & Geist, P. (1995). Hispanic library services in south Florida. *Public Libraries, 34,* 34–37.

du Gay, P., Hall, S., Janes, L., Mackay, H. & Negus, K. (1997). *Doing cultural studies: The story of the Sony walkman.* London: Sage Publications.

Durrenberger, E. P. (1996). Ethnography. In *Encyclopedia of cultural anthropology.* Vol. 2, pp. 416–22. New York: Henry Holt and Company.

Estabrook, L. S. (1997, February 1). Polarized perceptions. *Library Journal, 122,* 46–48.

Flores, W. V. (1997). Citizens vs citizenry: Undocumented immigrants and Latino cultural citizenship. In W. V. Flores & R. Benmayor (Eds.) *Latino cultural citizenship* (pp. 225–277). Boston: Beacon.

Flores, W. V. & Benmayor, R. (Eds.) (1997). *Latino cultural citizenship.* Boston: Beacon.

Gonzalez, C. (1997, April 23). *Santa Ana Public Library services to Latinos.* Paper presented at the Reforma, National Association to Promote Library Services to the Spanish Speaking, Orange County Chapter Conference, Fullerton College, Fullerton, California.

Hayes-Bautista, D. E., Schink, W. O. & Rodríguez, G. (1994). *Latino immigrants in Los Angeles: A portrait from the 1990 census.* Los Angeles: Alta California Policy Research Center.

Horton, J. (1995). *The politics of diversity: Immigration, resistance and change in Monterey Park, California.* Philadelphia, Pa.: Temple University Press.

Institute for the Future. (1996, April). *Entering the 21st century: California's public libraries face the future.* Sacramento, Calif.: California State Library.

Kanellos, N. (1994). *The Hispanic almanac: From Columbus to corporate America.* Detroit, Mich.: Visible Ink Press.

Lamphere, L. (Ed.) (1992). *Structuring diversity: Ethnographic perspectives on the new immigration.* Chicago: University of Chicago Press.

Luévano-Molina, S. (2000). Ethnographic perspectives on transnational Mexican immigrant library users. In S. Güereña (Ed.) *Latino librarianship: A handbook for professionals* (pp. 169–80). Jefferson, N.C.: McFarland.

Magaloni, A. M. (1993). The Mexican library revolution: Taking books to the people. *Logos, 4,* 81–83.

Marchant, M. P. (1991). What motivates adult use of public libraries? *LISR, 13*, 201–235.

Metoyer-Duran, K. (1993). The information and referral process in culturally diverse communities. *RQ, 32*, 359–71.

Monsivais, C. (1996, August 25). The immigrants' view of education. *Los Angeles Times*, p. M2.

Padilla, A. M. (1991). *Public library services for immigrant populations in California.* Sacramento, Calif.: California State Library Foundation.

Portes, A. & Rumbault, R. G. (1996). *Immigrant America: A portrait.* 2nd ed. Berkeley, Calif.: University of California Press.

Riskind, M. (1992, Winter). Library use as an economic indicator. *New Jersey Libraries, 25*, 4–7.

Rocco, R. (1997). Citizenship, culture, and community: Restructuring in Southeast Los Angeles. In W. V. Flores & R. Benmayor (Eds.) *Latino cultural citizenship* (pp. 97–123). Boston: Beacon.

Rosaldo, R. & Flores, W. V. (1997). Identity, conflict, and evolving Latino communities: Cultural citizenship in San Jose, California. In W. V. Flores & R. Benmayor (Eds.) *Latino cultural citizenship* (pp. 57–96).Boston: Beacon.

Scheppke, J. (1994, October 15). Who's using the library. *Library Journal, 194*, 353–357.

Smith, J. F. (1998, March 20). Mexico's dual nationality opens doors for millions. *Los Angeles Times*, pp. A1, A8–A9.

Smith, M. P. (1992). Postmodernism, urban ethnography, and the new social space of ethnic identity. *Theory & Society, 21*, 493–531.

Smith, M. P. & Feagin, J. R. (Eds.) (1987). *The capitalist city: Global restructuring and community politics.* New York: Basil Blackwell.

Sommerville, M. R. (1995, February 15). Global is local. *Library Journal, 120*, 131–133.

Urciuoli, B. (1996). *Exposing prejudice: Puerto Rican experiences of language, race and class.* Boulder, Colo.: Westview Press.

5

Santa Ana Public Library Staff Perceptions of Immigrant Library Usage

Kenneth M. Knox

INTRODUCTION

This article reports on the findings of a staff survey conducted at the Santa Ana Public Library (SAPL) in July 1996. The purpose of the survey was to document the perceptions, experiences, and observations of library staffers serving Latino immigrant populations in the years immediately following the 1994 passage of the nativist California legislation known as the "Save Our State Initiative" or Proposition 187. This legislation which passed by a wide margin but was later ruled unconstitutional would have eliminated numerous social services to undocumented aliens. This survey was conducted in conjunction with a community ethnographic study (Chapter 4 of this volume). The study directed by Luévano-Molina was designed to determine perceptions and usage of the SAPL among Latino immigrants in the SAPL service area. Like the staff survey, the unique focus of the inquiry was to explore the impact of a strong statewide anti-immigrant movement on community users.

METHODOLOGY

In order to conduct the survey, a letter of explanation was sent to the library director in April 1996. The full support and cooperation of Library Director Rob Richards followed a meeting with the principal investigator. With this commitment, plans were made for the in-house survey to be created and distributed to all staff.

The principal investigator designed the survey instrument. It consisted of a cover sheet outlining the purpose of the survey and its relation to the Luévano-Molina community study. The cover sheet emphasized the significance of the survey, the grant-based funding, and the confidentiality of all responses. The survey consisted of eleven multiple-choice questions. A final twelfth question was open-ended.

The survey topics included queries on length of service, community contact hours, bilingual or multilingual skills, and impressions of usage patterns among the targeted study population. As previously mentioned, the final question was open-ended. Respondents were asked to share any comments or ideas regarding the questions posed in the survey.

The concept, timeline, and goals of the survey were presented at a full staff meeting prior to the distribution of the instrument. Copies of the instrument were distributed to all in attendance. A commitment was made by the primary investigator to return and provide a full report to the library staff on the results, analysis, and possible applications of the survey.

It was decided that the most efficient method of conducting the survey, presented as several stapled pages, was to let staff members complete it at their own leisure, rather than to administer it personally on a one-on-one basis or as a group. Two weeks were allowed for the staff to obtain, complete, and return the surveys.

The distribution, completion, and collection went very smoothly. A collection box was located in the staff lounge. The return rate exceeded expectations. Of the seventy copies distributed, a total of forty-eight were returned. Only two forms were invalidated due to damaged or lost pages. The survey findings were analyzed using the Statistical Package for the Social Sciences (SPSS). The findings were then compared with the qualitative data gathered in the Luévano-Molina study.

The staff survey was conducted in July 1996. It was initially planned to present the results to the Santa Ana library staff in September or October. However, it was not possible to present the survey results to library staff until November 1996. Again, the presentation was made at a full library staff meeting.

At this meeting, the survey findings were presented. In addition, a PowerPoint presentation by Luévano-Molina provided an executive summary of the ethnographic study. A question and answer period followed. Nearly all comments and questions during this session were positive and constructive.

Limitations of the Study

No distinction was made in the survey between public service library staff and those normally not in contact with the public although one question did survey whether the staff were "normally" in contact with non-English speaking patrons. Thus, the survey included staff whose duties did not normally include serving the public, and may have had little or no involvement with the issues in question. Fortunately, the survey results indicated that three-quarters of the respondents worked in public service positions.

Staff was asked to infer the background (immigrant status) of the targeted population. There may have been cases in which users who they assumed were immigrants were in fact longtime residents and visa versa. However, given the large immigrant population of Santa Ana the error rate was not expected to dramatically alter the study findings.

FINDINGS

In order to establish a profile of the staff respondents, the first several questions focused on staff demographics. Most respondents, 70 percent, were longtime workers. Only 39.6 percent were full-time workers. A large majority (74.2 percent) was bilingual in Spanish, followed by 16.1 percent Chinese speakers and another 9.7 percent who spoke other languages. The high rate of bilingualism was not surprising given the fact that bilingualism is a required skill in the City of Santa Ana for all public services positions. It should be noted that many staff noted multilingual skills. Among those identified as Spanish speaking, 74 percent reported that they served Spanish speaking patrons "very frequently." Consequently, almost without exception the Spanish speakers were public services staff working with a linguistically similar population.

The key survey question asked if the passage of Proposition 187 in November 1994 appeared to have had an effect on the willingness of immigrant patrons to approach library staff for assistance. The majority, 79.5 percent, of respondents reported that immigrants were "somewhat more hesitant" to ask for help since the passage of Proposition 187. In response to the inverse choice, no staff member felt that immigrant patrons were more likely to approach staff.

Interestingly, the amount of help requested by immigrant patrons does not appear to have changed significantly since the November 1994 passage of Proposition 187. A full 81.3 percent of staff agreed that the amount of assistance requested from the targeted population had not changed. In addition, approximately 59 percent of staff noted "no change" in the number of overall patrons using the library since the "Save Our State" approval.

The staff had fairly cohesive perceptions about how non-English speaking patrons were served: 76 percent felt that non-English speakers were served either very well or fairly well by the library. A large number of staff (83 percent) reported that they had regular formal and informal discussions about users' needs. There was a high awareness of specialized services targeting Latino immigrants.

Two types of comments were collected in the open-ended question at the end of the survey. The first general area most frequently mentioned was a commitment to library services to immigrant populations in Santa Ana. Many staff stated that neither the passage of Proposition 187 nor any other legislation would impede them from the delivery of library services to anyone desiring to use the community library. Second, many staff was offended that the survey even raised the possibility of restricted or limited service to the immigrant community given the strong public service policies of the library and the City of Santa Ana. It should be noted that the city has a policy of ignoring the immigration status of Santa Ana residents when providing public services except when the services in question are regulated by an outside funding source.

CONCLUSIONS

The primary conclusion established by the survey is that immigrant patrons are more hesitant to approach a SAPL staff person or to verbally ask for assistance since the passage of Proposition 187. The highly bilingual staff perceives that the target population's use of the library has not declined during or after the height of the nativist movement in Orange County. Furthermore, the collected data indicated staff's commitment to the immigrant community in the pre- and post-Proposition 187 era. The survey documented that staff are knowledgeable and sensitive to the political issues that have marginalized immigrants in recent years. Many staff indicated that they actively discuss methods of improving services to the targeted populations without prompting from the SAPL administration. Many staff felt slighted that their public service commitment to all library users might be suspect.

The ethnographic study conducted by Luévano-Molina (Chapter 4 of this volume) found that immigrant library users like the public library because they could not only converse with the staff in their native language but also find Spanish language resources. The study also indicated that the vast majority of Latino immigrant users had never encountered any feelings of unwelcomeness either before or after the "Save Our State" legislation. On the contrary, the study participants found the public library staff to be consistently warm and inviting.

Yet despite the many positive experiences of immigrant users documented in the qualitative study, Latino respondents noted an increased amount of anxiety when using the public library and especially when asking for assistance. They feared that the prevailing anti-immigrant mood of the county and state might impact the level of service they received. This finding was consistent among all Latino immigrant library users regardless of their immigrant status. This data was also in accord with staff's perception of the increased reluctance of non-English speaking users to ask for help at public service counters.

In conclusion, the Santa Ana Public Library staff at all organizational levels exhibits a strongly ingrained public service attitude. The commitment of these highly professional workers to traditional library values as noted in the Library Bill of Rights was validated in both the survey and the qualitative study. The majority of staff are bilingual, sensitive to community needs, and regularly consider methods to improve services. Most notable, in the context of this study, was the staff's commitment to providing service irrespective of external political pressures or movements. Given the highly volatile nativist sentiments and legislative actions of the 1980s and 1990s, especially in politically conservative Orange County, these findings are highly commendable and quite astonishing.

6

Passport to Promise: Public Libraries as Intellectual Spaces for Immigrant Students

JoAnn K. Aguirre

INTRODUCTION

> If the misery of our poor be caused not by the laws of nature, but by our institutions, great is our sin.
>
> Charles Darwin, *Voyage of the Beagle*

In his chronicles of schools and children in the South Bronx in New York City, Jonathon Kozol decries recent funding cuts to school library budgets. "A child cannot be a child twice" he laments (2000, p. 66). Such cuts to sorely needed resources amount to what he refers to as "intellectual theft . . . aggressive and state-sponsored deprivation of a child by municipal denial is a crime that cannot be atoned for in a later decade when the child's childhood is gone forever" (p. 66).

In our ongoing infatuation with technology we tend to forget about the enduring value of public libraries and their significance as catalysts for broad community collaborations. This amnesia often leads to underutilization of public libraries and their services; consequently their worth is minimized when budgets are being developed. Yet, for those individuals for whom public libraries have become largely obsolete, there are that many more that rely on them for a number of services on a frequent and consistent basis. An example of these individuals would be the large immigrant populations who rely on the myriad services offered by public libraries, especially those that facilitate their citizenship status (Mylopoulos, 2000). It is precisely these individuals whose access to such services is threatened most by the persistent controversy surrounding anti-immigration legislation.

This chapter, based on two studies (Aguirre, 1999; Mirón, Inda, & Aguirre, 1998), examines the role of public libraries in developing cultural citizenship, as well as equalizing the playing field that in turn shapes academic identity and consequently academic success of Latino immigrant students. It is within the context of anti-immigrant movements in the 1990s—Propositions 187 and 227—that the role of public libraries is explored.

DISCOVERING THE PUBLIC LIBRARY SYSTEM

Mirón, Inda, & Aguirre (1998) conducted a qualitative study with twelve students from one high school in the Santa Ana Unified School District, the seventh largest in California. These students were enrolled in a summer language assistance program for newly arrived immigrants. The students participated in lengthy interviews that examined cultural citizenship and the politics of language in California. This was particularly timely in light of the controversy surrounding two major legal interventions affecting illegal immigrants: Proposition 187, the *Save Our State* initiative that was legislated in 1994 to deny illegal immigrants public services in the social, health, and educational arenas, and Proposition 227, the *English for the Children* initiative that proposed English-only instruction in California public schools. That study explored, through the notions of cultural citizenship,[1] how newly arrived Latino immigrant students in Santa Ana, California created social space.

In a subsequent study, Aguirre (1999) examined the histories and cultures of two other high schools in the same district and the communities in which they are situated. The unit of analysis in this study became the students themselves as they described, through in-depth narratives, their self-image and the role of schooling practices in the development of their sense of self. Whereupon the 1998 study was undertaken pre-Proposition 227, the data collection for the 1999 study took place after California voters overwhelmingly approved the *English for the Children* initiative in June 1998. In both studies student consensus on the value of school and the acquisition of the English language was not only unanimous; it also challenged common and enduring, but specious, intellectual and cultural deficit assumptions often ascribed to minority students.

What neither study expected to find was the significance of the public library to immigrant student academic success. As students consistently underscored the value of their public library, the research method took on a "grounded theory" approach (Glaser & Strauss, 1967), that is, the research efforts were grounded from the students' perspectives and voices as they were allowed to emerge. The data were then analyzed through a narrative analysis approach wherein "the analysis takes as its object of investigation the story itself" (Riessman, 1993). The centrality of this approach on human agency and imagination is well suited to studies of identity and was thus employed to systematically record and interpret immigrant students' interviews and accounts in order to reveal intersections within social, cultural, personal, and political contexts.

What ultimately emerged were compelling narratives focused on why new Latino immigrant students in Santa Ana, California viewed their public library as essential for their social, academic and future economic survival.[2] This information is significant because as Rios-Kravitz (Chapter 3 of this volume) has argued, little information exists on the "chilling effect" this measure would have on library access for immigrants. She states,

Public libraries have historically provided an avenue of socioeconomic advancement for all people, and efforts to limit library access thus threaten an important opportunity to help newcomers integrate into the community and become residents and citizens. (p. 38)

On the other hand, Martin (1998) saw the passage of Proposition 227 as an opportunity for public libraries to go where schools can't (p. 1). He states,

Although Proposition 227 has dismantled most bilingual education programs in public schools, public libraries—under no such restriction—are trumpeting these kinds of bilingual programs and working to offer more. (p. 1)

With these two perspectives in mind, this chapter presents brief contextual background on nativist rhetoric and public policies—Propositions 187 and 227—which have had an impact on Latino immigrants in general. This information is followed by a more focused portrayal of Latino immigrants in one of the largest urban inner cities in California, and the public library's role in serving their needs. The chapter closes with implications for communities and a final conclusion.

"NATIVISM": SOMETHING OLD SOMETHING NEW

The end of the twentieth century witnessed profound changes in the scope and character of immigration in the United States. The most fundamental change in contemporary immigration can be seen in the demographics alone. Following World War II, the majority of immigrants to the United States continued to originate from either Latin America or Asia in contrast to the first wave of primarily European immigrants (Hamamoto & Torres, 1997).

Such demographic changes have caused contemporary immigration issues to take on more complex hues—they are political, economic, racist, ethnic, and gendered, pitting even immigrants against each other with politicians on all sides advancing the interests of one group over another. As an example, U. S. Congressman Jay C. Kim (R-California), in response to Proposition 187, stated

It is an insult to law-abiding citizens and soon-to-be-citizens who patiently followed all laws and regulations to be lumped together in a bill with illegal aliens who have sneaked into this country and have knowingly and willingly broken U.S. law. (Wu, 1995)

Kim's self-aggrandizing remark was obviously directed at Latino illegal immigrants in an attempt to deflect potential criticism of Asian immigrants, while enhancing his own stature as a successful Korean immigrant and politician. Numerous reports of Asian illegal immigrants run counter to Kim's claims. Such is the case with the recent and unfortunate case of the fifty-eight Chinese who were found suffocated in a container after an attempt by Dutch smugglers to smuggle them into the United Kingdom where economic opportunities are at their highest (Montgomery, 2000). Still, the perceived erosion of values and the decline of the American educational system, along with society's many ills are often placed at the feet of Mexican, Central and South American illegal immigrants. While this is nothing new, it has become increasingly evident in the Southwest and especially in California where public policy tends to influence the entire nation.

Heated debate surrounding the anti-immigration controversy came to a head in the 1990s and spawned endless political commentary that continues even today. For example, the first frame of a political cartoon in the *Los Angeles Times* newspaper depicted a large white male (representing the State of California) angrily pointing a finger at a startled couple—presumably Latino illegals—and shouting at them, "I want you out of my schools, off my welfare rolls, away from my hospitals, and back to where you belong . . ." In the second frame, Mr. California (representing former Governor Pete Wilson) added, with a welcoming smile and benign gesture, "cleaning my kitchens, watching my kids, picking my crops!" (*Los Angeles Times*, 1994, B7). Such hypocrisy, contradiction, and ambivalence underscore the "split-personality" and "new" nativisim attitude of the United States on immigration issues (Chavez, 1996). This has changed little from the "old" nativism discourse characteristic of such movements of the late 1800s and the early twentieth century. It recycles with heightened passion especially during economic downturns. Yet, the rhetoric and public policy initiatives are continually targeted at immigrants (most recently from Mexico and Central and South American countries) as opposed to institutions and governments, and remain the same no matter the circumstances. The following comments spanning the eighteenth to the twenty-first centuries bear witness to this.

Benjamin Franklin in 1751:

Why should the Palatine boors be suffered to swarm into our settlements, and by herding together, establish their language and manners, to the exclusion of ours? Why should Pennsylvania, founded by the English, become a colony of aliens, who will shortly be so numerous as to Germanize us, instead of our Anglifying them? (Chavez, 1996, p. 251)

New York Times editorial, May 15, 1880:

We are willing to receive immigrants just as fast as we can make them over into good American citizens . . . [But] we are not in need of any more aliens at present. Foreigners who come here and herd together like sheep remain foreigners all their lives. We know how stubbornly conservative of his dirt and his ignorance is the average immigrant who settles in New York, particularly if he is of a clannish race like the Italian. (Chavez, 1996, p. 251)

Graham and Beck, *Los Angeles Times* columnists, 1992:

Weary conservatives and liberals have no shortage of explanations for the devastating Los Angeles riots. Yet a major focus has escaped serious discussion. It is immigration, currently running at unprecedented levels, that exacerbates the economic and social forces behind the riots. (Chavez, 1996, p. 250)

John Rocker, relief pitcher for the Atlanta Braves, 2000

Imagine having to take the 7 train to [Shea Stadium], looking like you're in Beirut next to some kid with purple hair, next to some queer with AIDS, right next to some dude who got out of jail for the fourth time, right next to some 20-year-old mom with four kids. It's depressing. (Newhan, 2000, p. A13)

While we continue to decry the presence of illegal aliens, Montgomery (2000) argues that we are collectively guilty of perpetuating the system that denounces them. Commenting on the consequences of immigration tragedies, Montgomery illuminated the vicious cycle of illegal immigration and the complicitous role we all play in this phenomenon. He states,

The next day . . . hopeful immigrants gather again, waiting their chance. The same employers looking for cheap labor are there, the same consumers looking for cheaper goods are there and the same poor countries supporting their finances with the hard currency sent back by illegals are there. It might be permitted to wonder whether anyone really wants the system to stop. (p. M6)

PROPOSITION 187: CALIFORNIA DREAMIN'

The passage of Proposition 187 *(Save Our State)* by California voters in November 1994 sent a clarion call to immigration opponents and proponents alike as well as the entire nation. An example of cyclical nativism, this initiative was fueled primarily by California's economic slump during the early 1990s. One of the key provisions of this legislation makes it unlawful for illegal aliens to receive public social services, public health care services, and public school education at elementary, secondary, and post-secondary levels. A secondary, but equally forceful provision requires service providers to report suspected illegal aliens to the California Attorney General's Office and to the Immigration and Naturalization Service.

While many saw the introduction of this legislation as an egregious form of political and economic hostility, a sufficient portion of the population considered the legislation as long overdue. The primary factors attributed to the support of this proposition by California voters included:

- the perception of a poor economy and/or one in obvious decline;
- the perceived threat to voters' economic stability, that is, illegal aliens stealing their jobs and thereby compromising their livelihoods;
- the economic stability of voters with lower educational levels;

- the perception of voters in Southern California that they are more directly affected by illegal immigration and thereby more vulnerable (Alvarez & Butterfield, 1997).

On December 14, 1991, much to the dismay of many across the nation, a Los Angeles federal judge issued an injunction against Proposition 187, preventing much of it from being enforced. As of this writing, the denial of public education to illegal children has been deemed unconstitutional; hence equal access to education for all young students in California stands as a result.

PROPOSITION 227—ENGLISH FOR THE CHILDREN

I remember being caught speaking Spanish at recess—that was good for three licks on the knuckles with a sharp ruler. I remember being sent to the corner of the classroom for "talking back" to the Anglo teacher when all I was trying to do was tell her how to pronounce my name. "If you want to be American, speak 'American.' If you don't like it, go back to Mexico where you belong.". . . . Wild tongues can't be tamed, they can only be cut. (Anzáldúa, 1987, pp. 53--54)

Responding to a class action suit brought by the parents of non-English speaking Chinese students, the U.S. Supreme Court found that the San Francisco Unified School District failed to provide English language instruction or other adequate instructional procedures to students of Chinese ancestry who did not speak English. The 1974 ruling — *Lau v. Nichols* (414 U.S. 563) —states in part,

Where inability to speak and understand the English language excludes national origin-minority group children from effective participation in the educational program offered by a school district, the district must take affirmative steps to rectify the language deficiency in order to open its instructional program to these students. (Mitchell, Destino, and Karam, 1997, p. I–1)

In response to this federal ruling as well as the needs of the overwhelming majority of students for whom English is not their first language, school districts throughout California, during the last twenty-five years, developed and implemented a number of special programs. These programs have grown in size as well as sophistication as the numbers of limited English proficient (LEP) students have grown.

The use of bilingual education can be traced to our early education system, yet the controversy surrounding the use of non-English languages escalated in the 1990s. The "new nativism" previously described by Chavez (1996) has produced a hostile climate stemming largely from the perception that immigrants threaten the integrity of the American nation because they are culturally and linguistically different.

Sensing a growing sentiment against the use of non-English languages, California businessman Ron Unz authored Proposition 227, which is now part of the California Education Code. The legislation banned most bilingual instruction in public schools in favor of English only, also known as "English immersion." However, the law contains a provision allowing parents to obtain waivers that allow students to learn in their native language. Since its passage, well-established bilingual education programs throughout California have been increasingly challenged to comply with the mandate.

DEMOGRAPHICS OF A YOUTH CAPITAL

But in a neighborhood like mine, with no bookstores and a lightly endowed school library, the sons and daughters of the working class were able to get a foothold on upward mobility, expand our heads, and dream the American Dream. (Suarez, 2000, pp. 64–65)

After decades of following crops around the American Southwest under the U.S. sponsored Bracero Program, numerous Mexican *colonias* or neighborhoods were reborn in Orange County, a key citrus producer in southern California (Gonzalez, 1994). Although today Orange County has evolved from a major agricultural region to a vibrant, highly technical industrial region, it remains a desirable economic gateway to many immigrants, particularly those from Mexico and other Latin American countries. Poised to be one of the most significant leaders in information technology in the nation, if not the world, Orange County is continually challenged to prepare individuals of every ilk to compete in highly technical job markets, locally as well as globally (Kotkin in Anderson, 1998).

Education 1st!

The City of Santa Ana is the largest in the County of Orange and the ninth largest in the state by population (California State Department of Finance, 2000) with an estimated 310,000 inhabitants. The 1990 U.S. Census projected that the population for the year 2020 will reach 350,000. In terms of population by city, approximately 11,245 persons per square mile reside in Santa Ana.

Much of Orange County's growth can be attributed to Santa Ana alone, whose population grew by 44 percent in the 1980s, much higher than the countywide rate of 25 percent (Cleeland, 1998). According to a U.S. Census Bureau report released in September 1998, Orange County "now has one of the fastest-growing Latino populations in the country, with a rate (28 percent) surpassing Los Angeles County's" (Garvey, 1998). This statistic was supported by Gordon (1998) who estimated that Orange County has 761,228 Latinos, the fifth highest number in the nation, reflecting an increase of 35 percent since 1990.

The 1990 U.S. Census also found Santa Ana to have the youngest median age of the 100 largest cities in the United States. Compared to Orange County's median age of 32.6 years, the median age for males is 24.6 and 25.5 for females. Today Santa Ana is referred to as one of two "youth capitals"[3] in the United States along with El Paso, Texas. In comparison to the 100 largest cities in the nation, Santa Ana can be described by the following characteristics:

- 2nd in number of students (per capita)
- 3rd in Hispanic population (percentage of total population)
- 6th in percentage of public school enrollment
- 52nd in total population
- 93rd in personal income (per capita)
- 98th in high school graduates (over age 25)
- 25th safest city in United States

(U.S. Census Bureau; 1996)

The motto of the City of Santa Ana—Education 1st!—is proudly displayed high on a water tower right off the Santa Ana Freeway and 17th Street, one of the city's major thoroughfares. To passers by unfamiliar with this urban inner city, it hints at a degree of academic prowess. But if one knows anything about the city or its school system—the Santa Ana Unified School District—the motto is an oxymoron as the district has historically been one of the lowest academically-achieving school districts in the County of Orange as well as in California.[4] One is left to wonder whether city officials coined this motto as a subtle motivation for the Santa Ana community to rise to the connotation, or whether indeed their intent was to make education the city's priority. In any case, it appears that neither has happened to the extent possible.[5]

Although the City of Santa Ana is in a stage of vigorous revitalization (state enterprise and federal empowerment zone status)[6], it is also the epitome of the inner city. Gangs, drugs, and crime plague many of its residents. A large number of its residents are immigrants or children of immigrants, and the majority speaks a first language other than English. Additionally, the Center for Demographic Research, (1998) noted a particularly disturbing problem: the city's unemployment rate is twice the county average. The location of Orange County along the Pacific Rim, coupled with recent state and federal funding initiatives promise to boost the local economy, yet the city continues to account for a large number of unemployed and underemployed individuals.

IMMIGRANTS AND LIBRARIES: SMALL WORLD LIVING

Newcomers live in their own "small world." We all live in our own "small worlds." It would make a significant contribution to everyday lives if it could be fully appreciated how libraries might make information more useful to 'small world living.' (Pendleton & Chatman, 1998)

In the city of Santa Ana—as in many similar settings across the nation—the large economically disadvantaged, limited English speaking, predominately Latino population seeks to be productive in a rapidly changing workforce that holds little promise for those who cannot read or write, who speak little or no English and/or who are technologically unskilled. Unfortunately, a comprehensive review of the Executive Summary for the Santa Ana Empowerment Zone made no reference whatsoever to the role of its public library in community redevelopment (1995). The review boasts a "Class 1" Fire Department, award-winning schools, numerous nationally-recognized youth programs and a Total Quality Management program among several other assets. But, what about the services offered by the public library? One has to wonder why no mention of its significant role was made if the primary focus of the city's strategic plan is "aimed at educating and training the youngest members of our community, specifically our immigrant population, to become productive members of our culturally rich and diverse community" (p. 2). Here again, it appears that the public library's role as a community player has been minimized.

Pendleton & Chatman (1998) precisely described a newcomer's narrowly defined life in the host country. Not surprisingly this was borne out by student narratives time and again. Thus, having been separated from the public library system since beginning doctoral studies in 1995, it appeared that a visit by the researcher to the Santa Ana Public Library was definitely in order. Having recently spent so much time in academic libraries within the University of California (UC) system—UC Irvine, UC San Diego, and UC Los Angeles—the researcher had unconsciously internalized a profile of a "typical" library user: middle- to upper-class college students and working professionals, primarily white and/or Asian (depending on the geographic location). Several more visits revealed three particularly surprising phenomena supported by Mylopoulos (2000), a Multicultural Services Specialist for the Toronto Public Library in Canada.

First, it was quite noticeable that the Santa Ana Public Library's constituency had changed from primarily White, middle-class, white-collar users to reflect the predominant population in Santa Ana—poor Latino working-class, blue-collar users, and not surprisingly, a good number of homeless individuals seeking shelter from the intense heat. Second, the cars in the parking lot were vastly different from the sleeker, newer, more expensive models parked at university and private libraries. Traffic patterns outside of the library revealed that more library users either walked to or rode the city bus to the library. Finally, whole families occupied various spaces within the library during after-school and especially during after-work hours as opposed to the usual individual user and mother-children types.

Other changes were also evident. For example, much like schools, the library has become a dispenser of social services information—pamphlets direct individuals to various resources for assistance in areas spanning the entire alphabet. Library information on virtually every subject is provided in various languages and of course, technological advances have added computers, videocassettes, audiocassettes, compact disks, and a computerized information locator system. Are these really the services that immigrants are seeking?

According to Mylopoulos (2000), it is this and much more that draws immigrants to public libraries. In his experience he has found they are interested in numerous topics such as:

information on employment and training, housing, the immigration process, family matters, age-related problems, health and living with illnesses, education, language learning, a variety of instruction classes, legal rights, welfare benefits, disabilities assistance, services for children and seniors, pensions, individual rights, and race relations. (p. 26)

Most immigrants who use the library come from countries where knowledge and practice of the English language is very limited if not nonexistent. Therefore, the library may be one of the first stops for an immigrant seeking to build cultural citizenship and acculturate to the laws, values, traditions, and nuances of the nation-state. This is a period of extreme hardship, fear, and adjustment for immigrants, especially if they are undocumented. Thus, they see the public library as a "service" organization; a community institution that will provide the information needed to satisfy their social needs.

Numerous references by immigrant students were made regarding their experiences with the Santa Ana Public Library. First of all, they found it to be more accessible than their own school libraries because of extended weekday and weekend hours thereby allowing families to visit. It also offered a wider selection of books to choose from and information regarding community resources and activities. Another advantage students mentioned was the ability to borrow audiocassettes and videocassettes without charge unless, of course, they paid fees for late returns. The public library also expanded their "small world living" because they were able to meet college students as well as students from other high schools within the district. In this regard, the public library served as a "neutral" space especially for those worried about any type of gang violence. The setting of the public library itself served their purposes well. Its location in the heart of the city's civic center facilitated accessibility as the central transportation center is within walking distance. Its proximity to the police department and other highly visible county and city offices served to ease fears of the surrounding neighborhood.

The Toolbox of Communication

Just as the way we perform changes, so should our sense of 'voice' . . . the engaged voice must never be fixed and absolute but always changing, always evolving in dialogue with a world beyond itself. (hooks, 1994, p. 11)

As students' values represent a powerful force within society there remains not only a responsibility, but also an opportunity to include them in the educational process. Both studies discussed earlier, from which the following student narratives were gleaned, were designed in a way in which students could freely engage in a discussion regarding their educational experiences. Acutely aware of the politics surrounding Propositions 187 and 227, immigrant students expressed their vulnerabilities as they confronted their major struggle—learning English. For it is the English language, they said, that is their passport to prosperity, the toolbox of communication.

These students—strangers to each other—represented vastly different experiences, yet learning to speak, read, and write English was the unifying goal in their lives. This passionate pursuit to learn English, many times against insufferable odds, begged the question, "Why?" Julio, a 17-year-old over-age 10th grade student, residing in Santa Ana for only six months at the time of the interview, put the question to rest with his impassioned response *"Es lo máximo!"* (To know the English language would be the greatest!). All of the students supported the notion that English is a highly sought after and contested commodity.

The following are profiles of three immigrant students who shared their stories (Aguirre 1999; Mirón, Inda, & Aguirre, 1998, pp. 670–76). Most students responded in the Spanish language as they were relatively new to the area and had very limited English speaking skills. Some spoke a combination of Spanish and English, commonly known as *Spanglish*. In either case translations of the Spanish responses are provided.

Julio - The Fugitive

Julio's story began with his pronouncement *"Soy fugitivo, ya no soy legal, se me venció mi pasaporte."* (I'm a fugitive, no longer legal, my passport expired.) Equipped with a three-month visitor's passport, 17-year-old Julio, an only child, arrived in Santa Ana approximately six months before our interview from the state of Morelos, Mexico where he had recently completed his second semester of *prepa*—the U.S. equivalent of the sophomore year in high school. His mother, a single parent, stayed behind working long, hard hours as owner of a *tortillería* to ensure that Julio's education is guaranteed, preferably in the United States. At the time of the interview Julio lived with a maternal aunt and her three children in Santa Ana. Although he would prefer to hold a part-time job to earn spending money, his aunt is adamant about his real job—learning English.

By all standards in Mexico, Julio and his mother were economically stable. Compared to other immigrant students, he received an above-average, consistent education. This was evident in Julio's mannerisms, his speech, his ability for critical reflection, and the way in which he articulated his thoughts. He is committed to staying in California, albeit illegally, at least until he gets his prize—a high school diploma.

Julio loves the English language. "Knowing it gives you the upper edge," he noted, speaking authoritatively. For example, he continued, "one can improve the overall quality of life, have a better job, earn higher wages, fit in socially in any kind of situation, well, there's so much more." Other than by taking English classes, Julio felt that watching movies is the best way to learn English as well as American culture. When asked if too much television or time spent at the theater was detrimental to his studies, he responded,

Absolutely not! English classes teach you by the book, but not really about fitting in here in America. For that you have to socialize or watch T.V. Because then you start knowing how Americans think. For example, I rent a lot of movies, like every three days and that's why I'm ahead.

"That sounds pretty expensive, especially if you go to Blockbuster Video," the researcher remarked. "Oh no," he replied, "I could never afford that. I rent from the library, well, not my school library but you know the big library in the city."

Finding this revelation surprising, the researcher continued to draw out information regarding the library topic. She asked, "So, Julio, you use the Santa Ana Public Library quite frequently?"

Oh sí, ¡es una necesidad! (Oh yes, it's a necessity.) Because, you see, I have so much homework for my classes. The school library doesn't have that much compared to this library and I don't have a computer at home. It's (school library) not open as much either. But the best is that I see so many people that want to learn. We are there so many of us learning new things all the time. I can check out videos all the time, but my aunt thinks I should read many more books. She's right, but you know . . .

Julio sees no barriers to his goals because as he puts it, *"A la escuela ni a la biblioteca no les importa que sea ilegal. Aquí me dan mi educación, sea como sea. Nos toman en cuenta"* (It doesn't matter to the school nor the library that I am illegal. Here they give me my education, regardless of who I am. They consider us.)

Javier—From Chicago to Mexico to Santa Ana

"¡Un día les voy a enseñar mi acta de nacimiento!" (One day I'm going to show my classmates my birth certificate!) Javier's inability to speak English belies his American citizenship. In sharp contrast to Julio, 14-year-old Javier, a ninth grader who was born in Chicago, knows little English. At age six, his family returned to Mexico, where they remained until four months prior to our interview when they made their way to Santa Ana. *"Podía hablar bien con mis hermanos."* (I could speak well with my brothers.) Javier remembered a time before leaving for Mexico when he spoke English with his brothers. *"Llegué a México y casi no hablaba español."* (I arrived in Mexico hardly speaking Spanish.) Recalling his arrival in Mexico knowing little Spanish, he pointed out the irony of finding himself in the same situation—this time in his place of birth—not knowing English. *"¡Se me olvido todo!"* He lamented that he forgot it all.

His immediate goal is to learn English, following the lead of his two older brothers who have excelled in their studies here. He thought that he too could be successful if he tried hard, *"hechándole muchas ganas"* (putting forth much effort), *"y estudiando en la biblioteca diariamente"* (and studying in the library every day). "Every day!" The researcher exclaimed. He explained that both brothers got a job at the city library through an after-school program.

His mother did not want him to run the streets and expected him to accompany his brothers. While they worked he studied...supposedly. *"Muchas veces no entiendo las palabras, ni en ingles ni en espanol, entonces me pongo a platicar con unas muchachas o veo libros con dibujos."* (Many times I don't understand the words in Spanish or in English so I talk to some girls or look at books with pictures.)

Javier turned wistful as he described his father's work in a factory where years of exposure to fiberglass have harmed his health. *"Lo está dañando mucho."* (It is causing him much harm.) He vowed to have a different type of job, one that requires working with his mind. *"Yo quiero trabajar con mi mente, quiero ser un maestro de historia."* (I want to work with my mind, become a history teacher.) Javier reasoned this would be safer and more rewarding. He also recognized that he needs to learn English not only because it is necessary, but as he pointed out, because one can have a better job.

Galia—Juggling Three Languages

Fourteen-year-old Galia, like Javier, is a legal resident. She was quick to point out that in Bolivia she was far more advanced educationally and that today she would be in her sophomore year instead of the ninth grade, but because she could not speak English, she was held back. The entire interview with Galia was conducted in Spanish. She spoke with the wisdom of a sage, articulate beyond her years, witty and very positive about her role in life. While telling her story, she freely dispensed opinions about everything from the educational system to the types of students it serves whom she found *un poco extraño* (a bit strange).

In addition to her struggle to learn the English language, Galia found herself immersed in an environment where culture, food, dress, and customs differed markedly from her more privileged environment in Bolivia. The challenge to learn English was compounded by the need to learn what she called *español Chicano*, a perplexing mix of English and Spanish, formal as well as slang. *"El primer día y el segundo sufría mucho porque decía ¿Qué quiere decir eso?*" Galia recalls how she suffered those first few days of school constantly asking, *"What does that mean?!"* Now she prided herself on having learned many of the expressions and being able to talk *como los mexicanos* (like Mexicans) at school and in the larger society, while reverting to formal Spanish with family and friends. Her desire to speak English like *los americanos* (Americans) remained her foremost goal.

Although Galia felt that the greatest barrier to living in the United States was not being able to speak English, she admitted that her school does the best to make immigrant students feel accepted by teaching them English and including them in other ways. Enthusiastic about her future prospects in the United States and how advantaged she will be by learning English, Galia nevertheless recognized the great sacrifices her parents have made so that she and her sister may learn English. Her father, a former university librarian and a part-time tailor in Bolivia, is now a legal resident, having lived in California with other relatives for the past fifteen years. Galia claimed he learned English by being in California so long. Exhausted after working twelve-hour days and double shifts cleaning hotel rooms, he nevertheless finds time to indulge his passion for books at the Santa Ana Public Library. Galia recounted how her father methodically planned his family's arrival to Santa Ana—where they would live, work, attend school. Since their arrival, the library has been like a second home, so much so that at times Galia tires of it. But her father persists, *"Tienen que ir a averigüar."* (You must go and investigate.) In the end, Galia proudly described her report on Rhode Island that could not have been prepared so well without library research. This particular narrative supports Mylopoulos' contention that "there are newcomers who know a lot about the public library. They regard it as a link to their new environment and make extensive use of its information services and resources" (2000, p. 26).

These three students spoke in great depth about their identities being tied, in large part, to their academic success. As another student, Adriana, stated, *"Yo quiero ser sobresaliente...como dicen aquí, una 'schoolie.' No quiero ser como muchos...que según ellos quieren estudiar pero no les hechan ganas y nada más vienen a calentar la banca."* (I want to be successful...like they say here, a *schoolie*. I don't want to be like those who say they want to study but they don't try and they just come to keep the seat warm.)

The preceding student narratives confirm Mylopoulos' statement that, "In large urban settings with a diverse population, goals and objectives of public libraries state that part of the services they provide to new immigrants relate to their information needs coming from the fact that they have just moved into a new country and are learning a new language" (2000, p. 26).

BUILDING A LEARNING (AND READING AND THINKING) COMMUNITY

People are hungry for community. Since libraries of all types are often at the geographic center of the communities they serve, they are naturally positioned to be community gathering places. (Long, 2000, unnumbered)

With demographics portending a continued increase of Latinos in the state as well as the nation, the importance of having solid literacy skills cannot be underestimated. Not long ago individuals could promote their personal as well as professional status through a solid foundation of the three R's (reading, writing, and arithmetic). However, rapidly changing innovations brought about by the technological revolution have changed virtually every aspect of society, especially the family, education, and work. Elkind (1995) describes this postmodern phenomenon as a downward push of accomplishment and sophistication at much earlier years than ever before. Hence, today's workplace requires a broader mastery of numerous and diverse skills. Witness the U.S. Department of Labor's SCANS report—Secretary's Commission on Achieving Necessary Skills (Lankard, 1995).

In 1991 the U.S. Department of Labor issued the SCANS report outlining the skills, competencies, and personal qualities required to succeed in a high performance workplace. Five broad categories that would facilitate a student's transition from school to postsecondary education and/or the workplace were identified in the SCANS report. These included:

- Resources—identifies, organizes, plans, and allocates resources

- Interpersonal—works with others on teams, teaches others, serves clients, excecises leadership; negotiates, and works with diversity

- Information—acquires, organizes, interprets, evaluates, and communicates information

- Systems—understands complex interrelationships and can distinguish trends, predict impacts, as well as monitor and correct performance

- Technology—works with a variety of technologies and can choose appropriate tool for task. (Lankard, 1995)

Critics of the federal School-to-Work program decry the emphasis of reports such as SCANS for their emphasis on "work," yet these skills clearly apply to any individual pursuing postsecondary studies and certainly would benefit library users of all levels. Additionally, the mastery of these skills, in addition to traditional skills, cannot be the sole responsibility of schools and teachers. Entire communities must be encouraged to assume responsibility for educating its youth (Meier, 1995; Sergiovanni, 1993; Starratt, 1994). This includes parents, schools, business and industry, and community resources such as public libraries.

IMPLICATIONS FOR URBAN INNER CITY PUBLIC LIBRARIES

Although the preceding student narratives indicated a degree of knowledge about the city's public library, and certainly a healthy respect for it, there are also many community members who regard the library with skepticism. According to Mylopoulos (2000), individuals who are faced with a language barrier as well as the inability to understand the complex nature of the information they might be seeking are particularly reluctant to approach public spaces in order to satisfy their specific needs. This being the case, libraries must evolve, just as the immigrant must, out of a "small world living" comfort zone in order to remain a viable player in the community. In other words, immigrants must constantly strive to build their knowledge base about their role in the larger community. Conversely, libraries should reconsider their ability to support their constituencies and sustain their effectiveness as providers of knowledge, information, and services.

Biggs (2000) advanced some critical questions regarding the structure of tribal libraries in her research of tribal library development. "Are the cultural values embedded in the framework of the library?" and "Who are the 'information keepers,' 'wisdom keepers,' or 'oral librarians' in the community?" (p.

21). That is, does the library develop and support a collection of culture-specific material, and could librarians learn from those who possess other "funds of knowledge?" (Moll & Greenberg, 1990). These questions may have implications for urban inner city public libraries in terms of nurturing a "relevant" and "safe" environment; relevant meaning that the library is able to meet the needs of its community, and safe meaning that all community members feel comfortable and accepted in an environment that is more than likely quite foreign to them.

According to Biggs' research (2000), libraries hold certain characteristics that either make a library accessible to its community or not. Based on some of these characteristics, the Santa Ana Public Library appears to be in an excellent position to serve the entire community. For example, it is geographically situated to optimize access; it is situated within or adjacent to various social service agencies; and, it serves as a hub or gathering place for socialization at different levels—young children, families, sole users, adults, senior citizens, school and college students, etc. Biggs' description of a tribal library may appropriately and presciently describe how the Santa Ana Public Library is evolving. She stated: "The sacred hushed environment and intellectual façade of a macroculture library is not to be found in a tribal library. This is not to say that patrons are not seeking information, but often this is a secondary purpose" (p. 21).

What then could all of this mean for the Santa Ana Public Library? With all of the state and federal funding being awarded the city, probably the most important action the city could take would be to collaborate closely with the library in order to optimize services to the entire community. It is obvious that it will have to keep pace with changing times and demographics. It is also obvious that it has quite a large customer base that would benefit from a more user-friendly public institution.

Harry Boyte, a political scientist and longtime community organizer divides community spaces into three types: public, private and what he calls "free" spaces. He argues:

For democracy to work, communities need free spaces, where the public and private realms come together. Here, citizens can work for individual and common goods rather than simply being served by government employees or focusing on private gain. (Watkins, 2000, p. 63)

This simply means that the public library can be a significant institutional player in the community of Santa Ana if given an opportunity. Today's public library must be able to transcend its "small world living" and that of their constituents as well.

CONCLUSION

Miller (2000) points out that the information technology age has created so many changes that have transformed public libraries into new areas of discovery. He states, "In some cities the library is a key part of urban revitalization" (p. 68). McNulty (2000) concurred with this assessment stating that:

Libraries of the future will be community centers that will be of special importance to those who have no access to computers (or to the more advanced ones) and/or who need assistance in finding their way in the World Wide Web and computerized data bases. (pp. 65–66)

Mylopoulos (2000) suggests numerous approaches in reexamining the delivery of community information services. Among these are an organization of resources, advisory services for users, a focused publicity and promotion campaign, resource networking or "one-stop" shopping, and most importantly, advocacy and collaboration.

Time and again, immigrant students recognized that library privileges, services, and resources are much like the English language—a prized commodity to be taken advantage of. This realization is borne out by a young high school student from Guerrero, Mexico: *"Sí, sí, desafortunadamente es cierto . . . soy ilegal."* "Yes, unfortunately it's true...I'm an illegal," the young boy admitted, staring down at his feet. Then he perked up, and with eyes widening he continued in Spanglish, *"Pero tengo todo lo que necesito para sobrevivir en este país. ¡Aquí tengo mi school ID, la mica y mi library card!"* (But here I have everything necessary to survive in this country—my school ID, my green card and my library card!)

Continued progress in our information and knowledge-based society necessitates focused measures in order to survive turbulent social and economic times. As immigration patterns transport the world to our doorstep, it will be essential for the City of Santa Ana's community institutions, including its public library, to make the leap from small world living to global thinking and living.

APPENDIX: AUTHOR'S REFLECTIONS

In elementary school (early 1960s) I had this beat up, unofficial looking card that said "City of Santa Ana Public Library" along with my name. My school's librarian arranged for students to have these so that we could check out books from the city library as well as my school's tiny library. I guarded that little card with pride for it was my escape to a world of knowledge found in books that a family of eleven could not dream of having at home.

Not until I began high school did I discover that my small bookmobile van that parked twice a month on Rosita and Hazard Streets in my Santa Ana barrio was not the Santa Ana Public Library. Imagine my shock to find out there was a main branch! It didn't matter though because there was no way to get there until I received my driver's license in my sophomore year.

My all-time greatest fantasy during childhood and well into adulthood was to own a leather-bound set of *Encyclopedia Britannica*. So as recently as 1994 I sat in my living room with an encyclopedia salesman. It was a preliminary step toward fulfilling this unrealistic fantasy of mine, but logic (and lack of funds) quickly overcame my impulse to buy these dinosaurs on the verge of extinction.

In 1995 when I embarked upon doctoral studies I purchased a new computer. Included in the array of "free" software was a compact disk for the *Grolier Multimedia Encyclopedia.* I still own this computer and to this day have never used the encyclopedic software. Two years ago I inherited a beautiful burgundy, leather-bound A-Z set of *1960 Grolier Encyclopedias.* I turn to this set quite often to feel and smell the richness of the leather, run my fingers over the embossed designs on the covers, and drink in that "library book" smell that evokes fond memories of my beloved bookmobile.

NOTES

1.   The process of acquiring the cultural capital necessary to function within an environment through acculturation to national traditions (Mitchell, 1977).

2.   For the purposes of this study, "new" immigrants were defined as those having lived in the country less than two years.

3.   The 1990 U.S. Census reported approximately 25,000 children under the age of 18 within a square mile of a particularly densely populated Santa Ana neighborhood.

4.   The pattern of academic underachievement in the Santa Ana Unified School District has been particularly strong since the influx of immigrants and refugees from Latin American and Southeast Asian countries. Although standardized test scores should not be used as the sole benchmark for success, they continue as the prevailing measure by which entire learning communities are judged.

5.   Numerous reasons con be attributed to the school district's academic underachievement such as the $1.7 billion loss suffered in the 1994 Orange County bankruptcy, the largest municipal financial crisis in U.S. history.

6.   In 1996 Santa Ana Unified School District received a $3.2 million five-year federal School-to-Work Opportunities grant. The City of Santa Ana is the only designated enterprise zone in Orange County and in 1999 the city was designated as one of several empowerment zones throughout the nation. This is a $100 million, ten-year award.

REFERENCES

Aguirre, J. K. (1999). Coming closer to their dreams: Psychological and philosophical theories as complementary lenses for understanding school reform. Unpublished dissertation. University of California, Los Angeles and Irvine. Los Angeles and Irvine, CA.

Alvarez, R. M. & Butterfield T. L. (1997, September 27). The resurgence of nativism in California? The case of Proposition 187 and illegal immigration. Retrieved May 5, 2000, from the World Wide Web: http://wizard.ucr.edu/polmeth/working_papers 97/alvar97d.html

Anderson, K. (1998, January/February). Santa Ana: OC's capital prepares for the future. *The CityLine, 2* (1), 1–2.

Anzáldüa G. (1987). *Borderlands: La frontera. The new mestiza.* San Francisco, Calif.: Spinster.

Biggs, B. (2000, March). Tribal libraries: And still they rise. *Multicultural Review, 9* (1), 20–23, 55–56.

Boyte, H. (2000, June/July). Union of libraries and communities. *American Libraries, 31* (6), 63.

California State Department of Finance. (2000). City of Santa Ana. Retrieved May 5, 2000, from the World Wide Web: http://www.cl.santa-ana.ca.us/

Center for Demographic Research. (1998). *Statistical report.* Fullerton, Calif.: California State University, Fullerton.

Chavez, L. R. (1996). Borders and bridges: Undocumented immigrants from Mexico and Central America. In S. Pedraza & R. G. Rumbaut (Eds*.) Origins and destinies: Immigration, race, and ethnicity in America* (pp. 250–62). San Francisco, Calif.: Wadsworth.

Cleeland, N. (1998, September 9). They have simple hopes for a complex problem. *Los Angeles Times,* p. A10.

Darwin, C. (1871). *The descent of man.* London: John Murray.

Elkind, D. (1995). School and family in the postmodern world. *Phi Delta Kappan, 79* (3), 241–46.

Garvey, M. (1998). Power in numbers. *Los Angeles Times,* pp. B1, B4.

Glaser, B. G. & Strauss, A. L. (1967). *The discovery of grounded theory.* Chicago: Aldine.

Gonzalez, G. G. (1994). *Labor and community: Mexican citrus worker villages in a southern California county, 1900–1950.* Chicago: University of Illinois Press.

Gordon, L. (1998, September 19). L.A. County leads U.S. by large margins in numbers of Latinos, Asians. *Los Angeles Times,* p. A24.

Hamamoto, D. Y. & Torres, R. D. (Eds.) (1997). *New American destinies: A reader in contemporary Asian and Latino immigration.* New York: Routledge.

hooks, b. (1994). *Teaching to transgress: Education as the practice of freedom.* New York and London: Routledge.

Kozol, J. (2000, June-July). Library cutbacks: A crime that cannot be atoned for. *American Libraries, 31* (6), 66.

Lankard, B. A. (1995). SCANS and the new vocationalism. *ERIC Clearinghouse on Adult, Career, and Vocational Education,* Digest No. 165.

Long, S. A. (2000, June-July). An initiative of the American Library Association. *American Libraries, 31* (6), unnumbered.

Los Angeles Times. (1994). Political cartoon, no author or date, p. B7.

Martin, H. (1998, November 22). Going where schools can't. *Los Angeles Times.* Retrieved May 5, 2000, from the World Wide Web: http://www.bcf.usc.edu/~cmmr/NEWS/L.A..Times_Nov22_98.html.

McNulty, R. (2000, June-July). The most exciting institutions. *American Libraries, 31* (6), 66.

Meier, D. (1995). *The power of their ideas: Lessons for America from a small school in Harlem.* Boston, Mass.: Beacon Press.

Miller, E. (2000, June-July). A writer's view: Journey to a sacred place. *American Libraries, 31* (6), 66.

Mirón, L. F., Inda, J. X., & Aguirre, J. K. (1998). Transnational migrants, cultural citizenship, and the politics of language in California. *Educational Policy, 12* (6), 659–81.

Mitchell, D. E., Destino, T., & Karam, R. (1997). *Evaluation of English language development programs in the Santa Ana Unified School District: A report on data system reliability and statistical modeling of program impacts.* California Educational Research Cooperative. School of Education, University of California, Riverside.

Mitchell, K. (1997). Transnational subjects: Constituting the cultural citizen in the era of Pacific Rim capital. In A. Ong & D. M. Nonini (Eds.) *Undergrounded empires: The cultural politics of modern Chinese transnationalism* (pp. 228–56). New York: Routledge.

Moll, L. C. & Greenberg, J. B. (1990). Creating zones of possibilities: Combining social contexts for instruction. In L.C. Moll (Ed.) *Vygotsky and education (319*–48). Cambridge, Mass.: Cambridge University Press.

Montgomery, P. L. (2000, June 25). All decry system of illegal workers, while all use it. *Los Angeles Times*, pp. M1, M6.

Mylopoulos, C. (2000, March). Tending to the city's needs, serving newcomer immigrants: The value of community information. *Multicultural Review_9*, (1), 24–27, 57–59.

Newhan, R. (2000, June 29). New York grids for the worst: Rocker's back. *Los Angeles Times*, pp. A1, A13.

Pendleton. V. E. & Chatman, E. A. (1998, Spring). Small world lives: Implications for the public library. *Library Trends, 46* (14), 732–51

Riessman, C. K. (1993). Narrative analysis. Newbury Park, CA Sage Publications.

The Santa Ana Empowerment Zone: Executive summary. (2000, June 15). Retrieved July 20, 2000, from the World Wide Web:s http://www.ci.santaana.ca.us/Departments/cda/empowerment/exec.html

Sergiovanni, T. J. (1994). *Building community in schools*. New York: Jossey-Bass.

Starratt, R. (1994*). Building an ethical school: A practical response to the moral crisis in schools*. Bristol, Pa.: The Falmer Press.

Suarez, R. (2000). Neighborhood library: Part of the public realm. *American Libraries, 31* (6), 64.

U. S. Census Bureau. (1996). *Statistical abstract of the United States* (116 th Ed). Washington, D.C.: Government Printing Office.

U.S. Census Bureau. (1991, June*). 1990 census profile: Race and Hispanic origin.* Number 2. Washington, D.C.: Government Printing Office.

Watkins, C. (2000, June-July). Union of libraries and communities. *American Libraries, 31* (6), 66.

Wu, F. H. (1995, November 10). Washington journal: Immigration disaster. *Asian Week*, p. 13.

7

Impact of Proposition 187 on Public Libraries and Elementary Education in Tucson, Arizona

Ninfa Almance Trejo

INTRODUCTION

This study involved a series of surveys administered to various groups to measure the impact of the California imitative known as Proposition 187 on the Latino community, on public library usage, and on elementary school education in Tucson, Arizona. In addition, this research sought to determine community sources of information for immigration legislation. The study populations included Latino immigrants, nonimmigrant Latinos, White non-immigrants, public librarians, and elementary school teachers who either lived or worked in targeted immigrant-populated areas of the city.

The hypothesis of this study was that the anti-immigrant legislation and mood of the country would reveal a negative impact on Latino immigrants' use of and attitudes toward the public libraries and schools in Tucson, Arizona.

BACKGROUND

Why this study? The public library's mission in the United States since 1856 has been to educate immigrants (Escolar, 1987, p.374). The public library's philosophy, starting with the Library Bill of Rights, has consistently maintained that libraries are for everyone, regardless of country of origin, religion, or primary language (American Library Association, 1965, pp. 7–12). Public libraries have traditionally provided new immigrants needed materials to learn the laws, systems, and the language of this country. In essence, public libraries have historically played a key role in the acculturation process of new immigrants.

According to the U.S. Immigration and Naturalization Service (1996), over 7,000 immigration bills have been introduced in the House of Representatives or the Senate since 1790. The congress has actually only passed 138 of these proposals into law. Of these federal immigration laws none has ever out-lawed educational opportunities for children of undocumented persons living within the United States.

An anti-immigrant movement has been gaining momentum since the 1970s, stimulating various anti-immigrant campaigns across the nation. The most notorious was Proposition 187, a California initiative that was approved by voters in November 1994. This legislation made it an illegal act, among other restrictions, to provide a public education to out-of-status immigrants. The constitutionality of this measure has been challenged and defeated in fed-eral court, as immigration law is a federal not a state mandate. This law fur-ther propelled anti-immigrant and xenophobic sentiments in the mid–1990s.

Voters in the State of Arizona contributed to this pattern. While Arizona has not proposed legislation mirroring Proposition 187, some legislation tar-geting immigrants, especially out-of-status immigrants, has been passed. For example, after an English Only Proposition passed in California during the early 1980s, Arizona passed copycat legislation known as Proposition 106 in 1986 (Tatalovich, 1995). After California passed legislation restricting un-documented persons from applying for a driver's license or a state identifica-tion card without proof of citizenship in 1994, Arizona enacted very similar legislation known as HB 2154–422R—H Ver in 1996 (State of Arizona, 1996).

It was feared that the passage of Proposition 187 would incite comparable legislation. In fact, "Save Our State" advocates from California were meeting with high profile state legislators in Arizona during the period this study was conducted. This fear was due in part to the existing and growing Mexican immigration population already in the State and in Tucson, in particular. Ac-cording to the 1990 U.S. Census Bureau (1996) statistics, the total population of the city of Tucson was 666,880, including urban and rural areas. The popu-lation of Hispanic-origin persons numbered 161,880 or close to 24 percent of the population. The vast majority (147,242) of this population was of Mexican origin. In addition, Tucson's close proximity to the Mexican border continues to make it a popular destination for Latino immigrants.

In conclusion, the period in which the surveys were administered was marked by fervent anti-immigrant attitudes in Tucson, the State of Arizona, and the nation. It would have been highly unlikely for Latino or White popu-lations or service providers such as librarians or elementary school teacher to be unaware of this pervasive mood.

METHODOLOGY

An Advisory Board was established to serve as a peer review panel. The primary role of the Board was to review the development of the project and as-sist with the interpretation of the collected data. Four professionals from Tuc-son agreed to serve as advisors on this project. They were: Dr. Leonard Busurto, Director of Bilingual Education, Tucson Unified School District; Frank De La Cruz, Librarian, Unit Supervisor at El Pueblo Public Library;

Bob Diaz, Assistant Dean of Libraries, University of Arizona; and Dr. Alfonso Morales, Assistant, Professor of Sociology at the University of Arizona.

Three questionnaires were developed in English and Spanish by the principal investigator. All surveys were administered by the principal investigator in the preferred language of the respondents between May and August of 1996. Instruments were designed for families (twenty questions), public librarians (ten questions), and elementary school teachers (ten questions).

The respondents included:

- A total of 15 families including ten undocumented immigrant Latino and five nonimmigrant families. Of the non-immigrant families two were White and three were Mexican Americans. The Mexican Americans had lived in Tucson for at least two and up to four generations. All immigrant respondents were interviewed in Spanish. All non-immigrant respondents were interviewed in English. Eleven families were traditional two-parent households and four were single-parent female households. Seventy-one family members were interviewed, twenty-six adults and forty-five children. Among the child respondents twenty-three were males and twenty-two were females. Child respondents were under the age of eighteen.

- Five public librarians who work with immigrant children or children of immigrantparents. Four of the librarians were bilingual in Spanish and English and one was a monolingual English speaker.

- Five elementary school teachers who work predominantly with immigrant children and children of immigrant parents in the targeted community. Of these participants four were bilingual and bicultural and one was not.

All immigrant participants were recommended by a teacher or librarian involved in the study. The teacher or librarian facilitated the contact. All immigrant respondents were perceived to be undocumented residents in the United States.

The immigrant respondents lived in densely populated Latino neighborhoods as identified by census track data (1996). The selected study areas in South Tucson corresponded with the following zip code numbers: 85701, 85706, 85713, 85714, 85745, and 85746. The census data for these areas also indicated that all residents were low income. It was determined during the interview process that all respondents were working class. At the time of the interview most were underemployed or unemployed. The predominant language in these homes was Spanish.

The nonimmigrant respondents were used as a control group to see how much, if at all, their responses differed from the undocumented immigrant population. The principal investigator identified and initiated contact with all non-immigrant families. The nonimmigrant participants lived in predominantly White middle class neighborhoods. All were gainfully employed at the time of the contact. The predominant language in these homes was English.

Initial contacts were made by phone. Librarians and teacher interviews were conducted in one-on-one situations while families were interviewed in group situations in which the entire family often participated. The questionnaires utilized a combination of open-ended and "yes" or "no" questions. Often parents and children within the same family had different responses. The qualitative findings were summarized and categorized. The Advisory Board reviewed the conclusions. Necessary changes and adjustments were made following these discussions.

FINDINGS

Families

When families were asked about their length and place of residency, it was found that families had lived in Tucson from 1 to 36 years, an average of 9 years per family, and a median of 5. Immigrant families had lived in the United States from 2 to 36 years, an average of 15 years, and a median of 10. These families have relatives that have lived in Tucson from 0 to 80 years, an average of 24 years, and a median of 13 years. These familial relations were often parents or grandparents. Within the nonimmigrant families interviewed in English, two were third generation Americans of Mexican ancestry.

All respondents indicated that their main source of information is television (Spanish or English), followed by newspapers, radio, library, family members, church, friends, and wire services. Inquiries regarding main sources of social service and educational information included here in ranked order were public schools, public libraries, learning centers, county health services, government offices, wellness centers, and referral services.

The respondents were asked about how long it had been since they had used a public library. Their responses varied from 0 to 30 years with an average of 8 years per family, and a median of 2.5 years. Only one male Latino immigrant indicated that he had never used the library.

All but one family was aware of the fact the Tucson Pima Public Library (TPPL) offers a free library card. Among the respondents eight families had TPPL cards and seven families did not. Despite the fact that some families (four) did not have library cards all families stated that they take advantage of services offered by TPPL and use them regularly. All nonimmigrant participants were library cardholders and users.

Respondents' general impressions of TPPL and its services included the following:

- A key information and resource provides.

- A great source for children's programs and services.

- A quiet sanctuary for study, personal development, and contemplation.

- An excellent source of reference services and computer technology.

Only one family perceived that the library had limited resources and that the collection was inadequate. This family used a small TPPL branch and continues to use this facility despite the limited resources.

The general comments about TPPL were positive including those from children. All families took advantage of the TPPL children's services to fulfill educational needs and because services are free. Children stated that they liked the TPPL learning activities and homework help. Parents expressed appreciation for the newspaper collection. Immigrant parents, in particular, enjoyed reading newspapers from their home countries. All respondents expressed their enjoyment of the fiction collection, citizenship information, videocassettes, and interlibrary loan services.

All library user families indicated that they have communicated with staff members when using the public library. Six Spanish-speaking immigrant families indicated that they only communicate with library staff in Spanish. Four families stated that they communicate with library staff in English and Spanish. Thirteen families responded that going to the library was always worth the trip.

Discussion about the Tucson Unified School District (TUSD) provided mixed data. A nonimmigrant family perceived that the TUSD was poorly administered even though their children had benefited educationally. The parents stated that middle- and upper-class children benefit more from the system than poor communities such as those in the study area. There was a perception that resources were not equitably distributed. This imbalance was perceived as intentional and discriminatory. Despite this one negative assessment most families, immigrant and nonimmigrant, were very happy with the schools their children attended. Some were concerned about various sorts of discipline issues. Others, particularly immigrants, were simply grateful for the educational opportunities.

Immigrant families articulated their feelings about living in this country. Most felt that they had adapted and considered themselves comfortable in both Mexico and the United States. A few immigrant families indicated that they have been made to feel that they do not belong in the United Stated or in the Tucson community. These families felt that their contributions to the community were not appreciated. Some parents indicated that they are often fearful, confused, and alienated. However, all immigrant respondents noted that the public schools have been instrumental in making them feel welcome.

The nonimmigrant White respondents felt very comfortable living in Tucson. The nonimmigrant Latinos did not indicate that they had suffered due to language, culture, or immigration status. All nonimmigrant Latino respondents empathized with the immigrant families, as their ancestors were also newcomers at one time.

When respondents were questioned about California's infamous Proposition 187, fourteen families responded that they were aware of the 1994 legislation. Only one immigrant family had not heard of it. The principal investigator volunteered to read the text of Proposition 187 or to further explain its meaning and context. Half of the immigrant families responded affirmatively to this request.

All respondents who were cognizant of California's anti-immigrant legislation, regardless of ethnic or immigration status, voiced concern regarding the injustice of the law which would prevent innocent children from receiving an education. Participants used phrases such as "unfair," "painful," and "racist," when describing their feelings about the legislation. Respondents felt that children should not be persecuted for the unlawful status of their parents. In general, there was serious concern regarding the discriminatory backlash of this legislation against legal and undocumented residents outside of California. With respect to other immigration laws, eight families were aware of laws that might have repercussions for immigrant families. Nonimmigrant families were better informed on these issues than immigrant families.

The respondents, regardless of immigration or ethnic background, were concerned about the possibility of a "Save Our State" law in Arizona. Participants expressed a desire for clear and consistent immigration policy in Arizona and on the national level. The respondents expressed a need for specific information on the implementation of any such legislation. Most participants were uneasy about the anti-immigrant frenzy. Even White nonimmigrant respondents felt bad even though this legislation would not directly affect them. Nonimmigrant respondents were most concerned about the impact on children and families in their communities. People, for the most part, indicated that they would be willing to fight against any proposition that might affect children's education, as educational attainment was perceived as the only way for their children to succeed in the United States.

Respondents were asked if they would continue to use the public library if future laws restricted use based on immigration status. Participants' reasons for wanting to continue using the public library were varied. Some participants indicated that using the public library was critical to completing school assignments for their children. Others stated that public libraries were necessary for improving themselves and maintaining their quality of life. The nonimmigrant families did not respond to this question, as they did not feel that this legislation, if passed, would affect them or their children.

Families felt that the library should not ask about immigration status in the process of conducing services to community residents. Library usage was viewed as a human right that should be available to all taxpayers regardless of citizenship status.

Similarly all families expressed a strong desire to send their or other families' children to school even if future legislation limited attendance based on immigration status. All participants indicated that their desire to live in a community of educated people, people who want to improve themselves, would improve the entire community. Education was seen as an avenue for maintaining a positive mind-set and discouraging negative or anti-social behavior such as gangs or drugs. Immigrant families stated that the education of their children as the major reason they came the to United States in the first place. These families noted a strong desire for their children to become proficient in English so that they could find a good job. Immigrant parents stated that they would find other means to educate themselves and their children regardless of institutional barriers. All families agreed on the importance of education and insisted that their children would be enrolled in school in spite of their immigration status or anti-immigrant sentiment.

The nonimmigrant respondents' answers were significantly different from the undocumented immigrants in some key area:

- There was no sense of fear or sense of exclusion by the dominant society.

- Nonimmigrant Latinos did not feel that anti-immigrant legislation would affect them or their children. They felt that their native-born status would protect them from prejudice.

- Nonimmigrants were better informed on all anti-immigrant issues than undocumented populations.

Public Librarians

Public librarians employed by the Tucson Pima Public Library and working in the targeted study area were interviewed. These five librarians have worked at TPPL from 9 to 23 years, an average of 16.6 years per librarian.

These respondents indicated that an average of 60 percent of their regular library users were Latino immigrants. Librarians agreed that the most common types of materials immigrants seek are: English as a Second Language (ESL) materials, followed by citizenship materials, *fotonovelas*, magazines, Spanish language children's materials, and English language materials to complete homework assignments. Nonimmigrant Latinos library users were most often observed requesting Spanish as a Second Language (SSL) materials, Mexican history, books on dreams, horoscopes, computers, nonfiction, videos, women's magazines and general education degree preparation guides.

Of the five librarians interviewed, all were aware of California's Proposition 187 and the possibility that similar legislation might be introduced in Arizona. Two librarians noted changes among Latino immigrant users including an increase in the circulation of citizenship and ESL materials. In addition, users were openly expressing an eagerness to become citizens as soon as possible. Immigrant users expressed fear about their noncitizenship status.

When asked about TPPL policies, all librarians agreed that the library should have proactive policies in place to assist staff in defusing rumors regarding immigrant legislation in the state of Arizona. One librarian stated that the library's commitment to public service as stated in the organizational mission statement should be emphasized to the public.

Respondents commented that the public library should serve as an information clearinghouse for important community issues such as proposed immigration legislation in Arizona or in the United States. Participants stated that the library's mission, as a public institution open to the entire community should continue to be emphasized and publicized. Librarians indicated that the proof of address required to secure a library card might be an indirect deterrent for potential immigrant library users. Librarians stated that some immigrants might feel discouraged if asked to present a permanent address, as their homes may be temporary or not registered in their names. Furthermore, some immigrants may perceive that this practice is a method of tracking their where-abouts given their undocumented immigration status. The respondents also felt that TPPL should be more vocal in promoting existing Spanish language collections, as well as holding public forums about immigration reforms or pending immigrant legislation.

In 1996 when this study was conducted, Arizona legislators and commu-nity leaders were meeting with the creators of California's Save Our State ini-tiative.

These meetings were highly publicized in the local media. Many respondents assumed that an anti-immigrant proposal(s) would soon follow. Respondents had been told of plans by the TPPL administration to educate staff regarding the library's positions on anticipated anti-immigration legislation in Arizona. Staff welcomed this training as they felt that librarians must be aware of any issue that so directly impacts community users. Fortunately, this legislation has not come to pass in Arizona.

Participants indicated that the Arizona Library Association and the Ser-vices to Spanish Speaking Round Table have sponsored programs and forums at state conferences, which examined both sides of the immigration debate.

Teachers

Teachers who were interviewed had worked with Tucson Unified School District (TUSD) and in the targeted communities from 6 months to 17 years, averaging 11 years of employment with the District. Four of the participating teachers were bilingual in Spanish and English.

The teachers' perception of the number of Latino immigrant children en-rolled in their school was from 40 to 100 percent, with an average of 79 per-cent. When respondents were asked to describe their immigrant Latino stu-dents they indicated that immigrant children and families were very apprecia-tive of the educational opportunities they received; a high percentage of chil-dren lived in homes where the parents' income was at or below poverty level; the percentage of gifted children was higher among immigrant children than majority children; and the percentage of learning disabled students among immigrant children did not differ from other ethnic groups or the dominant school population.

Not only were all respondents aware of Proposition 187 but two teachers responded that their students were also cognizant of California's anti-immigrant legislation. Four teachers noted negative attitudes from native-born students, parents, and teachers toward immigrant families. Non-immigrant pa-rental resentments appear to stem from the belief that immigrants are receiving undeserved social services.

The respondents stated their unanimous opposition to the "Save Our State" initiative and measures like it that might be proposed in Arizona. The teachers were most concerned about the denial of educational services to chil-dren. They predicted an increase in crime if the measure should ever be en-forced. The respondents expressed fear about how families could survive without basic health services and the health risks for teachers and other public employees who might be exposed to communicable diseases. The teachers agreed that the anti-immigrant propositions like Proposition 187, if implemented, would create a whole generation of uneducated adults with poor employment prospects. They indicated that the families that they serve have no intentions of returning to Mexico or other home countries. Some respondents expressed anger at the creators of Proposition 187 who have found undocumented residents an easy target during a weak economic period.

Besides viewing Proposition 187 as politically motivated the respondents noted a clear class breakdown among those that support anti-immigrant measures in Arizona. Elected officials, Democratic and Republican, from upper-middle-class orientations have been proponents of anti-immigrant proposals. However, all respondents stated that the deep seated antagonisms exhibited in California toward immigrants have not yet developed in Arizona. The participants felt that this was due to the strong binational economic ties with Mexico.

The respondents speculated on the position of the TUSD should an anti-immigrant measure pass, which might restrict education access to undocumented immigrants. Like the public library, the school district in-service training was planned pending the emergence of copycat legislation from California. The respondents hoped that their district would take a public stand against any such legislation if the proposed legislation should become state law. The teachers indicated that they would like to use their classrooms to promote tolerance and acceptance of difference.

The teachers also assumed that they would be forced to be more politically active if nativist legislation should ever come to pass in Arizona. The state teachers union, Arizona Education Association, had already issued a statement opposing any legislation that would limit educational access. The respondents felt that local school district administrations were responsible for providing the community with appropriate information about any upcoming immigration legislation.

ANALYSIS

From the responses of the families, librarians, and teachers, one can infer that there is a general awareness and high regard for the public library. Family respondents, regardless of immigration or ethnic status, were strong library supporters. All participants except one person were library users. The major factor in library usage appeared to be the presence of school age children in the home. The fact that some of the most frequently requested materials at the public library are English as a Second Language and citizenship materials indicates an interest and willingness of the non-English speaking immigrants to educate themselves and to become U.S. citizens. Immigrant and nonimmigrant users alike rated education as a top priority. The respondents were well aware of the importance of a quality education in building a better future for their children. They seemed determined to pursue these goals.

The census data reveals that the Latino population of the city is 24 percent. In the targeted communities immigrant children enrolled in public schools averaged 79 percent. Librarians perceived that Latino immigrants comprise an average of 60 percent of their regular users. This data indicates that not only is the immigrant population concentrated in the targeted areas but they are using the public library in large numbers, particularly families with school age children.

Librarians perceive that more families are seeking information on citizenship than before the anti-immigrant hysteria gained steam. However, the percentage of naturalized citizens in Tucson is very small. Only 3 percent of the population are naturalized citizens. One librarian respondent indicated that the fear generated by the new anti-immigration laws has added new interest in citizenship. If this is so, it poses a critical question for libraries, schools, and institutions of higher education. What strategies are these institutions using to reach out to Latino immigrant populations that are actively seeking incorporation and integration into U.S. society given the highly sensitive issue of immigration status in Arizona and the nation?

While interviewing Latino family respondents it was clear that mothers answered most of the questions and seemed to be more aware of their children's educational environment and needs. The Latino fathers were more passive and less informed on these issues. If mothers do in fact take the lead responsibility for their children's education it is important to determine how libraries and schools are reaching out to these immigrant mothers? How could libraries and educational institutions assist these female newcomers in acquiring the appropriate knowledge and skills to assist their children in succeeding in our complex and highly competitive society?

The findings indicate a fairly detailed knowledge in the community regarding immigration laws and policies. All respondents expressed a serious concern regarding anti-immigration laws in California and copycat proposals in Arizona. Families, regardless of ethnic background or immigration status, appear to be totally against it. Only one person that is employed in the public health field was supportive of immigration restrictions but even this family could not support the educational restrictions. Librarians and teachers appear united in their opposition to the kind of anti-immigration laws that have been adopted in California. Each group of respondents recommended steps to institute library and school district policies to defuse the anti-immigrant sentiment. Both the TPPL and the TUSD administrations were proactive in planning informational sessions for staff on policies and procedures in the event of new legislation targeting immigrants.

There were mostly positive impressions of Tucson's public schools and their services to immigrants. The family respondents felt that these services are critical to their childrens' personal development and provide a welcoming environment for parent involvement. There was a general consensus among families that Tucson public schools are good regardless of the overall anti-immigrant environment in the city, state, and nation. Most teachers work hand-in-hand with parents to help them help their children. Most teachers stated that immigrant children are more respectful and better behaved than nonimmigrant children. Teachers expressed their appreciation of these characteristics in immigrant students.

Librarian respondents were very active in disseminating the latest immigration related information to the community. They appeared willing to be proactive in informing other librarians and staff on how to tactfully handle the dissemination of immigration information. Some librarians expressed a need for a more activist role that would go beyond the dissemination of information on immigration legislation. Librarians and teachers suggested a more dynamic role for their respective professions and professional associations. In-service workshops, conference programs, and community-based public relations efforts sponsored by professional associations were most often listed as effective methods for raising the social consciousness of their membership and the community. Both groups of professionals agreed that they must ultimately impact the decisions of elected officials in dealing with these serious issues.

CONCLUSION

The hypothesis suggesting that there has been a negative impact from Proposition 187 on the Tucson community in the use of public libraries and attendance at public schools is rejected. Analysis of families' responses indicate a strong determination to improve and fight for, if necessary, educational opportunities for youth. Family participants are doing this now by utilizing public libraries and the public education systems regardless of external political factors. In addition, the librarian and teacher respondents exhibited a high public service commitment reflective of their respective professional ethics. It does not appear that anti-immigration sentiments or legislation would deter librarians or teachers in their efforts to contact and serve these immigrant populations. Even non-immigrant respondents were not in favor of educational restrictions for undocumented children.

Librarians and teachers agreed that there is a need to get involved in these critical issues. Library and education professionals must strive, "to make the connection between the classroom environment and the student's life environment to provide continuity of the learning experience," as stated by John Dewey in *Experience and Education* (1947, p. 16). Mothers are keenly aware of the issues related to their children's education. Librarians and teachers must continue to stimulate mothers' involvement in the educational development of their children.

Use of the home language was also a key factor in the relationships between librarians, teachers, and the immigrant families. The bilingualism of most of the professional staff made it possible to effectively alert the community to the opportunities and resources offered by their institutions and to provide the community with appropriate Spanish language material. It also allowed immigrants to communicate their needs, fears, and desires to these key service providers.

Librarians and educators must continue to draw Latino immigrants into the educational pipeline. These service professionals should collaborate on the following issues:

- Develop recommendations for improving the distribution and dissemination of information on immigration issues at libraries, schools, and other publicly supported agencies.

- Develop a public relations campaign, in Spanish and English, to help defuse an environment of anti-immigrant sentiment and to increase tolerance and understanding.

- Encourage universities and other institutions of higher education to implement needed outreach programs that will focus on immigrant populations including a program specifically directed at immigrant mothers.

- Develop coalitions among professional organizations that are committed to public education and oppose educational restrictions based on immigration status.

REFERENCES

American Library Association. (1965). American Library Association Policies. Chicago: American Library Association.

Dewey, J. (1947). *Experience and education*. New York: McMillan Company.

Escolar, H. (1987). *Historias de las bibliotecas*. Madrid: Ediciones Piramide.

State of Arizona. Secretary of State (1986). Arizona Ballot Propositions, 1986. Phoenix: State of Arizona.

State of Arizona. State Senate (1996). Session laws State of Arizona: Forty-second legislature. Phoenix: State of Arizona.

Tatalovich, R. (1995). *Nativism reborn?: The official English language movement and the American states*. Lexington: University Press of Kentucky.

U.S. Bureau of the Census. (1996, November). Census and you. Retrieved August 20, 1997, from the World Wide Web: http://www.census.gov

United States. Bureau of the Census. (1996, November). Immigration and naturalization legislation. Retrieved August 20, 1997, from the World Wide Web: http://www. usdoj.gov/legislativehistory/index.html

8

The Anti-Affirmative Action Movement in California: Implications for Public Library Services to Asian Immigrants

Xiwen Zhang

The contemporary assault on affirmative action in higher education in California has shocked many educators for its astonishing presumption that in barely thirty years we have successful resolved the nation' centuries of racial, ethnic, and gender contradictions. But this assault, certain to be imitated elsewhere, is symptomatic.

(Association of American College and Universities, 1995, p. xvi)

American society has been characterized by racial segregation from its inception. President Clinton has called on all Americans to help create "One America in the twenty-first century." He promoted "a diverse, democratic community in which we respect, even celebrate our differences, while embracing the shared values that unite us" (The President's Initiative on Race, 1997). California's anti-affirmative action legislation and the anti-immigrant movement of the past decade challenges this American commitment to creating a society of unity and equality.

The goal of this article is to examine the politically powerful anti-affirmative action movement in California, the judicial changes resulting from the passage of anti-affirmative action legislation known as Proposition 209, and the implications for California public libraries. In addition, this article will delineate Proposition 209's recent impact on a number of important issues, such as education and employment, with special reference to the situation of Asian Americans.

BACKGROUND

Affirmative action is a government policy designed to overcome historic and continuing ethnic and sex discrimination. In 1964 Congress passed the Civil Rights Act. Title VII of that Act prohibits employment discrimination based on race, color, religion, sex, or national origin in both private and public workplaces. After the passage of the Civil Rights Act of 1964, California and many other states adopted affirmative action policies and programs.

Throughout its thirty years of implementation, affirmative action has remained a controversial topic in California and the nation. Opponents contend that affirmative action is no longer needed and that most discriminatory actions have been remedied. They believe that affirmative action is a form of preferential treatment and that it constitutes reverse discrimination against White men. Those who hold this position promote a gender and colorblind policy that awards jobs, contracts, and admissions based on individual merit. Meanwhile, affirmative action supporters argue that while progress has been made, women and minorities still do not have equality of access to education, business, and employment opportunities. The affirmative action supporters believe that there is no better alternative to overcoming gender and race discrimination than well-developed affirmative action programs.

Years before the passage of Proposition 209, the Senate Office of Research (LaVally, Melendez, Sproul, and Vucinich, 1995) reported positively on the status of affirmative action in California. During the affirmative action era, affirmative action programs were operated at all levels of government in the state and encouraged governmental agencies to base some hiring and contracting decisions in part on race and gender. Educational institutions such as the University of California (UC), the California State University (CSU) system, and the California Community Colleges (CCC) had all adopted affirmative action programs to increase the representation of minority groups on campus. In addition, the state of California, Office of Compliance Programs monitored the minority hiring practices of 9,500 private sector employers who contracted with the state. The federal government required that nondiscriminatory programs be maintained. Monitoring and reporting to the U.S. Equal Employment Opportunity Commission was required of all California city and county government agencies.

Since the late 1970s California has utilized the ballot initiative to modify or change the state constitution. This popular electoral process has precipitated the legalization of many controversial proposals. Taylor states that the initiative process has become the most influential policy-making apparatus in California. Recently, the process has been widely manipulated by well-organized and well-funded interest groups. For example, the California Secretary of State reported that the "Yes on 209" group raised $5,239,287. Approximately $3 million came from individual donors who contributed at least $10,000 each (Taylor, 1999). The largest portion of the money went into a well-orchestrated media campaign.

The California Civil Rights Initiative, commonly known as Proposition 209, was passed on November 5, 1996, by a 54–46 percent vote. Unfortunately, Proposition 209's use of anti-discrimination language confused many voters in California. One-third of the Californians who voted for Proposition 209 said that they supported affirmative action and thought that they were voting for it (Paterson & Sellstrom, 1999).

In addition, the vote was divided along racial/ethnic lines with a majority of all ethnic minority groups voting 'no.' For example, 74 percent of African Americans, 76 percent of Latinos, and 61 percent of Asian Pacific Americans voted against 209. In some regions, the Asian American 'no' vote was even higher: 78 percent of Asian voters in the Koreatown/Pico area of Los Angeles rejected Prop 209. Asian Pacific Americans in the Los Angeles County region rejected the initiative by a 76 percent of 'no' votes (Rice, 1997). White voters were the only group supporting 209 with 63 percent voting 'yes' (*Coalition v Wilson*, 1996). Interestingly, only slightly over half (52 percent) of the female electorate voted against the proposition.

Proposition 209 amended the California Constitution under Article I, Section 31. The law now states: "(a) The state shall not discriminate against, or grant preferential treatment to, any individual or group on the basis of race, sex, color, ethnicity, or national origin in the operation of public employment, public education, or public contracting" (*Coalition v. Wilson,* 1996, p.1517). Spann (1997) highlights three things about the Proposition 209 language:

- It reaffirms existing law prohibiting racial and gender discrimination.

- It adds a new prohibition on affirmative action banning the state from giving preferences based on race or gender.

- It applies this new prohibition to government operations in public employment, education, and contracting.

Despite the passage of Proposition 209 it should be noted that federal affirmative action requirements remain intact. They must be followed as a condition to maintain eligibility for federal funds.

On November 6, 1996, the day after the election, a group of organizations representing the interests of racial minorities and women (including Chinese for Affirmative Action and the Asian Pacific American Labor Alliance) filed a lawsuit in the Northern Federal District Court of California to challenge the constitutionality of the new law. The Federal District Court issued a temporary restraining order on December 23, 1996, halting the enforcement of Proposition 209. The District Court ruled that plaintiffs had demonstrated a probability of success on two legal grounds:

- Proposition 209 has a racial and gender focus and places a substantial political burden on women and minorities. "Proposition 209 violates the Fourteenth Amendment's equal protection guarantee of full participation in the political life of the community" (*Coalition v. Wilson*, 1996, p. 1520).

- Proposition 209 would be an obstacle to the Congressional goal of promoting voluntary affirmative action by employers. "Congress intended to protect employers' discretion to utilize race- and gender-conscious affirmative action as a method of complying with their obligations under Title VII. Proposition 209 by eliminating the discretion to utilize race-and gender-conscious affirmative action contravenes this Congressional purpose" (*Coalition v. Wilson*, 1996, p. 1517).

On April 8, 1997, the Court of Appeals for the Ninth Circuit reversed the District Court decision and held Proposition 209 constitutional. The court found that Proposition 209 is not preempted by Title VII of the Civil Rights Act of 1964 and that "Proposition 209 does not violate the United States Constitution" (*Coalition v. Wilson*, 1997, p. 719). On November 3, 1997, the U.S. Supreme Court declined to review the Ninth Circuit decision. Thereafter, Proposition 209 went into effect.

The passage of Proposition 209 gave rise to a battle that remains intense and divisive. Opponents of affirmative action celebrated the victory. Sponsors of 209, such as University of California Regent Ward Connerly, prepared to ensure the enforcement of Proposition 209 and to promote anti-affirmative action measures throughout the whole country. Proponents supported by civil right organizations, racial minorities and women's organizations continue to fight against Proposition 209 and seek a legal solution.

THE IMPACT OF PROPOSITION 209

After the passage of Proposition 209, on September 9, 1997, Governor Wilson unveiled a hit list of more than thirty state statutes, which granted preferences based on race and/or gender. He called upon the legislature to begin the process of repealing or amending these statutes to conform to Proposition 209. "We now have the opportunity to establish California as America's first true color-blind society," Wilson said. The list of more than thirty California statutes was considered only "the starting point for identifying state statutes that violate the new provision of the California Constitution" (Governor's Office, 1997, p. 1). The removal of the statutes from the California Code has begun. However, it cannot be completed immediately since only court rulings can determine which statutes conflict with the new constitutional amendment.

The implementation of Proposition 209 has limited the ability of California state and local government agencies to prevent racial and sexual discrimination-based inequality in public education, employment, and contracting. Since court rulings on various affirmative action programs will take years to complete, the long-term impact of Proposition 209 on women and minorities is an evolving topic that deserves comprehensive study. Proposition 209 even prohibits governmental agencies "from taking voluntary action to remedy past and present discrimination through the use of constitutionally permissible race- and gender-conscious affirmative action programs" (*Coalition v. Wilson*, 1996, p. 1489). Whatever the outcome of ending affirmative action in California when "Proposition 209 is fully implemented, we could be left without any clear alternatives" (Ong, Garrett & Sirola, 1997, p. 4).

The following sections review what has happened since the passage of Proposition 209 and discuss the legislative and legal changes in the areas of public education and employment. Public contracting will not be discussed, as it is not relevant to the focus of this article.

Education

On July 20, 1995, even before the passage of Proposition 209, the University of California Regents passed resolution SP-1. The purpose of this resolution was to eliminate the use of affirmative action in admission, hiring, and contracting. On November 6, 1996, the day following of the passage of 209, Provost King of the University of California gave special written guidance to campus chancellors to comply with the law in the areas of admission, hiring, and contracting. To quote the letter, "in light of the passage of Proposition 209, effective immediately, campuses may no longer use race, ethnicity, sex or national origin as one of the supplemental criteria used to select admitted students from the pool of eligible students" (King, 1996, p. 2). University scholarships, tutoring, and outreach programs targeting women and minority students were also affected. The King policy required the suspension of all future financial aid awards where racial or gender criteria was used. The University's financial aid recruitment programs were also directed not to consider race and gender in their selection process.

Affirmative action admissions policies and programs had been successful in building a diverse student body at UC Berkeley. For example, at the University of California, Berkeley, one of the most prestigious schools in the nation, only 12 percent of the 1980 entering class belonged to underrepresented minorities. Affirmative action policies increased the rate to 28 percent of the 1988 entering class (Berdahl, 1998).

Since the implementation of SP-1 and Proposition 209 the negative effects have been immediate and definitive. The enrollment of minority students dropped drastically at the top University of California campuses. For instance, in 1998 the number of African Americans admitted to UC Berkeley dropped 66 percent and 43 percent at UCLA. New Latino freshman students dropped 53 percent at UC Berkeley and 33 percent at UCLA (Weiss and Curtius, 1998).

The drop in minority enrollment figures at the University of California has also been reflected at the most selective graduate and professional schools. In 1997, the admissions of Black students to law schools dropped 80 percent at the UCLA law school, 81 percent at UC Berkeley, and 26 percent at UC Davis. The declines for Latinos at UCLA and Berkeley law schools were 28 percent to 50 percent respectively (Gergen, 1997). UCLA Law School officials pointed out that fewer accepted minority students choose to attend. In 1999, 18 out of the 233 Blacks who applied were admitted but only two enrolled. Compare this to 1996, when 104 out of 399 Black students who applied were admitted and 19 enrolled (Pool, 1999). Even those few who were admitted felt like outcasts. Crystal James, one of the only two African American first-year law students said, "there are times I feel isolated and excluded" (Pool, 1999, p. B1).

Asian American students are not an underrepresented population in the UC system. Therefore, it must be noted that since the passage of Proposition 209, Asian American students have benefited through increased UC admissions. This gain should not be interpreted as proof that Asian Americans have no need for affirmative action. Rather Chin (1996) provides a more plausible interpretation in his book, *Beyond Self-Interest.* The author notes that since Asian Americans saw "no future in politics, sports, or entertainment, they turned their attention toward education" (1996, p. 18).

Top administrators, faculty, and students at the CSU and UC campuses reacted negatively to the passage of Proposition 209. The twenty-three CSU campus presidents attempted to act collectively in opposing 209 (Wallace, 1996). UC San Francisco Chancellor Joseph B. Martin, UC Berkeley Chancellor Chang-Lin Tien, and UCLA Chancellor Charles E. Young all resigned shortly after anti-affirmative action policies were mandated at the UC system (Wallace, 1997). The chancellors issued the following statement at a press conference in which they announced their resignations, "The passage of Proposition 209 will unquestionably alter the quality of the educational experience provided by our respective campuses by radically reducing the extraordinary diversity that they have managed to achieve" (Burdman, 1996, p. A1). UC faculty and students protested what they dubbed racial re-segregation. They "called on the UC system to refuse to comply with Proposition 209" (Lee, 1997, p. A13). A group of UC Berkeley faculty circulated a petition opposing resolution SP-1, a Regents' policy that was decided without consulting the UC faculty or chancellors. The petition argued that the Regents violated the UC tradition of shared governance. The petition was signed by 1,800 faculty members (Taylor, 1999). In February 1999 the Mexican-American Legal Defense and Educational Fund and other civil rights groups sued the Berkeley campus in federal court for discrimination in admissions that had reduced the number of underrepresented minority students at the UC campuses (Burdman, 1999).

In the face of declining minority enrollments, race-blind alternatives have been used to find a method to work around Proposition 209's ban on affirmative action. The UC Regents on March 19, 1999 passed the 4 percent admission policy. This initiative was strongly supported by Governor Gray Davis. Under the new policy, the top 4 percent of seniors from each California high school would be accepted into UC's undergraduate programs (Burdman, 1999).

California is not alone in utilizing a percentage system as a substitute for affirmative action. The University of Texas introduced a top 10 percent admissions policy after the Hopwood decision by the 5th U.S. Circuit Court of Appeals in March 1996, which banned affirmative action in the admission policies of the states of Texas, Louisiana, and Mississippi. The University of Michigan currently faces two lawsuits on this issue. The University is also considering switching to a percentage system (Gorman, 1999). Meanwhile, Florida's Governor Jeb Bush proposed a top 20 percent admission policy to replace affirmative action.

The outcome of switching from affirmative action to a percentage system in Texas was that Black and Hispanic freshmen increased by 1.7 percent at thirty-five public universities but dropped by 4 percent at the two most selective universities (Scott, 2000). UC officials estimated that, " 877 more Black and Hispanic students would qualify for UC under the 4 percent plan. That means the eligibility of Blacks and Hispanics to the UC campuses would still be a low 13.6 percent of the 32,000 California seniors eligible for UC" (Wildavsky, 1999). Berkeley Chancellor Robert Berdahl commented that the new 4 percent policy will have "no truly significant impact" on the percentages of underrepresented minority students at the Berkeley campus (Lochhead, 1999, p. A7).

Other race-blind alternatives, such as using socioeconomic status and the UC partnership with low-performing high schools are also under consideration. In any case, no better solution has yet been found to replace affirmative action in achieving educational equity in California public education.

Besides higher education, race- and gender-specific programs in California public elementary and secondary schools were also affected by Proposition 209. For example, in 1996, a Legislative Analyst for the state of California stated that 209 could eliminate, or cause fundamental changes to, voluntary desegregation programs run by school districts. Up to $60 million spent per year on the implementation of these programs could be affected (Secretary of State, 1996, p. 31). After the passage of Proposition 209, many sections of the California Education Code were found on Wilson's list of offending statutes that violated the new provision of the state Constitution, for example:

- California Education Code Section 8631 established the California Summer Science and Technology Academy that emphasizes female and minority participation in university-based research programs in science and math.

- California Education Code Section 52060–52065 established the American Indian Early Childhood Education Program. This program allows the allocation of state funds to school districts with 10 percent or more American Indian pupils.

The list states that, "the allocation of funding based on the percentage of a certain ethnicity in a school may run afoul of the prohibition on preferential treatment on the basis of race and ethnicity in the operation of public education" (Governor's Office, 1997, p. 3).

The impact of Proposition 209 has been immediate and severe. However, it will continue to impact generations of minority populations in years to come. As Chancellor Berdahl stated, "We meet at a time when, once again, the issue of race is central to American discourse...we may be in danger of becoming several nations, separate and unequal" (Berdahl, 1988).

What has happened in California attracted the attention of educational institutions nationwide. On May 29, 1997, the Board of Directors of the

American Council on Education adopted a statement reaffirming support for affirmative action in admission and employment in higher education. Several higher education associations, such as the Association of American Universities, the American Association of Community Colleges, and the American Association of State Colleges and Universities all issued statements supporting affirmative action in education (American Council on Education, 1997).

Employment

Affirmative action in employment is designed to reduce racial and sexual inequality in the workplace and to overcome discrimination. It became law in California after Governor Ronald Reagan signed Equal Employment Opportunity legislation (EEO) in 1974. California Education Code Section 44101 defines an affirmative action employment program as "planned activities designed to seek, hire, and promote persons who are underrepresented in the work force compared to their number in the population, including individuals with disabilities, women, and persons of minority racial and ethnic backgrounds" (Cal. Educ. Code § 44101, p. 259).

During this early period, the State Personnel Board (SPB) issued hiring guidelines for governmental agencies. The affirmative action employment programs that resulted have proven very successful in remedying the underutilization of women and minorities. SPB reported in January 1996 that "the state's work force was 97 percent consistent with the demographics of California's relevant labor markets" (LaVally et al., 1995, p. 9). Various studies on the impact of affirmative action have proved its effectiveness in reducing inequality. A study entitled *The Impact of Affirmative Action Policy on Ethnic and Sexual Inequality in Employment* found that "ethnic and sexual inequality in the California municipal workforce was reduced from 1975 to 1985. The indicators of this reduction were the changes in the minority and female employment representation and in the occupational segregation level between them and White men" (Espinosa, 1986, p. 35). In "The Impact of Affirmative Action on Public Sector Employment in California, 1970-1990," Badgett (1997) found that California equal opportunity laws and programs increased the employment of women and minorities in both private and public sectors. The study also found that minorities have "greater access to public managerial and professional jobs, suggesting a positive impact from affirmative action policies" (Ong, 1997, p. xiv).

Affirmative action employment policies and programs were the first line of attack under Proposition 209. Months before the passage of 209, Governor Pete Wilson filed lawsuits on August 10, 1995, challenging many state statutory programs. Wilson's hit list included Government Code section 19790, which relates to an affirmative action employment program administered by the State Personnel Board and Education Code section 87100 relating to an affirmative action employment program administered by the Board of Governors of the California Community Colleges (*Wilson v. State*

Personnel Board, 1995). In March 1998, the California Court of Appeal held that the State Personnel Board's affirmative action policy of "supplemental certification" to augment the eligibility of women and minorities in state civil service to be unconstitutional (*Kidd v. State of California*, 1998). This was the first court ruling in California to strike down an affirmative action employment requirement under Proposition 209. The *Los Angeles Times* reported that Governor Pete Wilson hailed the decision, because the ruling would serve as a precedent for his main lawsuit attacking other such statutes (Morain, 1998).

The University of California, Office of the President issued *Questions and Answers* regarding the impact of Proposition 209 on UC's employment practices. In response to the question "What is the University Permitted to do under Proposition 209 and Regents' Resolution SP-2?" It states that "UC must use race- or gender-neutral criteria in its employment practices." The University affirmed that race and gender could be considered only for maintaining eligibility for federal programs. Another answer notes: "Any use of race, ethnicity, or gender as criteria for selection in hiring, participating in training programs, or any other employment practice conflicts with the new constitutional amendment and SP-2" (UC Office of the President, 1997, p. 2).

Two years after the passage of Proposition 209, Schneider reported on the status of faculty diversity at California educational institutions. He noted that all affirmative action offices had experienced name changes. For example, the University of California, Berkeley renamed the "Faculty Assistant on Affirmative Action" position to the "Faculty Equity Associate." According to one sociologist at the University of California, Santa Cruz, the effects of the anti-affirmative action initiative goes beyond verbal changes. When participating in a job search, he said, "We have to prove that we're not paying attention to race." Another professor said, "the hiring of a person of color or a woman becomes tainted with suspicion and speculation. If you pick a minority applicant, that person had better be head-and-shoulders above the rest of the pool" (Schneider, 1998).

The *Los Angeles Times* reported that about 6,000 government agencies in California have been affected by Proposition 209. Public officials remain conflicted about how to promote diversity under the framework of the new law. At the local level, many government officials have turned to their lawyers and administrators seeking legal advice for new guidelines. While some cities are still struggling to keep their affirmative action programs active, some agencies have adjusted their policies to comply with the new requirements, others have attempted to find alternative methods to repair the damage caused by Proposition 209, and many municipalities have simply eliminated any trace of affirmative action (Lesher, 1997).

A hostile atmosphere toward equal opportunity programs now exists in California (Paterson, 1999). Those cities attempting to maintain some vestige of affirmative action have found themselves faced with lawsuits. For example, the City of Mountain View established a new hiring plan. It was the first local government to be sued in July 1998 for retaining affirmative action related hiring practices under Proposition 209 (Workman, 1998). Anti-affirmative action forces are closely monitoring local government reactions. The Sacramento-based Pacific Legal Foundation representing the sponsors of Proposition 209 has filed numerous complaints and lawsuits against local government agencies to enforce Proposition 209.

Even in this litigious atmosphere, cities, such as San Francisco, San Jose, Los Angeles, and Sacramento have tried to maintain their affirmative action programs. The City and County of San Francisco, for example, have expanded affirmative action programs in contracting. In response, the Pacific Legal Foundation filed a major lawsuit on behalf of a local graphics company.

With the elimination of affirmative action in hiring, cities and counties have no officially sanctioned mechanism to encourage the employment of women and minorities. This was underscored by the fact that both former Governor Pete Wilson in 1998 and current Governor Gray Davis vetoed a bill in July 1999 that would have allowed for the use of outreach programs to increase the number of women and minorities in public employment. Governor Davis, an opponent of Proposition 209, believed that the bill violated Proposition 209. He felt obligated to enforce the ruling and uphold the state law. According to Governor Davis, constitutionally permissible outreach programs can only be based on socioeconomic status, geographic area, or other race neutral characteristics (Gunnison, 1999).

Badgett suggested that the potential impact of eliminating public-sector affirmative action programs would be a reduced demand for women and minorities in the public sector. The shift of these workers to the private sector would result in lower wages. The study also suggested that "some individuals who would have been hired for managerial or professional jobs in the public sector will not be able to obtain comparable jobs in the private sector, resulting in underemployment for some female and minority managers and professionals" (Ong, 1997, p. 91).

Espinosa (1986) found that the majority of the progress in reducing workplace inequality occurred within the first three years following the initial implementation of the city's affirmative action policy. Subsequently, when there was less effort to continue the new policy, progress was slower. It seems clear that when a race- and gender-blind employment policy replaces affirmative action there will be little incentive to prevent discrimination and ensure equality. Everything will depend on the good will of employers. More troubling is the fact that there will be no way to monitor the underrepresentation of women and minorities in the workforce as data collection is prohibited.

Nationwide Impact

Bills similar to Proposition 209 were introduced in thirteen states during the first two years following its passage in California (Feldmann, 1998) In total, there are presently seventeen states which have attempted to eliminate affirmative action through legislation or the initiative process. Washington was the only state where the initiative process has succeeded. The voters of the state of Washington approved Initiative 200 on November 3, 1998. Initiative 200 was almost identical to California's Proposition 209.

In addition, the federal courts have begun to chip away at the legality of affirmative action. On March 18, 1998, the U.S. Court of Appeals for the Fifth Circuit ruled in the now famous *Hopwood v. State of Texas* case. The majority opinion states that the University of Texas School of Law discriminated in favor of blacks and Mexican Americans by giving racial preferences in its admissions. The Court concludes that race cannot be used as a factor in law school admissions (*Hopwood v. State of Texas*, 1998). This ruling was very important because it affects the states of Texas, Louisiana, and Mississippi that have large minority populations. In addition, it was a warning to other Districts that judiciary support for affirmative action was crumbling.

The connections between Initiative 200 and Proposition 209 are clearly visible. First, the ballot language is quite similar. The initiative was entitled the "Equal Rights Amendment" just like the California initiative. It should be stressed that the use of the term 'equal rights' misled many voters as to the true nature of the proposed law (Gildar, 1999). Furthermore, Ward Connerly, who led the fight against affirmative action in California, was also heavily involved in the state of Washington electoral process. His organization, the American Civil Rights Coalition, spent $178,000 to pay for signature collection that put the initiative on the Washington ballot (Balter, 1998).

Many prominent elected leaders such as Governor Locke, the nation's first Chinese American governor, opposed the measure. Major Seattle area corporations, including Boeing and Microsoft opposed I-200 (McMahon, P. 1998).

After the passage of Initiative 200, the state of Washington experienced similar enrollment decreases in institutions of higher learning as had occurred in California. There was a drop in minority enrollment at the University of Washington. Unlike California Governor Peter Wilson, Washington Governor Locke has preserved the data tracking of minorities and women (Brune & Varner, 1999). This is a significant difference, as it will eventually allow the state to generate data on the impact of the new law.

The banning of affirmative action in college admissions has occurred in different ways: by court order in Texas, by ballot initiatives in California and Washington, and by authority in Florida. The Florida Board of Regents approved Governor Jeb Bush's One Florida Initiative on February 17, 2000. This initiative eliminated race as a factor in college admissions and ended set-asides in state contracting. Instead the top 20 percent of each Florida high school class is guaranteed admission to an institution of higher education in Florida. The Florida branch of the National Association for the Advancement of Colored People has filed a lawsuit against the One Florida plan (Clary, 2000).

Viewed together, the initiatives, anti-affirmative action rulings, and executive orders in these three states will no doubt have a very chilling effect on government attempts to correct past wrongs related to race and gender.

Moreover, because these measures are based on legislative and judicial actions they will be extremely difficult to overturn. The wide-ranging impact of these rulings has undermined over three decades of progress on racial and gender equality.

AFFIRMATIVE ACTION AND ASIANS

The definition of "Asian" used in this discussion is adopted from Association of Library and Information Science Educators (ALISE): "Asian or Pacific Islander [is] a person having an origin in any of the original peoples of the Far East, Southeast Asia, the Indian subcontinent, or the Pacific Islands" (Saye, 1998, p. 5) Asians are one of the fastest growing American ethnic groups. In 1998, the estimated Asian population was 10.2 million, comprising 3.8 percent of the total population. In recent years, immigrants from Asia have comprised close to half of all legal immigrants. Since 1990, the Asian population has increased 35 percent. By the middle of the next century, it will reach 34 million and comprise 9 percent of the total population (Census Bureau, 1998). Moreover, "Asians" are a complex combination of more than twenty ethnic groups with different cultures, languages, religions, and economic levels. Asian Americans are one of the most diverse minority groups in the United States.

The Model Minority Myth

During the Proposition 209 debate, the stereotyped "Model Minority Myth" was used to claim that Whites and Asians are both victims of affirmative action. Opponents insisted that they object to affirmative action not only because it is unfair to White males but discriminates against Asian Americans as well.

A report by the American Council on Education described the Model Minority stereotype of Asians in the workplace as "hard-working, dutiful, well-represented in the professions, and economically successful, though lacking in the communication skills and leadership qualities necessary for higher level management positions" (Carter & Wilson, p. 53). The myth implies that Asian Americans are a homogenous ethnic group that has achieved the American dream of success. It assumes that since Asian Americans were successful even before affirmative action, that anti-discrimination programs can be safely eliminated. It infers that Asian Americans as a group have not been discriminated against and should not be considered disadvantaged. It, thereby, allows the majority culture to reprimand other minorities and encourages them to emulate the Asian American model.

However, the problem is that the Model Minority myth is simply not true. U.S. history documents much discrimination against Asian Americans. As an ethnic group, they have continually experienced racial discrimination. David and Lin (1997) presented a study on major Asian immigrant groups who have experienced and are continuing to face institutionalized discrimination and violence.

Asians are a combination of very different ethnic groups. On the one hand, there are highly educated U.S.-born Asian Americans who, due to their educational background, are more successful but have experienced the glass ceiling in promotion to managerial positions. "Less than 0.3 percent of senior executives in the United States are of Asian descent. U.S.-born Asian American men were between 7 and 11 percent less likely to be in managerial occupations than White men with the same education, work experience, English ability, religion, marital status, disability, and industry work" (Narasaki, K., 1998, p. 5).   Affirmative action opponents use the high representation of Asian students in education to illustrate the existence of equality and the absence of discrimination. In contrast, the American Council on Education reports that the high education participation rate of Asians is due to the role of racism and not to culture. The emphasis of Asians on education is based on their perceptions of "advanced schooling as an economic necessity and a protection against racial discrimination" (Carter & Wilson, 1997, p. 54). Recent studies found that the high educational attainment of Asians "has not resulted in income parity" compared with Whites or the U.S. population as a whole. Asians' returns on education are unequal compared with Whites. The experience of Asians has "demonstrated the persistence of racial discrimination and other barriers" (Carter & Wilson, 1997, p. 60).

On the other hand, there are large proportions of new Asian immigrants and refugees with limited English language skills. "Some Asian ethnic groups are at risk educationally, a fact that challenges the notion of the model minority" (Carter & Wilson, 1997, p. 69). Other studies indicate enrollment of Filipinos in higher education is very close to that of African Americans and Latinos. Asians stereotyped as a single entity, a "model minority," includes Southeast Asians, Pacific Islanders, and Filipinos.   There are significant disparities between a second or third generation Japanese student and a first generation Vietnamese refugee. The Model Minority myth misrepresents the true image of Asians. In *Asian American Attitudes Toward Affirmative Action in Employment*, the authors found differences in attitudes toward employment programs. The attitudes of Asians toward affirmative action are closer to that of Blacks and Hispanics than that of Whites.   Asians experience more workplace discrimination than Whites, about the same level as Hispanics, but less than Blacks.   The results of the study are clearly in conflict with the Model Minority myth (Bell, Harrison, & McLauglin, 1997).

Asians continue to face pervasive racial discrimination. Equal employment opportunity and affirmative action programs have protected Asians against discrimination at all levels of employment and public contracting. During the affirmative action era the employment rate of Asians in state jobs increased from 3 percent in 1975 to 10 percent in 1993 (Tokaji, 1996).

Asians and Discrimination in Libraries

As discussed above, racial discrimination against Asian Americans is still an obstacle to their full participation in American society and their enjoyment of the civil rights inscribed in federal law. Does the same problem exist in the library profession? *The Library Journal* published the results of a survey on employment racism as perceived among librarians of color. The survey, which targeted four-hundred librarians from four different ethnic groups, found that the majority of minority librarians believed that "racism in the library profession is as prevalent as in other professions" (St. Lifer & Nelson, 1997, p. 42). White respondents saw it differently. Almost two-thirds of Whites state that "racism in the ranks was less prevalent than in other professions" (St. Lifer & Nelson, 1997, p. 43). The survey also found that "four [out] of ten blacks, one-third of Asians and one-quarter of Latinos polled said they were discriminated against at their library at least occasionally" (St. Lifer & Nelson, 1997, p. 43) The survey showed that 33 percent of Asian librarians surveyed had experienced racial discrimination in the workplace. The rate is less than that of Blacks, but more than that of Latinos (St. Lifer & Nelson, 1997).

This study suggests that racism and racial discrimination exist in the library profession. Given this state of affairs it is clear that Asian Americans need legal protection as much as other librarians of color. Affirmative action is one important strategy to alleviate racial discrimination. Proposition 209, on the other hand, has disarmed Asian Americans in their fight against discrimination in the library profession.

Dr. Ling Hwey Jeng, the president of the Chinese American Librarians Association, gave a speech at the Asian Pacific American Librarians Association Annual Conference Program on June 28, 1999, entitled "Building Collective Esteem." In her speech, she shared some particularly flagrant examples of discrimination against Asian Americans in the library profession.

She told the story of Ms. B, an Asian American woman who has two master's degrees, one in comparative literature and another in library and information science. Despite her high academic qualifications she was only hired as a paraprofessional in an academic library. Her duties, however, were mostly at the professional level. When the library received funding to hire for a professional position, Ms. B was denied the opportunity to apply for the position despite letters from more than sixty faculty members who wrote recommendations on her behalf.

Mr. A is a middle-level manager in a community college library in the Southwest. When the position of library director opened up, Mr. A applied but was not considered a viable candidate for promotion by the selection committee. No reason whatsoever was given for this action. When he inquired, he was told that it would be better for him to find a job elsewhere (1999, e-mail message from Jeng).

In another case, an Asian American student of Dr. Jeng's, "was hired by a public library in the south and was promptly fired after three months because he was put in a situation from day one that made it impossible for him to succeed" (Personal communication, June 30, 1999). During a telephone interview with this person, he described the situation vividly. His supervisor took him to task from day one. She took detailed notes of mistakes he made, large or small, and enumerated them to him, one by one, on a regular basis. The hostile working environment made this employee so nervous and upset that it created an adverse effect on his performance. Finally, she told him to "stop working and leave immediately." He could not understand why the supervisor was so hostile, short of racial prejudice (Personal communication, September 16, 1999).

Rapid Asian migration has brought sociological change and racial conflicts to American society. The case of the Monterey Park Public Library sums up a host of problems illustrating this truism. Monterey Park, a suburb of Los Angeles, is a city that has experienced dramatic demographic changes in the last thirty years. Asian immigration has changed Monterey Park into an Asian-majority city (Hudson, 1989). According to the 1990 census, 56 percent of Monterey Park's residents are Asian.

The new Asian immigrants were not welcomed with open arms by the oldtime residents. There were many multicultural debates in the city during the 1980s regarding the delivery of public services to the new immigrants. Some of the controversies pertinent to this article regarded the development of foreign language collections and bilingual/bicultural staffing at the Monterey Park Public Library.

The city mayor at the time was Mayor Hatch. He was an outspoken anti-immigrant advocate. He was quoted in the *Los Angeles Times* as saying "The bottom line is we're losing our country. They're buying up our property. They're taking Western culture out and replacing it with eastern culture and Latin culture. They're taking us over. If their language is set up, all the rest will crumble" (Hudson, 1989, p. 5).

In 1989, a racial discrimination lawsuit was filed against the mayor. The court ordered Mayor Hatch and the city to reinstate three Monterey Park Public Library Board members who were fired by the Mayor for advocating the acquisition of foreign language books, particularly those in Chinese languages. The mayor was quoted as telling the city librarian that if library patrons wanted to read foreign-language books and periodicals, "they can go purchase books on their own." He urged the library not to enlarge its foreign-language collection, which included Chinese, Vietnamese, Spanish, and Japanese materials. Hatch said. "This is the United States of America. Monterey Park is part of it. Do you read me?" The *Los Angeles Times* reported that the Mayor "sees his battle for English as a rear-guard action against the decline of Western civilization" (Hudson, 1989, p. 1).

In 1994, the Monterey Park Public Library again became the center of media attention. The Library Board forced Jeanette Cheng, the city's first Chinese American librarian and a department head, to resign in April 1994. The Friends of the Library and library staff denounced the move, which was motivated by a "predominately white group of longtime residents of the city" (Winton, 1994, p. J2).

A few months later, an Asian American trustee named Marina Tse, one of two Asian Americans on the board, came under attack. The other trustees tried to oust Tse for opposing Cheng's resignation. The president of the Library Board said Tse was not suited to be a trustee and should take a "low[er] position until she can speak English" (Winton, 1994, p. J2).

Ironically, Ms. Tse is a teacher with a master's degree from the University of Southern California. In addition, the governor of California had recently appointed Tse to a special state education committee. The president of the Library Board not only made continued slurs against Tse but threw a cup of water at the self described Chinese American activist (Winton, 1994).

What this series of events illustrates is that even in a city where new immigrants are the majority, changing traditional services to meet the information needs of newcomers can be filled with political tensions and resentments by longtime residents. Despite the professions' historical belief in the Library Bill of Rights it does not necessarily follow that the majority residents will fully enjoy their right to the dissemination of information in a format that would be most acceptable to them. The new immigrants may not wish to assimilate as in previous historical eras but rather acculturate to their new environment while still mantaining ties to their home culture and language.

Given these new attitudes, immigrants need bilingual and bicultural library personnel who can help them in securing information and knowledge. Clearly they need materials in their native language that can assist them in acculturating to their new environment. Lastly, they need support from government agencies that will protect them from racial prejudice and discrimination in their attempt to settle in America. Given this perspective, we may say that Proposition 209 has made a bad situation even worse.

CALIFORNIA PUBLIC LIBRARIES IN THE POST-209 ERA

The California State Library has had a long-term commitment to serve the needs of California's ethnic groups. It has come to be known for its great efforts to recruit minority librarians and to improve services for ethnic communities. Like other library organizations it was guided by the principle that public libraries are to "freely offer all members of the community [library services] without regard to race, citizenship, age, education level, economic status, or any other qualification or condition" (American Library Association & Public Library Association, 1982).

However, under Proposition 209, the State Library can no longer employ race- and gender-conscious programs or policies. All government agencies in California including the State Library have had to adjust their policy and practice to comply with the new color-blind law.

Historical Review

California public libraries have attempted to respond to the demographic changes of the last three decades. For example, the California State Library has played a leadership role in recruiting minorities to the profession. The State Librarian, Gary Strong, approved $21,000 in 1986 to support the California Library School Recruitment Project. The focus of efforts was the recruitment of ethnic minorities (Katie, 1988). In 1987, there was a statewide recruitment campaign entitled "The Next Shortage of Librarians." There was also a broad array of statewide ethnicity-conscious programs to promote the equality of opportunities for historically underrepresented groups. An influential group called the Ethnic Services Task Force was also established to guide the State Library. Librarians from various ethnic communities comprised the membership of the group.

In May 1988, the State Library organized a conference titled "A State of Change; California's Ethnic Future and Libraries." As the result of the conference, a statewide program, "Partnership for Change," was created. Twenty-eight participating libraries were funded with Federal Library Services and Construction Act funds. The program lasted almost eight years (1988–1995). The mission of the program was to serve the changing needs of a diverse population. The program's purpose was to assist libraries in reaching out to their changing community populations, to better understand them and their information needs, and to restructure their services and policies to best meet the needs of these changing populations. The targeted populations were American Indian, Asian American, African American, and Hispanic (California State Library, 1988). A survey sent to the Partnership for Change participants in April 1999 indicates that the Partnership for Change program successfully developed the needed services, such as non-English language collection development, bilingual staffing, bilingual programming, and community linkages to ethnic communities (Keller, 1999).

Public Libraries Under Proposition 209

After the passage of Proposition 209, the California State Library made some notable program adjustments. The post-209 focus shifted to technology. The Library of California Act (1997) emphasizes technology: "Access to information is increasingly technology based. Technology is vital to the libraries serving Californians." In the paragraph on user services, one of the goals is to help libraries "to provide and improve service to the underserved" (Library of California Act, 1997). The term "ethnic minorities" was replaced by race neutral language such as "disadvantaged" and/or "diverse."

The Partnership for Change programs which targeted seven different Asian communities—Filipino, Cambodian, Korean, Vietnamese, Laotian, Japanese, and Chinese—are no longer possible for the State Library to support. The State Library vision statement (California State Library, 2000) does not reflect any future goals specific to the ethnic populations of California. Without this guidance and support from the state some public libraries may fail to provide services to certain ethnic communities that are linguistically or culturally different. As the census data indicate, most Asians are new immigrants with a large proportion of non-English speakers. The main barriers to information access are unawareness of available library services and lack of language skills. While technology-based information access is welcome, it may not be suitable for Asian immigrants who are most interested in survival needs. This may be especially true for less educated Asian immigrants and refugees.

The American Library Association (ALA) Office for Library Personnel Resources (OLPR) collected national data on race and gender among the library profession in 1980 and 1985 for affirmative action planning. The results were published in 1981 and 1986 under the title "Academic and Public Librarians: Data by Race, Ethnicity and Sex." The data contributed to many studies on recruitment, retention, and carrier advancement. Presently, more than ten years later, there is no compatible, similar data available.

In California, ethnic and gender data collecting is prohibited under Proposition 209. Governor Peter Wilson ordered state agencies to stop data collection in 1998 (Executive Order W–172–98). In addition, UC Board of Trustees member, Ward Connerly has called upon universities to stop gathering data about racial and ethnic background of students, faculty, and staff (Paterson, 1999). When I requested data on the number or percentage of Asian librarians employed at state, county, and city levels the response was mostly negative. The State Library told me that the data was not available (Personal communication, August 1999). Other libraries indicated that the collecting or reporting of employee ethnic background for any reason is very sensitive and not available to the general public (Personal communication, August 1999).

Ongoing monitoring and investigation of employment trends in the library profession need to continue. Data collection constitutes a powerful tool for identifying, documenting, and fighting racial discrimination. This lack of data will be a significant obstacle to research and litigation. Researchers and attorneys must rely on anecdotal evidence, which is easily dismissed.

In response to changes in state population, the center for Policy Development conducted a study in 1990 titled "Adrift in a Sea of Change: California's Public Libraries Struggle to Meet the Information Needs of Multicultural Communities." The study indicated that only 15 percent of California's public librarians in 1986 were minorities and emphasized the importance of having staff, which "reflect the racial and ethnic makeup and share the cultural values of the service community" (Carlson et al., 1990, p. 65). The State Library's commitment to building a workforce that reflects the population led to the creation of the Multi-Ethnic Recruiting Program Scholarship. The scholarship started in the late 1980s and has helped many minority library students at the University of California and San José State University library schools. After the passage of Proposition 209, the Library, as a State agency, was forced to eliminate the scholarship.

The University of California, Santa Barbara (UCSB) has a very successful "Minority Residency Program" started in 1989 to recruit new library school graduates from underrepresented ethnic groups. A major difficulty for new graduates entering the job market is a lack of work experience. It is more difficult for a minority student, especially a foreign-born student to have acceptable working experience. In seven years, nine minority students have gone through the UCSB program, and all were subsequently employed in academic libraries (Boisse, 1996). As the UC post-Proposition 209 guidelines prohibit any use of race, or ethnicity as criteria for scholarship practice, the UCSB program had to be changed to the "Library Fellowship Program." The program is now open to all applicants.

In spite of the ongoing recruitment efforts of the library profession, minorities are still underrepresented in the public library. This problem is more serious in California with its rapidly increasing population of foreign-born immigrants. Instead of increasing the recruitment effort, the elimination of minority recruitment programs will cause a further shortage of minority librarians in California public libraries.

The recruitment, retention, and promotion of ethnic minorities in the library profession have become pressing issues as the demographic reality of the society in the United States continues to shift. McCook (1993) cites "the profession's failure to recruit and retain a diversified workforce" as the single largest obstacle to realizing the dream of a multicultural service. According to "Academic and Public Librarians: Data by Race, Ethnicity and Sex" published in 1986, the racial and ethnic distribution of top management indicates that 93.4 percent of upper-level managers in public libraries are White. The percentage of Asian directors, deputy, associate, and assistant directors was only 1 percent in public libraries.

Yet in California today public library employment ads omit the term affirmative action or modify their applications to eliminate race- or gender-based affirmative action language. For example, a large Los Angeles public librarian job advertisement revised the phrase "An Equal Employment Opportunity/Affirmative Action Employer," to "An Equal Opportunity Employer." It states that "the City of Los Angeles does not discriminate on the basis of disability" (City of Los Angeles Personnel Department, 2000). "Disability" is not included in the preferential treatment category of Proposition 209. However, it is very clear that ethnic minorities and women are no longer considered protected groups by the city of Los Angeles.

Hiring is now based entirely on an examination (verbal interview) score. In this situation, a foreign-born candidate whose native language is not English is in a disadvantaged position, as they must compete with native speakers. Even where racial prejudice is completely absent linguistic prejudice may negatively impact the candidate. His or her bilingual or multicultural background may not even be taken into consideration, unless a particular job requires bilingual skills. During a telephone interview, a library personnel officer stated, "We only look at the score from the exam. No other qualifications are considered.   We give equal opportunity to everyone" (Personal communication, August 1999).

A bilingual library school graduate failed such an examination in 1997. His failure was not due to lack of library and information knowledge and skills but rather the fact that the verbal examination put him at a great disadvantage. It took him a long time to learn interview techniques. He finally passed the exam in the same library system after three years of practice.

Ms. Poon, head librarian in charge of the former Asian American Studies Library at UC Berkeley, shared the injustice she experienced after graduation. For six years, she failed to pass an entrance examination to be appointed as a professional librarian (Poon, 1998). It seems likely that such an exam will be skewed in favor of someone whose native language is English even if their library skills were not as competitive as other candidates.

Audit studies have found that "employers are less likely to interview and hire minority applicants" (Badgett, 1997, p. 64). In the post-affirmative action era library employers do not have a legal obligation to interview or hire a minority librarian. So it is often difficult for an Asian graduate who speaks English with an accent and lacks work experience in this country to get into the candidate pool for even an entry-level position.

INCREASING MINORITY LIBRARIANS IN PUBLIC LIBRARIES

ALISE statistics from 1999 revealed that the percentage of minority students awarded master's degrees was 9.4 percent of all degrees awarded that year.   Doctoral degrees comprised 1.7 percent of the total (ALISE, 1999). According to the new release of the American Association, the percentage of minority librarians in public libraries is 13.46 percent (Lynch, 1998).

In an effort to up the number of minority librarians ALA and other library organizations created the Spectrum Initiative to recruit and fund library school scholarships for minorities in 1997.   The three-year program that started in 1998 will provide fifty scholarships annually.   Neely discusses the need for national library science diversity initiatives for the recruitment, retention, and promotion of librarians from underrepresented populations. "It is important to realize that diversity efforts aimed at providing financial aid for educational programs to individuals from underrepresented groups are critical to ethnically diverse representation in library education and the profession as a whole" (Neely, 1999, p. 124).   ALA's Spectrum Initiative is the largest minority recruitment initiative within the profession. There was a total of $1.3 million allocated for the support of the initiative over the three-year period.

Since the passage of Proposition 209, similar recruitment efforts have become impossible at the state level. In the past, the California State Library played a leadership role in recruiting minorities to public libraries. This kind of leadership is no longer feasible. An e-mail message from a State Library employee states, "We currently do not have any 'targeted' grants programs specifically focusing on diversity. However, California libraries are eligible to apply for federal library Service and Technology Act grant funds to projects related to serving their diverse populations" (Personal communication, August, 1999). Proposition 209 will have a serious impact not only for the present, but also in years to come when California will have more than 59 percent minority population. The question, then, will be: "who will serve the information needs of this segment of the population?"

In order to serve the fast growing Asian population in California, the California public libraries face the important issue of the recruitment of Asian students to enter the library profession. Without the guidance and professional skills of Asian librarians public libraries will be hard pressed to provide effective and equitable services to Asian-language speakers in terms of Asian language collections, reference services, and special programs.

Comparing data over three time periods, the number of Asian librarians in public libraries nationwide has not changed much over an eighteen-year period. The percentage of Asian librarians in public libraries was 3.4 percent in 1980, 2.8 percent in 1985 (Guy 1986), and 3.93 percent in 1998 (Lynch, 1998). There was a decrease from 1980 to 1985 and an increase in 1998. In California, there is a shortage of Asian librarians. For example, Riverside and San Bernardino are two of the top five largest counties serving a population of over 500,000. These areas also have rapidly growing Asian populations. However, there are no Asian librarians or Asian material collections in the San Bernardino County system, and only one Asian librarian in the Riverside system. If an Asian patron wants to read Asian language material, he or she has to drive to the Los Angeles Public Library.

Asian American students, who are overrepresented at UC campuses, are primarily science and engineering majors. However, in the humanities and social sciences, they are underrepresented. In the library science field, the number of Asian American graduates from ALA-accredited master's programs had grown from 1.83 percent in 1984–85 to 3.44 percent in 1994–95 (McCook & Geist, 1997). In the fall of 1997 enrollment of Asian American students decreased to 2.49 percent (ALISE, 1998). Compared to 3.8 percent of the Asian population in the United States and 11 percent in California, Asian American students are underrepresented in library science schools. ALISE statistics indicate that there were no Ph.D.s conferred to Asian American candidates, while Asians who received master's degrees represented less than 5 percent of the total graduates at two California library schools (See Table 1). Although these numbers are higher than the national level (2.58 percent), compared to the demographics of California's Asian population, it is a rather telling statistic. It aptly contradicts the popular "overrepresentation" claim. According to census data, in the year 2025, Asians will be 15 percent of the California population. The prohibition of recruitment and outreach programs to minority communities mandated under Proposition 209 will only add to the critical shortage of Asian librarians in the future.

Table 1
ALA-Accredited Master's Degrees and Certificates Awarded by Ethnic Origin (1996–1997)

School	Number of Asian Students	Percentage of Asian Students	Total Graduates
UCLA	2	4.87%	41
San Jose	6	4.16%	144
Total (56 schools)	131	2.58%	5,068

Source: ALISE Statistical Report (Association for Library and Information Science Education, 1998)

CONCLUSIONS AND RECOMMENDATIONS

Proposition 209 is now a fact of life in California. It has long-range impacts on the state and the nation. The library issues discussed here are only a small part of the discriminatory consequences of this legislation.

Asian American voters in California were so concerned about these consequences that 61 percent of them voted against Proposition 209. Many Asian American professors and intellectuals called on all Asians to support affirmative action, and to recognize that racial discrimination against all non-European minorities continues to exist in America. Asian American library organizations are also committed to the continuation of affirmative action as an issue of national social justice. In a report to Congress on professional education, the Asian Pacific American Librarians Association opposed Proposition 209. The report notes that libraries must "continue diversity education in all types of libraries despite trends such as California's Proposition 209 which prohibits affirmative action as a factor in employment, education, etc." (Asian Pacific Librarians Association, March 8, 1999).

The library profession, in general, is to be commended for its concern with the affirmative action debate. Following are some specific recommendations that may assist the profession and all other concerned parties in promoting affirmative action or other reasonable remedies.

National Conference on Equal Opportunities in Libraries

It is important to educate the general public about the hidden damage legislation such as Proposition 209 and the similar Washington Initiative, I-200, can create. Once such propositions have amended state constitutions, their legislative and judicial power will be hard to derail. The American Library Association is to be commended for its concern and the support for affirmative action within the library profession. It is recommended that a conference addressing the impact on libraries related to anti-discrimination legislation, equal opportunities, and the anti-affirmative action movement be sponsored by ALA and/or other major library organizations including ethnic caucuses.

Data Collection of Racial Discrimination Against Asians

A 1995 report to President Clinton on federal affirmative action concluded, "discrimination and exclusion remain all too common" (Stephanopoulos & Edley, 1995, Section 4). As a racial minority group, Asian Americans have and continue to face racial discrimination. Asian American library organizations should continue to address discrimination issues and support funding for assessment research and the collection of data on the hiring and employment status of Asians in the library profession. More public voices, like the speech by Dr. Jeng cited above, must call attention to discriminatory employment practices in the library profession and document their findings in the library literature. Asian American librarians must learn to fight collectively for equal opportunities in hiring and promotion.

Matching Funds for Spectrum Recipients

The California State Constitution now prohibits any racial and/or gender based recruitment or outreach programs. Consequently, California public libraries and public library schools are unable to provide funds to match the ALA Spectrum Initiative scholarship programs to recruit minorities into the library profession. Other library organizations, such as the California Library Association and the California Academic Research Libraries, should institute matching funds for Spectrum recipients and recruit targeted minorities to library school.

Enforcement of Federal Anti-Discrimination Laws

Public libraries should maintain and reaffirm their commitment to recruit bilingual and bicultural members from minority groups whenever possible. Even states that have passed anti-affirmative action measures similar to Proposition 209 cannot override federal laws. For example, Title VI of the federal Civil Rights Act of 1964 prohibits any entity that receives federal funding from practicing racial discrimination (Paterson & Sellstrom, 1999). Even without the intention to discriminate, an employer is still liable under federal law for the discriminatory effects of its employment practices (Ong, 1997).

Hiring Criteria of Asian American Librarians

Proposition 209 has changed the public employment landscape in California public libraries. It is no longer possible to hire underrepresented minorities according to the demographic distribution or the need of ethnic communities. While there are no better alternatives for affirmative action employment, it is recommended that library hiring policies be reexamined. A candidate's merit should not only be based on an oral examination but also on the candidate's cultural background, on the composition of the ethnic communities within the library service area, and the candidates' bilingual skills. Furthermore, community service experience and commitment to serve the designate community should also be weighted. To broaden hiring criteria, a written essay addressing these issues should be included in the application process and carefully evaluated.

Recruitment

More federal or private funds should be allocated to provide internship programs similar to the UCSB Minority Residency program to help minority students without work experience to enter the profession. Historically, more attention has been given to recruiting minority students to library schools. Often, a minority graduate needs more assistance with job seeking and interview skills. Federal or private funds should be sought to support Asian American library school recruitment programs.

Mentoring and training programs should be available from professional associations. The Reforma/San Jose School of Library and Information Science META mentoring program and the UCLA, School of Information Studies, Diversity, Mentoring and Recruitment Committee are two excellent models that could be replicated in other settings. Moreover, during library conferences, experienced librarians should mentor and assist targeted library school students who are job hunting.

REFERENCES

ALISE. (1998). *ALISE statistical report 1998: Students chapter.* Retrieved July 12, 1999, from the World Wide Web: http://ils.unc.edu/ALISE/1998/students/tb2-3c5.html

ALISE. (1998). *ALISE statistical report 1998: Students chapter.* Retrieved July 12, 1999, from the World Wide Web: http://ils.unc.edu/ALISE/1998/Students/tb2-4a.html

ALISE. (1999). *ALISE statistical report 1998: Students chapter.* Retrieved June 23, 2000, from the World Wide Web: http://ils.unc.edu/ALISE/1999/students/tableII-3-a.html

American Council on Education. (1997, May 29). *Statement reaffirming support for affirmative action and diversity adopted by the Board of Directors for the American Council on Education.* Retrieved March 5, 2000, from the World Wide Web: http://www.acenet.edu/bookstore/descriptions/makingthecase/ACEAA/statement

American Library Association & Public Library Association. (1982). *The public library: Democracy's resource, a statement of principle.* Chicago: American Library Association, Public Library Association.

Association of American College and Universities. (1995). *American pluralism and the college curriculum--Higher education in a diverse democracy.* Washington, D.C.: Association of American College and Universities, p. xxi.

Asian Pacific American Librarians Association. (1999). *Report to congress on profession al education.* Retrieved August 12, 1999, from the World Wide Web: http://www.ala.org/congress/apala.

Association of American College and Universities. (1995). *The drama of diversity and democracy—Higher education and American commitments.* Washington, D.C.: Association of American College and Universities, p. xvi.

Badgett, M. V. L. (1997). "The impact of affirmative action on public-sector employment in California, 1970–1990." In Ong (Ed.) *The impact of affirmative action on public-sector employment and contracting in California* (pp. 71–93). Los Angeles: University of California.

Balter, J. (1998, November 1). I-200: Affirmative action tug of war—separating fact from fiction on this misleading measure. *Seattle Times,* p. B11.

Berdahl, R. (1998, January 23). *After Proposition 209: Addressing the fundamental issues of educational inequity.* Retrieved November 20, 1999, from the World Wide Web: http//www.berkeley.edu/ aboutucb/chancellor/speech_012398.html

Bell, M. P., Harrison, D. A., McLaughlin, M. E. (1997). Asian American attitudes toward affirmative action in employment: Implications for the model minority myth. *Journal of Applied Behavioral Science, 33* (3), 356–77.

Boisse, J. A. (1996). Serving multicultural and multilingual populations in the libraries of the University of California. *Resource Sharing & Information Networks, 11* (1/2), pp. 71–79.

Brune, T. & Varner, L. K. (1999, July 7). Affirmative action not dead here, it just morphed, most agree. *Seattle Times,* p. A1.

Burdman, P. (1999, February 8). Lawsuit against UC Berkeley claims color-blind admissions policy is unjust. *San Francisco Chronicle,* p. A13.

Cal. Const. Amend. Art. I, § 31 (West 1983 & Vol. 1A. 2000).

Cal. Educ. Code § 44101 (West 1993).

Cal. Pub. Cont. Code § 10015–10115.15, West 1985, Cumulative Pocket, 2000, pp. 43–50.

California State Library. (1988, December 9). *California State Library News.* Sacramento, Calif.: California State Library.

Carlson, D. B., Martinez, A., Curtis, S. A., Coles, J., & Valenzuela, N. A. (1990). *Adrift in a sea of change: California's public libraries struggle to meet the information needs of multicultural communities.* Berkeley, Calif.: Center for Policy Development.

Carter, D. J. & Wilson, R. (1997). *Minorities in higher education. 1996-97 fifteenth annual status report.* Washington, D.C.: American Council on Education, Office of Minority Concerns. (ERIC Document Reproduction Service No. ED 425 668).

Charles, J. (1999). Troubled by newcomers: Anti-immigrant attitudes and action during two eras of mass immigration to the United States. *Journal of American Ethnic History, 18* (3), 9–39.

Chiang, H. (1999, June 12). Challenge to Wilson ban on bias data loses. *San Francisco Chronicle,* p. A23.

Chin, G., Cho, S., Kang, J., & Wu, F. (1996, October 21). *Beyond self-interest: APAs toward a community of justice.* Retrieved July 24, 1999, from the World Wide Web: http://www.sscnet.ucla.edu/ aassc/ policy

Clary, M. (2000, March 7). Jeb Bush's anti-affirmative action plan ignites firestorm. *Los Angeles Times,* p. A5.

Coalition for Economic Equity v. Wilson. 946 F. Supp. 1480, 1520–21 (N. D. Cal. 1996).

David, G. & Lin, J. (1997). Civil rights and Asian Americans. *Journal of Sociology and Social Welfare, 24* (1), 3–24.

Espinosa, D. J. (1986). *The impact of affirmative action policy on ethnic and sexual inequality in employment.* Unpublished master's thesis, University of California, Santa Barbara.

Executive Order No. W–172–98, Executive Department, State of California. Retrieved March 20, 2000, from the World Wide Web: http://www.osmb.dgs.ca.gov/prop209/execorder.htm

Feldmann, L. (1998, May 13). Drive stalls to end affirmative action. *Christian Science Monitor, 90* (117), 1.

Gergen, D. (1997, June 2). The end of affirmative action brings unexpectedly drastic results. *U.S. News & World Report,* p. 78.

Gildar, W. (1999). Key words for equality. *ABA Journal,* p. 64. Retrieved March 13, 2000, from Lexis/Nexis (Academic Universe) on the World Wide Web: http://web.lexis-nexis.com/universe

Gorman, S. (1999, March 20). The 4 percent solution. *The National Journal, 31* (12), 79.

Governor's Office. State of California. (1997). *Wilson unveils list of thirty offending statutes.* PR97:331. Retrieved January 8, 2000, from the World Wide Web: http:// aaad.english. ucsb.edu/docs wilson.997.html

Gunnison, R. B. (1999, July 29). Bill backing outreach for women, minorities vetoed. *San Francisco Chronicle,* p. A17.

Guy, J. (1986). *Academic and public librarians: Data by race, ethnicity and sex.* Chicago: American Library Association, Office for Library Personnel Resources.

Hi-voltage Wire Works, Inc. v. City of San Jose. 72 Cal. App. 4th 600, 1999. Cal. App. Retrieved March 6, 2000, from Lexis/Nexis (Academic Universe) on the World Wide Web: http://web. Lexis-nexis.com/universe

Hopwood v. State of Texas, 999 F. Supp. 872, 1998 U.S. Dist. No. A 92 CA 563 SS. Retrieved March 6, 2000, from Lexis/Nexis (Academic Universe) on the World Wide Web: htpp://web.lexis-nexis.com/universe

Hudson, B. (1988, December 8). Judge denies latest bid to reinstate 3 to library posts. *Los Angeles Times,* p. 1.

Hudson, B. (1989, April, 6). Star 'melting pot,' getting fed up with the publicity, *Los Angeles Times,* p. 5.

Izumi, L. T. (1999, January 1). State of the state. In *California Journal.* Retrieved August 13, 1999, from Lexis/Nexis (Academic Universe) on the World Wide Web: http://web.lexis-nexis.com/universe

Katie, S. (1988, October 15). Meeting the need for librarians: the California library school recruitment project. *Library Journal, 113* (17), 44.

Keller, S. (Ed). (1999, June). *Partnerships for change guidelines, branch and participant surveys.* Sacramento, Calif.: California State Library.

Keller, S. (Ed) (1998) *Harmony in diversity—Recommendations for effective library service to Asian Language speakers.* Sacramento: California State Library.

Kidd v. State of California. (1998) 62 Cal.App.4th 386, 72Cal. Rptr. 2d 758.

King, C. J. (1996, November 6). Letter from Provost C. Judson King to UC Chancellors, Re: *Guidance on implementing Proposition 209.* University of California, Office of the President. Retrieved July 24,1999, from the World Wide Web: http://www.ucop.edu/ucophome/commserv press/kinglet.htm

LaVally, R., Melendez, M., Sproul, K., & Vucinich, N. (1995*). The status of affirmative action in California.* Retrieved July 24, 1999, from the World Wide Web: http://www.sen.ca.gov/sor/ economy/afact395.txt

Lee, H. K. (1997, April 29). Violent protest at Cal campus cops spray, hit UC students opposing Prop.209. *San Francisco Chronicle,* p. A13.

Lesher, D. (1997, November 4). Government steps unsurely toward 'colorblind' goal; Prop. 209: Ruling prompts municipalities to begin retooling programs. Opponents promise further battles. *Los Angeles Times*, p. A1.

Library of California Act. (1997). An act to add chapter 4.5 to Part 11 of the Education Code. Retrieved November 16, 1999, from the World Wide Web: http://www.leginfo.ca.gov/pub/97-98/bill

Lochhead, C. (1999, June 3). UC Berkeley Chancellor raps 4% admissions policy. *San Francisco Chronicle*, p. A7.

Lynch, M. J. (1998). *Racial and ethnic diversity among librarians: A status report.* Retrieved November 16, 1999, from the World Wide Web: http://www.ala.org/ors/racethnc.html

Marlon, M. (1999, November 21). Florida action on quotas attacked. Chorus of critics: Jeb Bush's plan is the latest in varied Southern attempts to mesh court rulings and college admissions. *The Atlanta Journal and Constitution*, p. 4A.

McCook, K. P. & Geist, P. (1993). Diversity deferred: Where are the minority librarians? *Library Journal, 118* (18), 35.

McMahon, P. (1998, October 21). Affirmative action fight hits Wash. state foes; paint initiative as Calif. invader. *USA Today*, p. 3A.

Monterey Mechanical C. v. Wilson, 138 F.3d 1270, 9th Cir. (1998)

Morain, D. (1998, March 21). Appeals court ends hiring preferences for state jobs. Prop. 209: Judges cite mandate by voters in ruling affecting women and minorities. Gov. Wilson hails decision. *Los Angeles Times*, p. A19.

Narasaki, K. (1998). Discrimination and the need for affirmative action legislation. In G. A. Lew (Ed.) *Perspectives on affirmative action* (pp. 5–8). Los Angeles: Asian Pacific American Public Policy Institute.

Neely, T. (1999). Diversity initiatives and programs: The national approach. *Journal of Library Administration, 27* (1/2), 123–24.

Nwadiora E., & McAdoo H. (1996). Acculturative stress among Amerasian refugees: gender and racial differences. *Adolescence, 31* (122), 477–87.

Ong, P. (Ed.) (1997). *The impact of affirmative action on public-sector employment and contracting in California.* Los Angeles: University of California.

Ong, P., Garrett, M. & Sirola, P. (1997). The impact of affirmative action on public-sector employment in California. In P. Ong (Ed.) *The impact of affirmative action on public-sector employment and contracting in California* (pp.3–10). Los Angeles: University of California.

Paterson, E. & Sellstrom, O. (1999). Equal opportunity in a post-Proposition 209 world. *Human Rights: Journal of the Section of Individual Rights & Responsibilities, 26* (3), 9.

Pool, B. (1999, October 22). Protest over UCLA law school 'resegregation'; education: students and professors in the department walk out of class and seek action to reverse a steep drop-off in the admissions of minority students. *Los Angeles Times*, p. B1.

Poon, W. (1998, October). *The life experience of Chinese immigrant women in the U.S.* Paper presented at the International Symposium on Women's Education and Development in the 21st Century, Beijing, China.

President's Initiative on Race. (1997). Building on American for the 21st century. Retrieved May 5, 1999, from the World Wide Web: http://www.whitehouse.gov/initiatives/oneamerica.html

Rice, C. (1997). Toward affirmative reaction: California's Prop 209 failed as a racial wedge issue—but here's what it means. *Nation, 264* (2), 22.

Rojas, A. (1998, April 3). Minority contract statistics ban fought Governor's order angers civil rights groups, prompts suit. *San Francisco Chronicle*. p. A21.

Saye, J. (1998). *ALISE statistical report 1998: Students*. Retrieved July 12, 1999, from the World Wide Web: http://ils.unc.edu/ALISE/1998/Students/tb2-4a.html

Schneider, A. (1998, November 20). What has happened to faculty diversity in California? *The Chronicle of Higher Education, 45* (13), pp. A10–A12.

Scott, K. H. (2000, February 21). College affirmative action ban undergoes vote in Florida. In *Gannett News Service,* Retrieved June 12, 1999, from Dow Jones Interactive database on the World Wide Web: http://nrstg2p.djnr.com/

Secretary of State. (1996, November 5). California Ballot Pamphlet. General Election, p. 31.

Smith M. P., & Tarallo, B. (1993). California's changing faces: New immigrant survival strategies and state policy. Retrieved March 9, 2000, from the World Wide Web: http://www.ucop.edu/cprc/smith.html

Sellstrom, O. (1999). Equal opportunity in a post-Proposition 209 world. *Human Rights: Journal of the Section of Individual Rights & Responsibilities, 26* (3), 9–12.

Spann, G. (1997). Proposition 209. *Duke Law Journal* (47). Retrieved March 8, 2000, from the World Wide Web: http://www.law.duke.edu /journals/ dlr/articles/DLR 47P187.htm

St. Lifer, E. & Nelson, C. O. (1997). Unequal opportunities: Race does matter. *Library Journal, 122* (18), 42–46.

State of California, Department of Finance (1999, June). *Legal immigration to California in federal fiscal year 1996.* Sacramento, Calif. Retrieved March 9, 2000 from the World Wide Web: http://www.dof.ca.gov/html/Demograp/inssum.htm

Stephanopoulos, G. & Edley, C. Jr. (1995, July 19). Affirmative action review. Section 4. Justifications. The White House. Retrieved September 27, 1999, from the World Wide Web: http://www.whitehouse.gov/ WH/EOP/ OP/aa-lett.html

Taylor, U. (1999). Proposition 209 and the affirmative action debate on the University of California campuses. *Feminist Studies, 25* (1), 95.

Tokaji, D. P. (1996). The club: Asian Americans and affirmative action. *A Journal of Opinion*. Retrieved March 15, 2000, from Lexis/Nexis database (Academic Universe) on the World Wide Web: http;//www.democracyweb.com/model minority.com/law/ prop209.htm

University of California. Office of the President. (1997, November). Implementation of Proposition 209: How it impacts UC's employment practices. Retrieved November 13, 1999 from the World Wide Web: http://www.ucop.edu/humres/policies/sp-2.html

U.S. Census Bureau. (1996). *California's population projections: 1995 to 2025.* Retrieved March 20, 2000, from the World Wide Web: http://www.census.gov/population/projections/state/9525rank/caprsrel.txt

U.S. Census Bureau. (1998). Census bureau fact for features. Retrieved July 24, 2000 from the World Wide Web http://www.census.gov/press-Release/ff98-05.html

Wallace, A. (1996, September 11). CSU heads warned on Prop. 209 remarks; politics: Chancellor urges them to be neutral on anti-affirmative action measure. *Los Angeles Times,* p. A14.

Wallace, A. (1996, November 9). Prop. 209 to have immediate effect on UC applicants; education: Decision to drop race and gender as admissions criteria speeds up timetable by several months. Campuses expect difficulty in maintaining diversity. *Los Angeles Times,* p. A1.

Weiss, K. R. & Curtius, M. (1998, April 1). Acceptance of Blacks, Latinos to UC plunges. *Los Angeles Times*, p. A1.

Wildavsky, B. (1999, March, 22). Whatever happened to minority students? *U.S. News & World Report*, p. 28.

Wilson v. State Personnel Board, et al., Cal. Sup.Ct., Sacramento, 1998.

Winton, R. (1994, July 28). Accusations of racism plague Monterey Park library board. *Los Angeles Times,* p. J2.

Workman, B. (1998, July 22). Suit alleges city slow on Prop. 209; Mountain View may be first targeted since law. *San Francisco Chronicle,* p. A15.

9

Immigrants, Global Digital Economies, Cyber Segmentation, and Emergent Information Services

Richard Chabrán

BRING ME YOUR HANDS: IMMIGRANTS & HIGH TECH MANU-FACTURING

"The movement of people from Latin America to the United States during the 1970s will be a historic moment in the history of immigration." I still recall this statement by Leo Estrada, a demographer that I had invited to make a presentation at UC Berkeley in the late 1970s. This movement of people has continued. Since that time our understanding of the movement of people within the Americas has greatly increased. As a librarian struggling to identify, acquire, and make accessible information on the Latino population I have had an opportunity to witness multiple discourses on immigration which range from simplistic racist statements to complex and empowering historical, social, and economic narratives. Two recent important contributions to the study of immigration are Saskia Sassen's *Globalization and Its Discontents: Essays on the New Mobility of People and Money (1998)* and Frank Bonilla's *Borderless Borders: U.S. Latinos, Latin Americans, and the Paradox of Interdependence (1998)*. In *Globalization and Its Discontents* and later writings, Saskia Sassen places the rise of the digital economy within a process of globalization. She describes key aspects of globalization as spatial dispersal of economic activity and centralization of top-level management within global cities and the role of immigrants within these global cities. *Borderless Borders* provides more specificity to this picture by documenting how Latinos are not just objects of global economies but also active subjects.

In "The Commoditization and Devalorization of Mexicans in the Southwest United States: Implications for Human Rights Theory and Practice," Carlos Velez-Ibanez (forthcoming) extends Sassen's argument. He states "technological innovation and devalorization of traditional industrial wages create: first, those labor markets dominated by fast-developing technologies that demand lots of hands and few thoughts and few hands and lots of thoughts, and

devalorized occupations which decrease in wage value. Or—technological innovations in finance, administration, material production, and agriculture develop the market dynamics in which the devalorization of traditional labor
markets and makes necessary many hands and few ideas and their mirror re-
versal." (NA) This bifurcated process is key to understanding inequality and
the role of Latino immigrants within our economy. The commonly held view
is that immigrants are not taking part in the new economy. It is more accurate
to describe them as participants in the new economy, which are overrepresented in sectors that are not valued and which require their hands not their
minds. Velez-Ibanez provides a manner for locating Mexican immigrants in
the new economy. For too many Mexicans, innovations in high technology
have meant the need for many hands and few ideas. Elsewhere Velez-Ibanez
has used the example of strawberry workers who now carry computer chips,
which are used to monitor the harvesting process. The manufacturing of
motherboards or microchips at *maquiladoras* where Mexican women constitute the majority of the workforce is another example of this process (Hossfeld, 1988). We need to contest the images on television that suggest that *high
tech equals many ideas*. Let us consider another view of innovation and digital economies that offers a different set of opportunities.

THE QUEST FOR LIVING WAGE JOBS

Today there is a whole range of digital devices that contain computers
within them. For example, we presently have bank debit cards, digital assis-
tants, such as Palm Pilots, pagers, and cell phones that are digital. Soon we
will have digital television. This is just the beginning. Many people are fore-
casting that digital devices will become part of the clothes we wear. *The point
is that many of us already live in a digital world.* And what is more we live in
a digital world that is connected to the Internet. The Internet is a computer-
based worldwide information network that allows people to communicate and
share information and resources with each other. The Internet is also becoming an important entertainment medium and a digital marketplace.

In Computers in Our Future's *Policy Agenda for Community Technology
Centers* (2000), a project funded by the California Wellness Foundation, the
authors note, "The use of computers and the Internet is rapidly changing the
skills employers expect, the way students learn, the way people get jobs, and
the way communities solve problems" (p. 1). Additionally, the authors state
that, "Growing evidence demonstrates the impact of information technology
on the changing world of education, work, and health:

- The majority of jobs today require technological skills—whether for young
  people entering the job market, people transitioning off of welfare, or workers looking to advance their careers;

- Over the next seven years, more than one million new jobs will be created in
  computer-related fields alone;

- People who use computers on the job earn 43% more than other workers;

- Employed Californians who use a personal computer report significantly better health status and significantly lower depression levels than employed Californians who do not use a personal computer;

- Less than two-thirds of Californians who are employed, but do not use a personal computer, have health insurance" (p. 1).

High tech in this context refers to opportunities in knowledge-based jobs. However, the new economy is also creating new divisions that we refer to as cyber segmentations.

CYBER SEGMENTATION

All too often the term digital divide fails to note these connections. The digital divide is a term used to describe populations who do not have access to new technologies. The term has gained widespread use since its adoption by the Clinton administration. We would like to suggest another term—cyber segmentation, which refers to a process rather than a state. This allows us to see new inequities in relation to a global process. Our working definition of the cyber segmentation refers to the inequalities that exist with regard to the material capacity, acquired skills, and differential use of digital technologies that can either improve or diminish the quality of life. This definition allows us to explore both challenges and opportunities that the new digital economy holds out for our society.

What do we know at the national level about Latino computer ownership, Internet access and use? A 1999 report by the National Telecommunications and Information Administration entitled *Falling Through the Net: Defining the Digital Divide* found:

- By 1998, 46.6 percent of the Anglo population had computers compared to 23.2 percent of African Americans and 25.5 percent of Latinos. This persistent and widening divide comes at a point when computer prices have plummeted.

- The gap is wider among low-income people and individuals with lower educational attainment.

- By 1998, Anglo-households with online access had risen to 29.8 percent while African American and Latino households were only 11.2 percent and 12.6 percent respectively.

Latinos have lower computer ownership, less access to the Internet, and use these in lower proportions than other populations.

Similar results are echoed in a California Research Bureau report entitled *Profile of California Computer and Internet Users* (Moller, 2000) that found:

- Compared to other race/ethnic groups, Whites and Asians are more likely to have computers at home in both California and the United States, while Hispanics are less likely to have a computer at home than other groups.

- In California, there are 2.7 million Hispanics that do not have home computers. The low proportion of home computers for Hispanics should not be that surprising since Hispanics tend to have lower income and education than other groups, as well as a younger age structure. However, a statistical analysis that takes this all into account still indicates that race/ethnicity is very important in the explanation of availability of computers at home.

- Compared to other races/ethnic groups, Hispanics have the lowest proportion of persons who use the Internet at home as of December 1998. In California, where the percent of Hispanics is about three times higher than the rest of the country, the number of Hispanics using the Internet is slightly lower than the national average, where Hispanics represent about 11 percent of the population.

A regional survey conducted in 1999 for the Center for Virtual Research at the University of California, Riverside entitled *Cyber Access in the Inland Empire* found that 65.9 percent of Anglos owned home computers compared to 41 percent for Latinos. It further found that 45.4 percent of Anglos had access to the Internet compared to 20.8 percent for Latinos (Neiman & Chabrán, 1999).

A 1999 survey by the Public Policy Institute entitled *Californians and their Government,* notes that Latinos are less likely to gather information about elections on the Internet than other groups (Baldassare, 1990). Finally a study by the Henry J. Kaiser Foundation entitled *Kids & Media @ the new Millennium* also found that African American and Latinos have significantly less access to computers than Anglo children (1999). These studies also suggest that there is a correlation between computer ownership, Internet access, and race/ethnicity, education, and income. While these studies do not report on immigrants, other socio-economic indicators suggest that immigrants most likely have lower computer ownership and Internet use than U.S.-born Latinos. *In other words, the cyber segmentation is related to a preexisting ethnic/racial, immigrant status, education, and income divide.* In any case Latinos find themselves on the wrong side of the digital divide.

The relation of education to Latino economic achievement is the topic of an important new report entitled *Education = Success: Empowering Hispanic Youth and Adults* (Carnevale, 1999), jointly published by the Educational Testing Service and the Hispanic Association of Colleges and Universities. Its major findings are:

- Latino access to college is increasing.

- Latino youth still trail non-Latino White youth in educational achievement.

- Latino students are significantly underrepresented on today's college campuses.

- Underrepresentation on campus equals underrepresentation in good jobs.

- Underrepresentation on campus also translates into lower earnings.

In their conclusion, the authors note that "The bottom line is that we must improve educational attainment and achievement among Hispanic youth who are academically at risk if they are to be ready for postsecondary education. And an even larger proportion of Hispanic adults, especially recent immigrants, need academic remediation and job related education and training if they are going to get and keep good jobs" (pp. 8–19).

FROM THE FIELDS & MAQUILA TO LIVING WAGE JOBS: THE ROLE OF LIBRARIANS IN COMMUNITY INFORMATION CENTERS

The *CTCNet Center Start-Up Manual* starts each chapter with the mantra "It's about people—not computers" (Chow, 1998 p. 1). This theme is extended in Bonnie Nardi and Vicki O'Day's *Information Technologies: Using Technology with Heart* (1999) where the authors explore the importance of different contexts in which technologies (habitations) are deployed. They use libraries as an example of an information ecology, borrowing Edward O. Wilson's concept of keystone species to describe librarians (Nardi & O'Day, 1999). Wilson contends that the disappearance of some species can cause the disappearance of other species on which they depend (Wilson, 1992). The authors explore the many ways librarians are critical to healthy information ecologies from framing questions, to developing strategies, to evaluating results. They show how the librarian's role has become even more critical in the digital age (Nardi & O'Day, 1999). We need to go even further in this analysis. Of course, it is not just that librarian's skills and expertise are becoming more critical in the traditional places we call libraries, but that librarians are extending their role as a keystone species in untraditional information ecologies such as community information centers.

Libraries, of course, have a rich history in the United States. The impact of technology on libraries is explored in *Civic Space/Cyberspace* (Molz & Dain, 1999). Interestingly, this new summary of American libraries is largely silent on the challenges and contributions of Latino librarians and libraries not to mention the contribution of Latinos to cyberspace. Historically libraries have been described as purveyors of culture, depositories, and promoters of literacy. More recently some libraries and librarians have become part of the community technology movement. Community technology centers, which may be located in schools, libraries, or community-based organizations, offer a wide range of services in communities. A National Science Foundation sponsored study found:

- Centers are an important resource for women and girls, people of all ages, and members of racial and ethnic groups;
- Centers offer a range of opportunities to use computers and other technologies in classes as well as in self-directed activities;

- Centers are a valuable resource for obtaining job skills and learning about employment opportunities;

- Centers had a positive effect on participants' educational goals and experiences;

- Centers fostered a sense of community and personal effectiveness, and allowed for real community building to occur. (Chow, 1998; Servon, 1999)

The definition of a community technology center is fluid at the present time. Some offer access, others offer access and training. Training can be introductory or very sophisticated.

My own experience is instructive. I received my training in libraries first from an urban planner. Later I attended the UC Berkeley, School of Library and Information Studies. My original training emphasized information systems rather than a strict adherence to established library practices. My library career has been focused on the development of alternative libraries—Latino library collections at Berkeley and UCLA and now in cyberspace. My work at developing Chicano/Latinonet benefited greatly from my location within the Chicano Studies Research Library at UCLA (Salinas, 2000). However, my work in cyberspace drew me outside of the University to low-income communities in Southern California that were largely immigrant who did not have access to new technologies (Salinas, 1996). These journeys lead me to the University of California at Riverside (UCR) where we developed the Community Digital Initiative.

The UCR Community Digital Initiative (CDI) is one of eleven sites funded by the California Wellness Foundations Computers in our Future (CIOF) Program that is part of a larger Work and Health Initiative. CIOF represents a unique attempt to develop community technology centers. Essential aspects of the CIOF model are: a physical computer center located in a community which offers open access to residents, educational and training programs, links to employment services, and an emerging effort to engage the local communities in policies which would support community technology (Furedi & Chabran, 2000).

CDI established a computing center in the heart of a predominately Latino and African American community in the Eastside of Riverside. Its physical location is at the César Chávez Community Center in the Bobby Bonds Sports Park complex. The César Chávez Community Center is an old middle school built in the 1930s. The Center was named after the Mexican American labor leader and the park complex was named after an African American baseball star. CDI targets youth and works in partnership with local community-based organizations and institutions. CDI provides access to computer and information literacy training to a sector of society that otherwise would not have access.

At CDI we work with individuals, the majority of whom are immigrants. We have witnessed the impact that centers such as CDI may have not only on levels of technological fluency and critical literacy but in building a sense of self-empowerment (Computer Science and Telecommunication Board, National Research Council, Committee on Information Technology Literacy, 1999). CDI offers a space that is different than traditional libraries or schools because we are not constrained by the same limitations that exist in many public institutions. We strive to teach our youth how to empower themselves and their local communities by providing them a space where they can use technology to create different types of projects to express themselves. We encourage them to explore methods of self and community documentation through technology. For example, they create web pages for nonprofit community organizations, a process that helps identify and catalog community resources and contributes to the Riverside Community Online. These products and expressions have a clear connection to who they are and where they live. In this case CDI has provided the forum for people who otherwise would not have the means for contributing content to the information world of the World Wide Web. For example, CDI participants contributed to an evaluation of web resources, such as the State of California Ethnic Resource Center Healthy Mothers/Healthy Babies web site. This site provides multilingual multimedia health resources to low-income communities.

IMMIGRANT VOICES

Bethany is a high-achieving student in a local Riverside high school. Her parents bring her to CDI on a regular basis. She summarizes her experience in a recent article in the following manner:

For a teenager like me, going to school and trying hard to get good grades to become *alguien en la vida* (as my parents say) or "someone in life," is very important. I come from a working class background. Both my parents' work for the little we have. My little brother and I see the hardships my parents go through in trying to make ends meet. Only a few years ago, it was rare for a teacher to demand a typed paper with certain fonts and special indentations from one day to the next. Today students like me are required to conduct research on the Internet and do other assignments that require access to a computer. My current college prep high school coursework requires me to do a series of typed reports. I know personally that all these reports would not have been possible without a computer. CDI gave me access and assistance in learning how to use the technology. . . CDI has helped me tremendously, not only in my academics, but in my social life as well. Through the skills that I learned at CDI, I have been able to help my church using a program called Creative Writer that allows me to do my church's newsletter. I still remember when I learned how to use e-mail and sent a message to one of my friends who had moved to Oregon. The neat thing about it was that it was so cheap. I can still recall that awesome sensation of using e-mail for the first time. (Alvarez, 2000, p. 1)

Luis is a guard during the day. In his spare time he does landscaping. Back home in Guatemala, he had developed a horticultural background. His family still lives in Guatemala. As a regular CDI participant he shops online, using a credit card for food, supplies, and toys that are delivered to his home in Guatemala. He says, "It gives me piece of mind to know that I am providing for my family thousands of miles away." We promoted information fluency and Luis learned how to use the Internet effectively to address his needs.

I am not advocating for every librarian to develop a community computing center but only to suggest that we, as librarians, can create opportunities that can address cyber segmentation in low-income and immigrant communities. We need to extend our concept of libraries to include community information centers and clients to community information producers and users.

INFORMATION FLUENCY AS A HUMAN RIGHT

Albert Fong and Josh Senyak, my mentors in community technology, recently wrote, "People are not poor because they lack access to the Internet. They lack access because they're poor" (Fong & Senyak, 2000, p. 2). Libraries like to claim that since they are accessible to everyone they help level the playing field. I have even heard that since libraries are purchasing licenses to all kinds of digital databases and they have a few computers for public access that they are bridging the digital divide. Never mind that the databases they are licensing might not document the Latino experience, or that they are available only in English, or that they might not have training programs targeted toward immigrant communities—somehow, by virtue of being a library, they are bridging the digital divide.

Bridging the divide will require addressing the root causes of poverty and racism in this country. Services to immigrants must be targeted to fit new information ecologies. Foundations and granting agencies have a special role to play and it is not looking at the font size in proposals that seek to bridge the divide. It is in understanding and bringing people and institutions that care together to dialogue about solutions. We need to support initiatives that support lifelong learning. This support begins with birth and continues through life. We need to support our schools, colleges, and universities, community technology centers, and libraries. Our youth need to dedicate themselves in schools. We need to provide computers and Internet access to our youth so they can become technologically fluent and connect to new worlds. We need to make sure that our schools and libraries are digitally connected and that teachers and librarians know how to use and teach with new digital tools in a culturally relevant manner. We need to support existing and new community technology centers that provide support for both lifelong learning and a link to better jobs. This will require public/private partnerships, which together will provide the monetary and moral support required for success in a digital world. Finally we need to articulate the need for and advocate legislative measures that will provide the resources to carry out this work (Reforma: Information Technology Committee, 2000). Our struggle to assist immigrant workers become information fluent, and indeed information producers, is part of a struggle for human rights.

REFERENCES

Alvarez, B. (2000, Spring). For a teenager like me. *CIOF News*, p. 1.

Baldassare, M. (1990). The digital divide. In Public Policy Institute of California, *PPIC statewide survey: Californians and their government*, pp. 24–26. San Francisco.

Bonilla, F. (1998). *Borderless borders: U.S. Latinos, Latin Americans, and the* paradox of interdependence. Philadelphia, Pa.: Temple University Press.

Carnevale, A. P. (1999). *Education = success: Empowering Hispanic youth and adults*. Princeton, N.J.: Educational Testing Service.

Chow, C. (1998). *Impact of CTCNet affiliates: Findings from a national survey of users of community technology centers*. Newton, Mass.: Education Development Center.

Computer Science and Telecommunication Board, National Research Council, Committee on Information Technology Literacy. (1999). *Being fluent with information technology*. Washington, D.C.: National Academy Press.

Computers In Our Future. Policy Group. (2000). *A policy agenda for community technology centers: Assuring that low-income communities benefit from technological progress in the information age*. Los Angeles: Author.

Fong, A. & Senyak, J. (2000). *One more river to cross: Why bridging the digital divide won't save the world (and why it's still worth the fight)*. Los Angeles: Computers In Our Future.

Furedi, D. & Chabran, R. (2000). Telling the CIOF story to policymakers. *CIOF News*, 6.

Henry J. Kaiser Family Foundation. (1999). *Kids & media @ the new millennium*. Menlo Park, Calif.: Author.

Hossfeld, K. (1988). *Divisions of labor, divisions of lives: Immigrant women workers in Silicon Valley*. Unpublished doctoral dissertation, University of California, Santa Cruz, Santa Cruz, CA.

Larson, A. & Wilhelm, T. (1996). *Latinos and the super information highway*. Claremont, Calif.: Tomas Rivera Policy Institute.

Moller, R. M. (2000). *Profile of California computer and Internet users*. Sacramento, Calif.: California Research Bureau.

Molz, R. K. & Dain, P. (1999). *Civic space/cyberspace: The American public library in the information age*. Cambridge, Mass.: MIT Press.

Nardi, B. & O'Day, V. (1999). *Information technologies: Using technology with heart*. Cambridge, Mass.: MIT Press.

National Telecommunications and Information Administration. (1999). *Falling through the net: Defining the digital divide*. Washington, D.C.: Author.

Neiman, M. & Chabrán, R. (1999). *Cyber access in the Inland Empire*. Riverside, Calif.: Center for Social and Behavioral Science Research, University of California.

Reforma. Information Technology Committee. (2000). Information Technology Agenda.

Salinas, R. (1996, May). Building virtual communities: Latino organizations in an urban setting. *Community networking conference proceedings*, pp. 121–124. Taos, N.M.: La Plaza Telecommunity Foundation.

Salinas, R. (2000). CLNet: Redefining Latino library services in the digital era. In S Güereña (Ed.) *Library services to Latinos: An anthology* (pp.228–40). Jefferson, N.C.: McFarland.

Sassen, S. (1998). *Globalization and its discontents: Essays on the new mobility of people and money*. New York: The New Press.

Servon, L. (1999*). Creating an information democracy: The role of community tech-
    nology programs and their relationship to public policy.* New Brunswick, N.J.:
    Center for Urban Policy Research.
Velez-Ibanez, C. The commoditization and devalorization of Mexicans in the south-
    west United States: Implications for human rights Theory. In C. Nagengaust &
    C. Velez-Ibanez (Eds.) *Human rights, power, and difference: Expanding contem-
    porary interpretations of human rights in theory and practice.* Washington D.C.:
    Publications of the Society of Applied Anthropology. Refereed and Submitted,
    January 2000. Accepted for Publication, December 2001.
Wilhelm, A. (1997). *Buying into the computer age: A look at the Hispanic middle
    class.* Claremont, Calif.: Tomas Rivera Policy Institute.
Wilhelm., A. (1997). *Out of reach? Latinos, education and technology in California.*
    Claremont, Calif.: Tomas Rivera Policy Institute.
Wilhelm. A. (2000). *Democracy in the digital age: Challenges to political life in
    cyberspace.* New York: Routledge, 2000, p. 37.
Wilson, E. (1992). *The diversity of life.* Cambridge, Mass.: Harvard University Press.

10

The Practice and Politics of Public Library Services to Asian Immigrants

Xiwen Zhang

Who are the new Asian immigrants? What is unique about their information-seeking methods? Why are libraries important to Asian immigrants? Why does it matter to the larger Asian community how they are run and who they employ? To answer these seemingly innocent yet politically laden questions as well as to investigate the actual practice of public library services to Asian immigrants, I visited Los Angeles area public libraries serving Asian immigrant communities. The visited libraries included Chinatown, Little Tokyo, Korea Town, and Monterey Park. The experiences and observations of librarians in these community libraries form the basis of this article. In addition, the political dimensions of community-based library services are explored.

CULTURAL AND LINGUISTIC CHARACTERISTICS OF NEW ASIAN IMMIGRANTS

According to the 1990 census of the 4.1 million Asians five years old and over, 56 percent did not speak English very well and 35 percent were considered linguistically isolated. Furthermore, 65.2 percent of Asian American speak an Asian or Pacific Islander language at home. While it is true that some Asian immigrants come to America with higher educational backgrounds, their lack of English proficiency often prevents them from quickly integrating into American society.

In addition, there are twenty-two separate Asian ethnic groups, which have come to America during different immigration waves (U.S. Census, 1990). The earliest large-scale immigration occurred between the 1840s and 1930s. Following the new immigration policy of 1965 and the Southeast Asian conflict, large numbers of new Asian immigrants came to the United States. With the passage of the Amerasian Homecoming Act in 1987, there has been another increase in Asian immigration from Vietnam and Cambodia.

More than one million war refugees came from Southeast Asian between 1975 and 1990. Besides refugees who arrived with exceptionally low educational levels there are approximately 200,000 highly educated Asians who came between 1972 and 1988 under the immigration preference policy.

Due to this continuing immigration trend the Asian population will grow to more than 11 million and represent 4.1 percent of the nation's population by 2000. By the middle of the twenty-first century, it is expected to reach 34 million and represent 9 percent of the nation's total (U.S. Census, 1990). In 1996, 55.4 percent of the nation's Asians lived in the West and 94.2 percent resided in metropolitan areas.

NONTRADITIONAL SERVICES FOR NONTRADITIONAL USERS

Asian immigration continues to transform the ethnic composition of the United States. Traditional library services are not adequately designed to meet the special information needs of the diverse Asian immigrant community. For example, the major challenges faced by most newcomers are primarily in the areas of communicating in English and finding and maintaining gainful employment. Most new immigrants, especially in the Los Angeles area, live in ethnically segregated communities due to language and cultural differences that divide them from mainstream society. Therefore, just in Southern California alone, there is a Chinatown, Korea Town, a Little Tokyo, and a Little Saigon.

Los Angeles area librarians serving immigrant Asian communities indicate that these populations are most often seeking survival type information about their new environment. For example, common requests include information on acquiring English language instruction; English language study materials, either audio or video; immigration forms and requirements; study guides for citizenship tests; and information on locating housing, finding jobs, health care, and social welfare benefits.

Meeting these information needs for Asian-language speakers is a huge challenge for public libraries. How can information be provided in a language a patron can understand? How can a reference librarian conduct a reference interview with a patron without understanding what the patron is asking? How can multicultural services be provided to the twenty-two ethnic groups within the Los Angles service area? How can minority librarians be recruited from the various Asian backgrounds to better serve these communities?

INFORMATION-SEEKING BEHAVIOR OF ASIAN-LANUGAGE SPEAKERS

The information-seeking behaviors of the new Asian immigrants are directly related to both experience and culture. In most Asian countries there are no free public library services. Generally speaking, libraries are associated with academe or government agencies. The use of the facility and the materials is limited to their own members.

Libraries are merely places for storing books. Lending is conducted on a very limited scale. The evaluation of a library in Asian is based on the number of volumes in the collection. Quality of the library has nothing to do with public services.

On a personal level, when I was growing up in China I never experienced anything resembling an American public library either as a student or as a librarian. Reference services, even at an elite research institute in Beijing, were unheard of. A Chinese librarian's job is to purchase books and maintain the card catalogue.

When I came to America to study at a University of California campus, I mistook the reference desk as a site for general information about the library. Consequently, I never used reference services for research assignments. Only when I entered library school was I pleasantly surprised to learn of the existence of library services. In 1997, I gave a series of lectures on American public libraries and the services offered by American public libraries in Yunnan, China. My Chinese counterparts were very impressed by the services offered by American public libraries and their commitment to serving their communities. This story illustrates the lack of awareness among Chinese librarians to traditional reference and public services. If Chinese librarians were so uninformed, one can imagine the attitude of the general Asian public.

This lack of insight by Asian immigrants into the functions and services of a public library was corroborated by librarians in the Los Angeles area who serve these populations. The librarians in Little Tokyo, Chinatown, and Monterey Park who serve primarily Chinese and Japanese users indicated that many new Asian immigrants only know that the library is a place for borrowing books. If the library does not have books in their native languages, most immigrants would never go the library.

The new Asian communities are simply not aware of the reference services offered by public libraries and the vast amount of information that could be culled from these collections. Consequently, when Asian immigrants have information questions they do not go or call there nearest public library. Instead Asian immigrants rely on family or friends for necessary information. Familial networks in particular are the primary sources of information dissemination within the new Asian populations.

Moreover, in general, culture dictates that new Asian immigrants will not complain about the lack of services or bilingual staff. These populations do not want to stand out or make a fuss as harmonious relations are highly valued and dissonance is frowned upon. Consequently, if the library does not have books or newspapers in their native language they will most likely blame themselves for not speaking English.

Even when immigrant users may become informed about the existence of reference services they often cannot communicate without the assistance of bilingual personnel. If no bilingual staff is available, their questions will remain unanswered. In addition, due to poor English proficiency most immigrants are often just too shy or too intimidated to ask any questions to begin with.

Mr. He is a case in point. He is the vice-president of the World Association of Chinese Artists and a former art professor in China who now lives in San Bernardino. I interviewed him for the specific purpose of verifying these points. According to him, at least 95 percent of the members of the Association are Asian-language speakers and recent immigrants. Many of them came to the United States under new immigration laws as distinguished artists. All have college degrees and they were accomplished artists in one way or another in their home country.

However, most of the artist immigrants have not been financially successful in the United States. They have experienced high levels of unemployment and underemployment. Those that are self-employed can hardly make ends meet. Not only are they linguistically isolated but they do not know how to market their work, communicate within the art and business worlds, how to identify or apply for grants, or how to participate in American art competitions. In essence, they do not know what is going on around them or how to operate in the U.S. economy. As a result, some very talented artists are underemployed and exploited in the workplace. For example, Mr. He indicated that some artists were hand-painting T-shirts at a rate of $ .50 per piece or painting portraits on the street for $10 to $15 each. Some artists who have failed to make a living in the United States have moved back to China.

Mr. He, a monolingual Chinese speaker, was not aware of the various types of assistance the local public library might provide him. As a well-educated person, he loves to read and purchases books directly from China. He frequently drives an hour or more to the Monterey Park or the Chinatown library to check out Chinese books and videotapes. He also indicated that occasionally he goes to the University of California, Riverside library to browse the art collection (Personal communication, August 24, 1999).

The implications of these cases are threefold. First, immigrants like Mr. He have every intention of integrating into mainstream society. They just don't know how to do it yet. Their limited English language skills and unfamiliarity with U.S. public library services and programs further isolates them from the general population. Although these immigrants try very hard to learn English, without effective help, their progress is limited. Second, had appropriate assistance been provided, Mr. He and most immigrants would have been most happy to utilize various public library services. In so doing, not only would their intellectual activities have been broadened tremendously but also their financial situation would have been improved to boot. Third, adult immigrants are often more isolated than families with school age children as schools often provide a space where immigrant families feel comfortable and can begin to seek out assistance for themselves or their children.

EFFECTIVE LIBRARY SERVICES FOR ASIAN IMMIGRANTS

As discussed above, the Asian community is a complex combination of ethnic groups who are linguistically, educationally, culturally, and economically diverse. The following service recommendations should be considered in communities of new Asian immigrants and refugees who are linguistically isolated and live in segregated communities. The recommendations are based on the experience of public libraries serving majority Asian populations in Southern California (Personal Communication, August–September 1999).

Asian Language Collections

The majority of Asian immigrants are educated in their native countries and arrive in the United States without English proficiency. Therefore, collections in their native languages are critical to serving these non-English speaking patrons. Librarians in Southern California who serve majority Asian populations in Los Angeles' Chinatown, Little Tokyo, Korea Town, and in Monterey Park stressed that Asian language collections are indispensable in attracting and meeting the information and literacy need of immigrants. All four of these libraries have extensive Asian language collections. For example, 60 percent of the library collection at the Little Tokyo branch is in the Japanese language. More than 60 percent of the Korea Town branch collection is in the Korean language. Chinese language materials make up over 40 percent in the Chinatown library and over 50 percent in the Monterey Park Public Library. All the librarians of these facilities reported the exceptional attraction of the foreign language collections for their non English speaker patrons. Users come from all over Southern California including Orange and San Diego counties to utilize these materials. Even the limited space of the Chinatown branch had not deterred the 18,000 to 22,000 visitors per month that visit the library each year. In fact, the Chinatown library has one of the highest circulations of materials in the Los Angles Public Library (LAPL) system.

Collection Purchasing and Cataloguing

Collection development and cataloguing of Asian materials are a problem for libraries with limited human resources. The Riverside City Library, for example, has a very small Asian language collection. Book ordering and processing are outsourced to a commercial vendor. The result has been a collection of low quality. One branch of the San Bernardino County Library which received donations of Asian language books left them on a shelf for in-library browsing due to a lack of cataloging.

Given the tremendous challenge of cataloging the diverse Asian languages which are spoken by the new immigrants it seems that collective efforts in ordering and cataloguing would be an effective way to solve the problem. For example, LAPL has sixty-three branches. Not every branch maintains a large non-English collection. The LAPL main library coordinates the foreign language purchasing, cataloging, processing, and delivery of non-English language materials. All branch purchases of foreign languages items are coordinated through the Multilingual Services Department. Librarians throughout the system with special language abilities are asked to participate in the collaborative collection development process. A minimum materials allocation commitment of $5,000 per language is required for a branch to establish or continue a language collection. Branches with minimal language usage can use the central library's long-term loan program (several months). All new non-English materials are delivered to the cataloguing department for processing and then delivered to branches as quickly as possible. This cooperative method is very effective.

At present, most library catalogues use Roman script to retrieve Asian language materials. This is confusing not only for patrons, but also for bilingual librarians trying to find Asian books using phonetic data. A reference librarian in Chinatown library told me that it is almost impossible for a patron to use the online catalog to find books. Most LAPL users tend to ignore the online catalogue and go directly to the shelves to browse by subject. When a patron has a specific title or author, he or she would come to the reference desk for help. Any librarian knows that this is not the most efficient method of searching the collection. To solve this problem Monterey Park Public Library is trying to develop its own Chinese character online catalogue.

Library cataloguing in both the romanization and Asian language characters is strongly recommended to better serve Asian users. The technology needed to make this service a reality is available on the market. A good example is OCLC's CJK 3.2 software that supports efficient cataloguing of Chinese, Japanese, and Korean (CJK) materials with CJK characters. Library users can search and access local library records displaying both the romanization and Asian language characters. Los Angeles Public Library and Chicago Public Library, as well as several university libraries with large Asian collection are using OCLC CJK software to catalog their collections (OCLC Newsletter, 1999). The OCLC international database provides over half a million Asian language records. The LAPL cataloguing department has started using OCLC CJK software to produce an online catalog which contains bibliographic records in romanization and characters of Chinese, Japanese, and Korean languages. Presently, LAPL is working on displaying of Asian language characters on their local system. The OCLC solution is one very excellent method that can be used to overcome the staffing problems associated with foreign language original cataloguing.

Networking

For libraries located in areas with small numbers of Asian immigrants and no bilingual staff, networking is one way to better serve Asian immigrants. For example, the Los Angeles County Public Library system effectively uses its multilingual staff resources by maintaining a system-wide network of bilingual library staff. This networking makes it possible for librarians to assist non-English speaking users through the telephone.

The multitype library network is a model for resource sharing within large geographic areas. All types of libraries (public, academic, special, and school libraries) in California are grouped into seven regions by the State Library. This structure allows users to have greater access to the resources in the region (California State Library, 2000).

In addition, another way of networking is by joining ethnic library organizations such as the Asian Pacific Library Association or the Chinese American Library Association. These organizations are affiliated with the American Library Association and conduct national and regional programming.

Bilingual Staff

Communicating with Asian immigrants is a major barrier for monolingual librarians in providing services to non-English Asian speakers. Primary Asian languages used in Los Angeles include Korean, Chinese (Mandarin and Cantonese), and Vietnamese. The availability of bilingual staff accounts in large part for the heavy use of the above libraries by Asian immigrants. In fact, Chinatown and Little Tokyo have 100 percent bilingual staffing. With such rich multilingual resources, reference services and programs have been designed specifically for non-English Asian speakers. For example, English as a Second Language classes, citizenship classes, and instructions on the Internet given by bilingual librarians and community volunteers are highly successful.

Community Partnerships

Outreach activities and partnerships within the Asian immigrant community are strongly recommended. Although this type of activity is labor intensive it has proven to be an effective way to promote library services to immigrants, obtain financial contributions, and raise social consciousness and volunteer support.

For example, before 1977 Chinatown did not have a public library. The urgent information needs of the Chinese community led to a fund-raising effort which netted $500,000 to build a public library on public school grounds. The result is the only permanent LAPL branch which is housed rent-free on public school land. After being open for only two months, the library achieved permanent status after meeting the required 30,000 annual volume circulation. Many community organizations have continued to raise funds for the library. So far they have paid for a 15-unit computer classroom within the library and nine scholarships for high school students and Chinese library school students. For several years the Chinatown branch has offered very successful weekly English conversation classes and citizenship test preparation classes. Volunteers from the community conduct the classes. Without community support, the library would not be able to provide these services. The Chinatown branch is one of the busiest branches in the LAPL system.

The Little Tokyo partnership was modeled after the Chinatown effort and has been similarly successful. It has created a heavily used Japanese heritage collection. Community support continues because of the large multilingual collection, bilingual librarians, and classes staffed by community volunteers. All these factors ensure quality services to local users.

Public Relations

Promotional materials in different Asian languages are needed for promoting library services to Asian immigrants. The LAPL launched a multilingual, multicultural campaign to increase usage of the central library and branch libraries throughout the city. The campaign included the creation of printed and electronically promoted material in different languages. Monterey Park Public Library, a municipal city public library, developed a close relationship with the local Chinese media. The library was subsequently able to generate free advertising services and programs on Chinese language television and radio stations.

POLITICS OF CREATING NEW MODELS OF SERVICE

Why are libraries important to Asian immigrants? The simple answer to this question is that specialized multilingual services, collections, and outreach efforts can change the information-seeking behavior of Asian immigrants as demonstrated at the public libraries in the Los Angeles area. These services can be transformative experiences that could more quickly integrate Asian immigrants into American society. In fact, I would venture to say that all immigrant users regardless of their ethnic/racial background would benefit from these types of targeted services. As a result, the library could become the center of the community where immigrants can find survival information, acculturate to their new surroundings, and launch contacts with the outside world.

On a more profound level, public library use is a political endeavor that suggests issues of individual and group agency. Ultimately authentic community-based library services will not only provide self-improvement but social transformation aimed at creating the conditions for oppressed minorities to overcome material, ideological, and psychological forms of domination while reviving and expanding the fabric of democratic institutions.

Why does it matter to the larger Asian community how their local public library is run and who they employ? If you accept the notion that public library service is not simple a methodology but a social theory whose aim is the liberation of individuals and groups through a critical education process, then you become interested in the leadership that will oversee this transformation (Freire, 1973).

The role of the librarian usually includes helping users get involved in personal and/or collective education. Freire is very clear about the fact that political struggles are won and lost in those public spaces, such as the public library, that connect everyday experience with the force and power of institutional domination (1973). Any librarian who serves the community as an advocate must embrace the concept that they can help shape the historical context and the political projects of that community.

Consequently, providing appropriate library services to Asian communities can be viewed as much more than a technical procedure. Immigrant communities care deeply about the staff that leads the community institutions in their cultural milieu. The right staff will take seriously what it means to link political struggle, such as the anti-immigrant movement, to teaching and learning that reflect the marginalized groups in question and allows them to develop their own cultural agenda fashioned to meet their personalized sense of political and cultural agency. The nature of work in an Asian immigrant community is about public education and an attentiveness to the interconnections between knowledge, language, culture, and everyday lived experiences.

Our capacity to think politically about public library work is not often discussed. Yet community-minded librarians must often struggle within their organizations to access and regulate the distribution of resources that make it possible to service immigrant communities. The cultural wars in public libraries often come down to ordering and cataloguing multilingual materials and hiring the bilingual staffs that are essential to serving immigrant communities. In addition, the challenge of providing multicultural services requires the training and recruitment of future librarians and library staff. This task has always been difficult in and of itself. In the present anti-affirmative action era the problem has become almost intractable.

However, the role of the public library and the librarian, as part of a broader political practice for democratic change, cannot be viewed as an easy political fix with a set formula of accommodation. Rather, each communities' activities must be specific and contextual to that service area but ultimately related to the ongoing global, historical, social, and economic struggles.

Public libraries can be part of a community process of critical consciousness that promotes critical thinking skills. This thinking goes beyond uplifting the communities' self-esteem, that is, making them feel good about themselves and their culture. Librarians are the "teachers" who provide users or "students" with forms of information that will create individual and social change. However, in order to be successful it is essential that community librarians be convinced of the ability of ordinary people to bring about social change.

While librarians must never impose their views on users, they must develop service patterns and practices grounded in existing concrete realities and social problems. The critical role that librarians and the public library can play is to emphasize the importance of developing a worldview that is based on a rigorous examination of the ideas on any topic while highlighting the social nature of learning and struggle in a democracy. In short, public libraries must continue to equate themselves with the practice of freedom.

CONCLUSIONS

The success of the librarians in the Los Angeles area in serving their Asian immigrant communities embodies a vibrant and dynamic quality that all library service providers should emulate. However, successful public library work is rooted in the specific needs of particular communities. The linguistic, cultural, economic, and transnational conditions of new immigrants mandate that nontraditional services be deployed. Additional ideas on serving Asian immigrant users can be found in *Harmony in Diversity—Recommendations for*

Effective Library Service to Asian Language Speakers (Keller, 1998).

The theoretical work of Paulo Freire is recalled to provide a basis for rethinking the crucial connection between the educational mission of public libraries and social change. The public library can provide a much-needed public space for the development of individual public intellectuals and critical social consciousness. Both individual and social interests intersect at the public library to create a forum for democracy to flourish. The public library can serve as that critical institution that links the everyday life of Asian immigrants with broader social movements for progressive social change.

The anti-immigrant attitudes that have paralleled the growth of Asian immigrants during the 1980s and 1990s have been difficult for all Asians and Asian Americans living in the United States. The backlash of the nativist movement has created additional barriers for all Asians. During difficult times, the public library remains one of the few public institutions where all members of the community can experience democracy. Yet even public libraries are mandated by state laws to recognize English as the official language and to eliminate all affirmative action programs that might assist the library in the recruitment, training, and employment of multicultural personnel. Consequently, the Asian and Asian American communities in collaboration with all progressive groups must even be more steadfast in their defense of these services and staff. The preservation and expansion of multicultural library services can greatly enhance the democratic spirit of the ever-growing Asian immigrant community.

REFERENCES

California State Library. (2000). Regional library development. Retrieved September 12, 2000, from the World Wide Web: http://www.library.ca.gov/loc/regional/index .html

Freire, P. (1973). *Pedagogy of the oppressed.* New York: Seabury Press.

Keller, S. (Ed.) (1998). *Harmony in diversity—Recommendations for effective library service to Asian language speakers.* Sacramento, Calif. California State Library.

OCLC Newsletter. (1999, January/February) No. 237. Retrieved November 14, 1999, from the World Wide Web: http://www.oclc.org/oclc/new/n237/product/02product .htm

U.S. Census Bureau. (1990). *1990 We reports.* Retrieved July 22, 1999, from the World Wide Web: http://www.census.gov/pubinfo/www/apihot1.html

U.S. Census Bureau. (1990). Census Bureau fact for features. Retrieved July 24, 1999, from the World Wide Web: http://www.census.gov/press-release/ff98-05.html

11

Some Basic Issues of Diversity:
A Contextual Inquiry

Ling Hwey Jeng

It's about recognizing that a consensus does exist, and that there is a standard that all Americans can rely on that assures that their individual heritage can be respected.

Bob Calahan, *The Big Book of American Irish Culture*

WHY DIVERSITY?

There has been a significant but limited amount of writing on diversity in library and information science (LIS) in the past few years (for example, Josey, 1993; Peterson, 1994; and Welburn, 1995). Diversity has also been a topic of thought for more than a decade in LIS, as evident in the frequent discussions of minority recruitment among practitioners, faculty, and students in LIS education programs. But, has the scholarship on diversity issues or subsequent discussions made a visible impact on minority recruitment in the field?

Recent statistics show that ethnic minorities made up 26.4 percent of the U.S. population but comprised only about 10 percent of LIS graduates in 1995 (De la Pena McCook & Lippincott, 1997). White majority professionals account for 87.8 percent of academic and public librarians in 1991, representing an insignificant decrease from 88.2 percent in 1981.

The LIS profession has for more than a century been largely a female workforce managed by overwhelmingly male administrators. Only in the past two decades has the profession finally begun to see an increase in women library administrators. The average salary of these women academic library directors, however, is still lower than that of their male counterparts. Diversity education has made little, if any, impact on the integration of minorities or women librarians over the past decades.

Three major factors contribute to the lack of success of diversity education in library and information science. There is a general absence of concern for or interest in the issue in the LIS field. Many librarians assume that diversity is merely one of the many academic subjects they have to deal with some-how some way. The dispassionate disconnection to a perceived academic topic of thought is completely divorced from the daily reality of marginalized people across the United States. Interpreting issues of difference as merely in-tellectual abstractions insulates librarians from the urgency and the frustration of the issue. It also makes them powerless to become part of the solution.

A more prevailing problem is the unwillingness of librarians to acknowl-edge the diversity problem in many workplaces. As St. Lifer & Nelson (1997) documented, minority librarians overwhelmingly express feelings of alienation amidst the prevailing white European culture in their workplace. Meanwhile, many LIS practitioners and educators argue that white librarians are just as well equipped, without any particular diversity education and training, to serve multiracial and multicultural user groups. The real issue, it seems to many of the majority in LIS, lies in the need for the minority groups to learn the major-ity culture. By defining diversity as an issue only for the minority, the major-ity among LIS practitioners and educators fail to acknowledge their own role in contributing to the problem and their responsibility for seeking solutions.

Furthermore, there is the perception that diversity does not belong in the LIS curriculum. This argument is both a philosophical and a practical one. The philosophical argument is almost always based on the notion that social and political issues have no place in the academy. The practical argument originates largely from the fact that most LIS degree programs require only 36 credit hours of course work and thus cannot accommodate yet another course in the already crowded curriculum. The perception that diversity can only be delivered as a separate academic course ignores the fact that the success of di-versity education can only be achieved when it is integrated into the entire cur-riculum.

Given the dismal statistics of minority recruitment to the field and the re-sistance and lack of knowledge about diversity issues among many practitio-ners and educators, diversity education in LIS still has a long way to go. This paper will now explore some contextual aspects of the topic of diversity. Baseline definitions of diversity will be provided, and in the end, some sugges-tions for promoting diversity education will be offered.

DEFINING DIVERSITY

One of the difficult points surrounding the diversity debates centers on its scope of definition. The American Library Association (ALA) established its first Diversity Council several years ago to address racial diversity concerns within the organization. The participants quickly learned that the definition of diversity based on race alone could be easily challenged by other marginalized groups, for example, lesbians and gays. The original definition of diversity based solely on race had to be expanded to include gender and sexual orienta-tion.

The contemporary notion of diversity has evolved from very different per-spectives over the years in American history. As Rudenstine described in his report: Many nineteenth-century educators tended to think of diversity in terms of ideas, differences in opinions and views in all the areas of life where actual proof was impossible to achieve (Rudenstine, 1996). Citing scholars such as Milton, Mill, and Newman, Rudenstine traced the earlier definition of diversity to the value of eliciting different opinions and ideas by the presence of people from different geographical areas.

It was not until the Civil War era, according to Rudenstine, that diversity was linked with the concept of removing prejudices. This change was attributed to the social struggles between different racial and religious groups and the women suffrage movement. More significantly the influx of immigrants from southern and eastern Europe who arrived in the United States with different language, culture, and economic status elicited fears and anxieties among the earlier Anglo-Saxon settlers. The rise of White supremacist groups during the twentieth-century and the political debates on traditional American family values in recent years reinforce the notion of diversity as one defined entirely by race, gender, language, and religion.

Given the modern predominate definition of diversity as removing prejudices against race, gender, language, and religion, it is essential to address the various facets that contribute to chauvinistic attitudes. These include social issues such as discrimination and population migration; political issues such as affirmative action and immigration-related laws; and basic concepts of prejudices such as stereotyping, proportional representation, and nativism.

DISCRIMINATION

What constitutes discrimination? Although the social context of discrimination is a complex one, discrimination almost always entails behaviors of members of a certain group against those of different groups. A society rift with discriminatory attributes interprets the different languages and the various living styles of its minority populations as intellectually and culturally inferior. In a society that discriminates, the demand on racially and culturally inferior groups to assimilate to the culture of the dominant group is paramount. Such demands are usually followed by the majority's observation that the inferior group fails to do so. Furthermore, those from the perceived inferior groups are often considered as threats to, and freeloaders of, the economic market of the dominant group. This usually prompts the majority group to conclude that the inferior groups are a burden on public services and the government.

Discrimination can occur in almost all facets of a society. The causes can be attributed to race, ethnicity, religion, gender, sexual orientation, language, age, economic status, or physical characteristics. Discrimination manifests itself in many different forms, ranging from psychological or physical harm against individuals to actions against the entire group, such as persecution and genocide, immigration limitations, language restrictions, employment restraints, and social practice confinement.

To reduce individual acts of discrimination, it is easy for a society to propose laws that define specific acts of discrimination as crimes and punish individuals who are caught committing such crimes. What's harder to deal with in discrimination is the act committed by one social group against another social group. When a group act of discrimination occurs, members of the guilty group are often charged with collective moral guilt and are mandated to pay long afterwards for the historical injustice done by their group members to those of the victim group. The assignment of collective guilt and demand for the reparation of historical injustices often result in intensified resentments among different social groups.

This resentment may not be without merit if one considers the distinction between social responsibility for discrimination and individuals who act to discriminate. Discrimination may be the result of governmental laws hostile to particular groups and in many cases is condoned by the cultural norm of certain conservative social groups, yet the acts of discrimination are ultimately committed by individuals and targeted toward individuals. As Goldhagen (1997) says, "I reject the notion of collective guilt. The thrust of the charge of collective guilt is that a person is guilty merely by dint of his membership in a collectivity. Only individuals are to be deemed guilty. . . for their own individual deeds. The concept of guilt should be applied to an individual only when that person has committed a crime for the term carries with it all the connotations of legal guilt, namely guilt of a crime. It is essential to recognize both social and individual responsibilities in any discussion of discrimination. More importantly, the distinction between the two is critical to the society's quest for solutions."

POPULATION MIGRATION

Migration is a natural phenomenon that has as long a history as the existence of living organisms on earth. It is a survival skill for animals to avoid extraordinary hardship in their homeland and to search for a better environment in which to live. Population migration in human beings becomes a problem when it occurs across the artificial construct of nations and nationalities. When a nation is created by people of one race, language, and religion, the immigration of people of different races, languages, and religions becomes a visible, often tremendously politically threatening, situation to the earlier settlers.

The use of nationality to justify immigration restrictions in the United States is evident in political arguments of traditional American family values over the years. Although the United States is a nation of immigrants, the fact that the nation is bound only by a constitution created by people of a particular race, language, and religion more than two centuries ago has often been used to justify the call for exclusion of immigration by groups with different races, languages, and religions.

Political attempts to restrict immigration abound in American history. The Alien Act of 1798 represents one of the earliest political actions to establish America as a nation of the Nordic race. The Chinese Exclusion Act of 1882 and the Gentlemen's Agreement of 1907 were designed to exclude particular minority groups that did not conform to the cultural and religious beliefs of the group in power. The National Origins Act passed by the Congress in 1924 further solidified the definition of the United States as a country of people from Western and Northern European origins.

Using the notion of nationality in restricting population immigration is a political act with roots that go much deeper than just public laws. Most of the laws of immigration restriction are established with the help of social conservatives who justify discrimination based on minority inferiority. Some conservative scholars, such as Carl Brigham (1923) and Richard Hernstein and Charles Murray (1995), have gone to extraordinary lengths to provide scientific impressions by using social constructs such as IQ or language tests to define biological characteristics that distinguish the superiority of the majority group from the inferiority of groups that do not conform with the original concept of nationality.

The fact that the supposed scientific studies were largely the result of social constructs is evident in the treatment of Southern and Eastern European groups in different studies. The same Southern and Eastern European groups, including Polish and Italian immigrants who were the targets of social discrimination during the turn of the century, were declared inferior in Brigham's 1920s study, but described as brave, hard-working, imaginative, self-starting—and probably smart by Hernstein and Murray (1995) at the end of the next century when Eastern and Southern European immigrants were no longer targets of social discrimination in America.

NATIVISM

While nationality is an essential notion behind the motives of immigration restriction, the issue of immigration restriction cannot be fully explained without an understanding of the concept of nativism. *Random House Dictionary* defines nativism as the policy of favoring native inhabitants as against immigrants. This definition is however a very narrow one. To put it in a larger social context, nativism is but a means to define a majority by distinguishing superior insiders with power and control from inferior outsiders. In the realm of politics, nativism is the laws that define legitimacy for social and political entitlement.

The criteria used in differentiating powerful and controlling insiders from inferior outsiders often change according to the perceived strengths of the insider group. They often have no direct relation with the nativity of inhabitants of the land. Criteria used by people who claim majority nativism include not only length of settling history, but, more often, legal residency, citizenship, race, culture, or the degree of assimilation. Thus even though Native American Indians are the earliest settlers of the American land, they are not considered superior insiders for they have never assimilated to the White cultural group. African Americans have had a long history of occupying the land yet race and culture have largely prevented them from becoming part of the entitlement majority.

The practice of nativism is alive and well in today's political arena, where speakers often choose to define the term based on whatever criteria fits the political agenda. When presidential candidate Bob Dole, campaigned on the "traditional American family values" platform in 1996, it was apparent that he defined nativism as the predominate culture and religion of earlier White Anglo-Saxon Protestant settlers in the New England area. But, when Peter Brimelow (1995) warns about the threat of today's immigrants as being "virtually all racially distinct visible minorities," he apparently defines nativism as racial conformity. He does not view his own European immigrant accent as an obstacle to his membership in the entitlement group.

The Congress wrote nativism into its 1996 welfare reform bill by singling out legal residents without citizenship and reducing public services and benefits that was part of their entitlement. The English Only laws in almost half of the United States seek to define the language used by recent immigrants from non-English countries and to limit the educational and literacy programs needed by these immigrants to succeed.

The politics of nativism rises and falls in society with a predictable pattern. It is most active when a society experiences economic anxieties, as evident in the United States during the Great Depression of the 1920s and again in the 1990s. As people experience particular social discontent, such as higher crime rates, nativism becomes a prevalent issue. Politicians' exploitation of these issues also helps revive the politics of nativism, as has been seen during the Reagan and Bush administrations and, since 1994, when the Republican party took over the Congress.

PROTOTYPING, STEREOTYPING, AND PREJUDICE

As cognitive psychologists, including Eleanor Rosch (1978), demonstrate in their studies on cognition and categorization, humans learn to identify objects by grouping them into categories. A prototype is created for a category of objects as a result. Prototyping is done by isolating common attributes from individual objects and formulating a model of a typical object in a category, called internal structure of the category or a prototype. Some objects in the category share more common attributes with the prototype whereas some other objects may not share as many common attributes with their prototype in the category. Once a prototype is established, human beings rely on the description or image of such a prototype to reduce the need to memorize individual objects and the time and efforts to identify (that is, to learn) new objects. Prototyping is an essential step in the human learning process.

When comfortable with the use of a prototype to represent a group of objects, an individual may rely more and more on the "model of typical object" in a category as the basis for learning about the environment. An individual may even begin to use the model of typical object to interpret newly encountered objects and to infer potential consequences of such encounters. This is the process of stereotyping. A stereotype is the same model of typical object that results from the prototyping process. However, it is used as the sole basis for interpreting unfamiliar objects from different group surroundings. A person's heavy reliance on stereotypes and a lack of flexibility in recognizing differences in individual members of an unfamiliar group typically leads to fears and thus prejudice against all members of that group.

Prototyping is a positive human learning process that reduces information overload. Stereotyping carries a chilling effect for it generates fears of the unknown and unfamiliarity. Yet, like prototyping, stereotyping, as Devine (1989) shows in her study, is an automatic categorization process used to infer knowledge of human group characteristics. When facing ambiguous objects or behaviors of a different group, people automatically activate stereotypes to reduce ambiguity. Devine found that people with little prejudice learn to handle automatically activated stereotypes and replace them with thoughts reflecting equality and open-mindedness. Devine's research clearly demonstrates that prejudice is a learned behavior that often begin with stereotypes, but stereotypes do not always lead to prejudice. One has to learn to hate and fear and to become prejudiced just as one has to learn to suppress stereotypes in order to remain fair and impartial.

Scholars believe that education is the key attribute among people who are capable of suppressing their stereotypes. People with high prejudice learn to reinforce their own stereotypes by uncritically accepting assumptions and perceptions put forth by their families, friends, and the media. Shanto Iyengar, a UCLA professor studying television news crime reports, found that when the media disproportionately show nonwhite suspects in television crime stories, viewers begin to believe they see a nonwhite male suspect even when the report says nothing about a suspect. When media provides biased reporting on crime stories, it becomes a reflex for people to automatically associate a crime story with a nonwhite suspect.

KEYS TO DIVERSITY EDUCATION

Given the discussion of some of the basic issues of diversity, how do we go about promoting diversity in the LIS field? To address a society's prejudice and discrimination and promote diversity, one must first realize that assigning historical guilt and past injustice to the entire social group, even if justifiable, does little to help reduce discrimination by individuals. To hold the society responsible for fighting discrimination, one must focus on building healthy social norms in which individuals are allowed to critically challenge actions of nativism based on the culture and religion of the powerful, controlling majority, and are given equal opportunities for the pursuits of social privileges and personal achievements.

The notion of equal opportunities is paramount in a minority's quest for social and political success. Many opponents of equal opportunity policies argue for replacement of race and gender by social and economic classes in policies such as affirmative action. This is an argument of ideology lacking a sense of reality. While social or economic status could be a determinant for individual education and employment opportunities, it is important to recognize the intricate relationship between race and social/economic status throughout history which put most minority races at a greater disadvantage in obtaining social privileges in education and employment that were inherited by people of the majority group. A sanitized system that does not consider the inherited disadvantages of race and gender of minority groups only further preserves the inherited social, economic, and cultural privileges of the well-to-do majority.

In combating discrimination, one must be aware of the danger of blaming the gene. Defining majority by declaring biological superiority among the powerful insider group and inferiority of minority groups ignores the limits of biology in human development. It wrongfully assumes no difference between life development of human beings and that of animals, and ignores the crucial roles of culture and education in shaping human development.

The social problem of prejudice can only be addressed through lifelong learning on the part of individuals. Although education is the key to lessening prejudice, education per se does not guarantee prejudice-free individuals. To be successful in reducing prejudice, one must be sensitized, through learning, to the need for critically evaluating prejudiced messages in the environment and to recognize the automatic activation of stereotypes and one's own active role in suppressing these stereotypes.

THE SPIRIT OF DIVERSITY

Diversity is about recognizing differences. It is about making individual cultures and heritages visible and celebrating their coexistence. Diversity is an ongoing process of diversification in a society in which individuals of different groups accept the need to learn from one another. It is about building sensitivity and respect for individual personalities. Diversity is a matter of open-mindedness and positive attitudes. Ultimately a diverse society is a friendly society for all.

REFERENCES

Brigham, C. C. (1923). A study of American intelligence. Princeton, N.J.: Princeton University Press.

Brimelow, P. (1995). *Alien nation: Common sense about America's immigration disaster*. New York: Random House.

De la Pena McCook, K. & Lippincott, K. (1997, April 15). Library schools and diversity: Who makes the grade? *Library Journal, 122*, 30–32.

Devine, P. G. (1989). Stereotypes and prejudice: Their automatic and controlled components. *Journal of Personality and Social Psychology, 56*, 5–18.

Goldhagen, D. J. (1997). *Hitler's willing executioners: Ordinary Germans and the Holocaust*. New York: Vintage Books.

Hernstein, R. & Murray, C. (1995). The bell curve: Intelligence and class structure in American life. New York: Free Press.

Josey, E. J. (1993, Fall). The challenges of cultural diversity in the recruitment of faculty and students from diverse backgrounds. *Journal of Education for Library and Information Science, 34*, 302–11.

Peterson, L. (1994). Teaching the practitioners: one professor's attempt at library education and sensitivity to multicultural diversity. *Reference Librarian, 45/46*, 23–38.

Rosch, E. (1978). Principles of categorization. In E. Rosch & B. B. Lloyd (Eds.) *Cognition and Categorization* (pp. 27–48). Hillsdale, N.J.: L. Erlbaum Associates.

Rudenstine, N. L. (1996). The President's report: diversity and learning. Retrieved July 20, 1996, from the World Wide Web: http://www.harvard.edu/presidents_office/home.html

St. Lifer, E. & Nelson, C. (1997). Unequal opportunities: Race does matter. *Library Journal, 122* (18), 42–46.

Welburn, W. C. (1995). Moving beyond cliche: Cultural diversity and the curriculum in library and information studies. *Public & Access Services Quarterly, 1*, 97–100.

12

Anti-Immigrant Literature:
A Selected Bibliography

Evelyn Escatiola

It is said that the United States is a nation of immigrants. Almost everyone, with the exception of the native-born population, has come from somewhere else outside of what we recognize as the United States. In fact, this country has been built, literally, with the blood and sweat of immigrant laborers. It has also been said that America has had a love-hate relationship with its immigrant population. This has been quite evident during the last three decades as there have been numerous anti-immigrant proposals set up to stop the flow of what has been called by some, the "illegal alien invasion." In this essay and bibliography, I have sought out important materials on the new nativism published since 1990. These sources discuss the issues and controversies related to the late twentieth-century anti-immigrant period. In addition, I have chosen to highlight the literature on two recent specific propositions, 187 (Save Our State Initiative, 1994) and 209 (California Civil Rights Initiative, 1996). These two initiatives, both of which have their foundation in California, have had a profound impact on the rest of the United States.

HISTORICAL BACKGROUND

Consider some of the historical events that have taken place in the United States as they relate to immigrants. In 1882, Congress passed the Chinese Exclusion Act, which forbade all Chinese laborers from entering America. For the next sixty-one years, fourteen different exclusion acts laid down a federal barrier designed only for the Chinese. One prohibited women from immigrating. Another nullified all the visas held by Chinese who had temporarily returned to China, preventing their return (Takaki, 1995). "Prior to 1965, probably over 90 percent of the Chinese population came here illegally" (Paton, 2000, p. 3). During the early part of the 1890s the nation was in the midst of an economic depression. Henry Cabot Lodge, an U.S. senator was instrumental in the movement to limit the entry of "undesirable" immigrants into the United States. In addition, organizations such as the Immigration Restriction League were formed in Boston in 1894 for the purpose of limiting the number of foreigners who could come into the United States (Espenshade & Hempstead, 1996). A literacy test was proposed and passed in the Senate in 1896. It insured that unskilled and uneducated immigrants would be denied entry. The following year this legislation was vetoed by President Grover Cleveland (Espenshade & Hempstead, 1996).

In 1931 a repatriation program to deport Mexicans took place. Thousands of Mexicans, legal and illegal residents of the United States, were sent en mass to Mexico. In 1942, the "Emergency Labor Program" was initiated. This program brought Mexican laborers to work in the agricultural fields and railroads on a temporary basis, as low paid laborers. They were imported into the United States from 1942 to 1947. Then in the 1950s, the United States' "Operation Wetback" took effect. Thousands of Mexicans were again deported, including U.S. citizens. Ironically, many of those deported were those same laborers and their families that were brought to the United States in the 1940s. Massive raids took place and created a climate of fear within the Mexican and Mexican American community.

The McCarran-Walter Act of 1952 was a further blow against immigrants (Acuña, 1981). Unfortunately, those most suspect as subversives were largely people of color. In the 1980s Central American refugees who were seeking asylum in the United States were routinely detained. Many were deported to their home country despite the civil wars that raged in the area.

During the latest economic depression of the early 1990s, the integrity of the nation's border with Mexico became a national concern. Vigilante groups formed to protect the United States' border with Mexico, sometimes taking the law into their own hands. Increased funding of the Border Patrol and the construction of a fence became the solution to what was perceived to be the nation's immigration problem.

PROPOSITION 187

In 1994, Proposition 187, the "Save Our State" initiative, was placed on the ballot in California and passed by 60 percent of the voting public. The intent of this initiative was to prohibit undocumented immigrants from receiving any medical, educational, or social services. From the ballot box to the courtroom, the battle was waged. In a 1998 decision Federal Judge Pfaelzer invalidated the initiative as she deemed the provisions to be unconstitutional. However, Peter Schey, one of the attorneys who filed a suit against the state of California stated, "I think in many respects we need to understand that we may have won the battle but [former Gov.] Pete Wilson won the war . . . we won a tactical victory but they injected many of the standards of 187 in federal law" (Hernandez, 1999, p. 24).

Not only were proponents of Proposition 187 successful in integrating legal standards into federal law, they were equally successful in creating a climate of fear and distrust within immigrant communities of California. Supporters of the initiative made many negative statements during the campaign. The polarization is evident in the following statements made by two prominent supporters of Proposition 187. Howard Ezell, a retired Immigration and Naturalization official stated, "The people are tired of watching their state run wild and become a third world country" (Johnson, 1997, p. 178). Betty Coe, an Orange County resident and leader of the Save Our State organization stated, "You're dealing with Third World cultures who come in, they shoot, they beat, they stab and they spread their drugs around in our school system" (Johnson, 1997, p. 179).

What fuels contemporary American attitudes against immigration? According to an article written by Espenshade & Hempstead, in which they analyzed a poll conducted by CBS/*New York Times* in June 1993, they found that the respondents' views were related to such events as the health of the U.S. economy, feelings of social and political alienation, and isolationist sentiments concerning international economic issues and foreign relations. Proposition 187 is but the latest episode in a resurgence of anti-immigrant sentiment that began in the United States in the 1970s (Espenshade & Hempstead, 1996). In 1994, California was witnessing a period of economic stagnation and repeated state budgetary problems. In addition, the school system was impacted by population growth and lack of an infrastructure to provide improvements that were desperately needed (Kadetsky, 1994). It was no wonder then that the voters of California placed blame on the undocumented immigrant. They had reason to believe that these poor people were the cause of their problems.

Undocumented immigrants face many hardships including employer exploitation, racial/ethnic discrimination, and sub-standard living conditions. They come to this country in the quest for survival and self-improvement. The undocumented worker is willing to sacrifice whatever it takes to feed his/her family.

The labor market situation of undocumented Mexican workers is frequently a difficult one. Although illegal immigrants can buy fraudulent identification papers that allow them to find some jobs in the mainstream labor market, those who cannot afford those papers are forced to work in a shadow labor market that is itself illegal. The lack of documents, and the fear of detection by the INS, puts the workers in a radically subordinate position relative to their employers. The result is exploitation and subhuman working conditions . . . Thai and Hispanic undocumented garment workers were forced to toil in a compound ringed with barbed wire for less than US$ 1 an hour (when the minimum wage was US$ 4.25). (Rivera-Batiz, 2000)

PROPOSITION 209

Proposition 187 is one of the most dramatic examples of the immigrant hysteria of the 1990s. However, in 1996 another anti-immigrant initiative hit the California ballot box. Proposition 209, officially entitled the California Civil Rights Initiative, was passed by 54 percent of the voting electorate. According to the proponents of 209, it was introduced to stem the reverse discrimination that was occurring against Whites.

The civil rights movement of the 1960s paved the way for the Civil Rights Act of 1964 which outlawed discrimination. President Johnson declared at the time, "You do not take a person who, for years, has been hobbled by chains and liberate him, bring him up to the starting line of a race and then say, 'You are free to compete with all the others,' and still justly believe that you have been completely fair" (Mueller, 1999). In 1978, Allan Bakke filed a discrimination suit based on the premise that he was denied admission into the University of California, Davis, Medical School because preferential treatment was being given to minority applicants. He claimed reverse discrimination and was granted admission.

Despite the fact that the Bakke decision chipped away at the foundations of affirmative action, the policy remained functional. Supreme Court Justice Lewis Powell stated that the University of California could take race into account and that a diverse student population was a "constitutionally permissible goal" which can benefit students by leading to a "robust exchange of ideas" (Mueller,1999). In 1995, Governor Wilson and the University of California Board of Regents passed two resolutions directing the University of California (UC) system to end the use of racial, religious, sexual, and ethnic considerations when it came to admissions. In 1996, Proposition 209 was placed on the ballot in California. Its passage totally eliminated racial considerations in all public agencies. Presently universities and colleges are attempting to find other methods to admit a racially diverse student population in order to comply with the federal law which still permits affirmative action programs and the State of California which does not. The reality is that with the scaling back of equal opportunity programs, such as affirmative action in the UCs, there have been lower enrollments of minority students. For example, African American students suffered admission declines of 36 percent at UC Davis, 19 percent at UC Irvine, and 46 percent at UC San Diego for the fall of 1998. Latino students dropped by 20 percent at UC Davis, 9 percent at UC Irvine, and 31 percent at UC San Diego in the fall of 1998 (Aftermath, p. A8).

Many universities are attempting to address the need for racial diversity in alternative ways and still comply with the law. New admissions policies have been developed which consider participation in outreach programs, standardized test scores, grade point average, and the completion of advanced placement courses (Gorman, 2000). Nationally California ranks 49th in educational spending. Many schools with minority majorities are negatively affected by this fact. "Black, Hispanic and Filipino-American students are unfairly penalized in the competition because more than half of California's high schools don't even offer advanced placement courses" (Price, 1999, p. 4).

Unfortunately, immigrants and people of color will continue to be disenfranchised by the effects of negative propositions such as 187 and 209 far into the next century. The fear tactics used to successfully pass these propositions will surely continue to work within our country to discourage immigrant populations from participating to the best of their ability in the democratic process. We must continue to remind ourselves as library professionals, citizens of the

United States, and human beings that we live in a global village in which we must all learn and live together.

PUBLIC LIBRARIES

As librarians who work in the public sector, we are a part of the establishment. During nativist periods the governmental status of libraries and library staff may cause immigrant populations to view these institutions and staff with skepticism and distrust. However, many public libraries have formed unique relationships with the communities they serve. Positive events such as adult literacy programs and children's reading programs have helped to create a positive bond between the library and the community. Essentially, it does not matter what we, as individual librarians, decide to do with our vote, what matters is how the library as a public institution, founded on the idea of providing free access to information to the general public, chooses to behave.

In Amado Padilla's excellent report, *Public Library Services for Immigrant Populations in California* (1991), he cites important factors and recommendations regarding how public libraries should work with the immigrant population. He states, "many immigrants, even those in possession of considerable education, come to this country with different perceptions and expectations of public services including libraries. It is important for professional librarians to understand and validate these perceptions and expectations. These newcomers and their offspring constitute the "new" Americans and they need to be as informed as possible to meet the "old" Americans on an equal footing. California public libraries can be instrumental in this process" (Padilla, 1991, p. 48).

Obviously, public libraries can play an integral role in the lives of all its constituents. It is important to avoid becoming part of the divisiveness that overshadows programs that bring the library and the immigrant communities closer together. When given the opportunity, people will strive to improve their quality of life. The public library can offer such an opportunity.

THE SELECTED BIBILOGRAPHY

The bibliography of sources that is included here is but a sample of the wealth of literature on the topic of immigration and immigrants in the United States since the early 1990s. Bibliographic citations regarding Propositions 187 and 209 have been included due to the national impact of these initiatives. While the majority of articles relating to immigration are critical of nativist movements in the United States, several articles favoring immigration restrictions have also been included.

For a collection of important essays which discuss the topic of migration into the United States from Mexico see David G. Gutierrez's, *Between Two Worlds: Mexican Immigrants in the United States* (1996). Essays in this volume analyze the push-pull factors that encourage migration, including the active participation of the United States' business interests. For a view of the integral role that the nativist agenda has had on our perception of immigrants and the consequences of this migration on the history of the United States see Juan F. Perea's collection of essays entitled *Immigrants Out! The New Nativism and the Anti-Immigrant Impulse in the United States* (1997). Within this volume Johnson offers an excellent chapter that is often cited in the literature entitled "The New Nativism: Something Old, Something New, Something Borrowed, Something Blue" (Johnson, 1997, p. 165–89). For perceptions of American citizens on immigration see "Contemporary American Attitudes Toward United States Immigration" (Espenshade & Hempstead, 1996). These authors are the leading experts in this area of study. The results of their 1993 poll are the basis of the article's findings. This is an extremely important article as it addresses the basic question, "Why do anti-immigrant attitudes exist?" Valuable tabular data is highlighted. *Migration News*, an online publication of the University of California, provides the latest analysis of international migration issues and current research by migration scholars.

The Asian perspective is very important to any discussion of immigration and the immigrant experience in the United States. The following are some important sources that specifically focus on these immigrants and the unique identity issues faced by Asian immigrants. In *Strangers at the Gates Again: Asian American Immigration After 1965*, Takaki (1995), the highly respected ethnic studies scholar, writes about the diversity of Asian groups and their entry into the United States. Kitano and Daniels analyze 1990 census data and "minority-majority" interactions in *Asian Americans: Emerging Minorities* (1995).

Latinos and Asians make up the largest migrant groups in the United States of the last three decades. There are a number of myths that are common to both groups. For example, immigrants are often perceived as taking jobs away from Americans, as well as being a drain on public assistance programs. In *The State of Asian Pacific America: Reframing the Immigration Debate* (Hing & Lee, 1996), these myths are discussed and dispelled. The reader is further informed regarding the contributions of Asian immigrants to the greater society. Asian immigrant economic contributions and their business practices are discussed as well. Dale Maharidge, a Pulitzer Prize author, has written a book about the need to recognize our commonalities in the face of dramatic demographic and social change. In his book *The Coming of the White Minority: California and America's immigration Debate* (1996), the author shares four in-depth interviews with individuals from various ethnic and racial backgrounds. Maharidge stresses that the population transformation of California is inevitable. Readers are encouraged to not only accept but embrace the social reality.

Much has been written about the impact of Proposition 187 on the immigrant population at large but a unique video shows what happened to a specific group of immigrant families in Los Angeles. Director and former Los Angeles school teacher, Laura Angelica Simon, created and produced *Fear and Learning at Hoover Elementary* (1997). What did undocumented immigrants feel about Proposition 187 and how did it affect them? These questions are confronted in the video. This film profoundly illustrates the heart wrenching experiences of immigrants from their point of view.

Many excellent articles have been published prior, during, and after the highly controversial California initiative, Proposition 187. Some informative contributions include "Bashing Illegals in California" (Kadetsky, 1994). In this article the author writes about the diversity of Proposition 187 supporters. Phillip Martin provides an interesting transnational perspective in "Proposition 187 in California" (1995). The Proposition 187 campaign, as well as United States and Mexican reactions are discussed. Martin offers valuable insights into why people migrate from Mexico in the first place. Linda Chavez, an author known for her conservative views on issues of immigration, bilingual education, and English only programs, provides an anti-undocumented immigrant perspective that is well worth reading. She maintains a web site that regularly addresses these issues. In "What to do about immigration" (Chavez, 1995), pp. 29–35, Chavez discusses the relationship between national identity and immigration, intermarriage rates among immigrants and the general impact of immigrants in the United States. Also, the Center for Equal Opportunity web site, a conservative think tank headed by Linda Chavez, offers viewpoints in favor of curbing immigration. Readers that want to see the fulltext of the Proposition 187 initiative including arguments for and against, analysis by a legislative analyst, and voting returns, should see the *1994 California Voters Information* (http://ca94.election.digital.cdm/e/prop/187/home.html).

It is hoped that the reader will find this bibliography useful in determining credible information about the issue of immigration and affirmative action. Unfortunately, only a few references were found that directly related to libraries. For those who desire additional citations and hard to find government documents see *Immigration Issues: A Bibliography* (http://www-lib.usc.edu/~anthonya/imm.html). This online web site is updated on a regular basis by A. Anderson, a government documents librarian at the University of Southern California.

REFERENCES

Acuña, R. (1981). *Occupied America: A history of Chicanos.* 2nd ed., New York: Harper & Row Publishers, pp. 158–60.

Aftermath of Prop. 209 hits UC campuses. (1998, April 18). *Los Angeles Sentinel,* p. A8. Retrieved October 13, 1999, from Ethnic NewsWatch on the World Wide Web: http://www.slinfo.com/ ethnic.htm

Anderson, A. (1997). *Immigration issues: A bibliography.* Los Angeles: University of Southern California. Retrieved January 25, 1998, from the World Wide Web: http://www.lib.usc.edu/~anthonya/imm. html

Chavez, L. (1995, March). What to do about immigration. *Commentary, 99* (3), 29–35.

Chavez, L. (1997). *The new immigrant challenge.* Washington, D.C.: Center for Equal Opportunity. Retrieved January 25, 1998, from the World Wide Web: http://www.ceousa.org/strang.html

Espenshade, T. J. & Hempstead, K. (1996). Contemporary American attitudes toward U.S. immigration. *The International Migration Review, 30* (2), 535.

Gorman, S. (2000, April 18). After affirmative action. *National Journal, 32* (15), 1120–24.

Gutierrez, D. G. (Ed.) (1996). *Between two worlds: Mexican immigrants in the United States.* Wilmington, D.E: Scholarly Resources.

Hernandez, S. (1999, September 2). The life after death of Proposition 187. *Black Issues In Higher Education, 16* (14), 24–25.

Hing, B. O. & Lee, R. (Eds.) (1996). *The state of Asian Pacific America: Reframing the immigration debate: A public policy report. Executive summary.* Los Angeles: University of California, Los Angeles, LEAP/Asian American Studies Center.

Johnson, K. R. (1997). The new nativism: Something old, something new, something borrowed, something blue. In J. F. Perea (Ed.) *Immigrants out! The new nativism and the anti-immigrant impulse in the United States* (pp. 165–98). New York: New York University Press.

Kadetsky, E. (1994, October 17). Bashing illegals in California, the "Save Our State" initiative. *Nation, 259* (12), 416–22.

Kitano, H. L. & Daniels, R. (1995). *Asian Americans: Emerging minorities.* Englewood Cliffs, N.J.: Prentice Hall.

Maharidge, D. (1996). *The coming of the white minority: California and America's immigration debate.* New York: Times Books.

Martin, P. (1995, Spring). Proposition 187 in California. *International Migration Review, 29* (1), 255–63.

Mueller, T. (1999, January 31). What's the solution? The affirmative action debate is hotter than ever—all in the name of civil rights. *Diversity Monthly, 11,* p. 23. Retrieved October 13, 1999, from Ethnic NewsWatch on the World Wide Web: http://www.slinfo.com/ethnic.htm

Padilla, A. (1991). *Public library services for immigrant populations in California.* Sacramento, Calif.: California State Library Foundation.

Paton, D. (2000, January 25). Immigrants take ever more perilous routes to America. *Christian Science Monitor,* p. Op3.

Price, H. B. (1999, February 3). Color-blindness equals exclusion. *Asianweek, 20* (22),4.

Rivera-Batiz, F. L. (2000, Spring). Underground on American soil: Undocumented workers and U.S. immigration policy. *Journal of International Affairs, 53* (2), 485–501. Retrieved June 5, 2000, from Proquest on the World Wide Web: http://www.proquest.umi/pdqweb

Simon, L. A. (1997). *Fear and learning at Hoover elementary.* VHS. Color. 54 min. Los Angeles: Transit Media.

State of California. Attorney General. (1994). 1994 California Voter Information. Retrieved November 2, 1994, from the World Wide Web: http://ca94.election.digital.com/e/187/home/home

Takaki, R. (1995). *Strangers at the gates again: Asian American immigration after 1965.* Broomall, N.Y.: Chelsea House Publishers.

University of California. (1997). *Migration Dialogue.* Davis, Calif.: Author. Retrieved January 25,1988, from the World Wide Web: http://migration.ucdavis.edu

SELECTED BIBLIOGRAPHY: ANTI-IMMIGRANT LITERATURE

Asian Immigrants

Barkan, E. R. (1992). *Asian and Pacific Islander migration to the United States: A model of new global patterns.* Westport, Conn.: Greenwood Publishing Group.

Daniels, R. & Kitano, H. H. L. (1995). *Asian Americans: Emerging minorities.* New York: Prentice Hall.

Foner, P. & Rosenberg, D. (Eds.) (1993). *Racism, dissent and Asian Americans: A documentary history.* Westport, Conn.: Greenwood Publishing Group.

Gardner, R. W. (1992). Asian immigration: The view from the United States. *Asian and Pacific Migration Journal, 1,* 64–99.

Goldberg, C. (1996, March 31). Asian immigrants help bolster U.S. economy, new report says. *New York Times,* pp. A1, A32.

Hamamoto, D. Y. & Torres, R. D. (Eds.) (1997). *New American destinies: A reader in contemporary Asian and Latino immigration.* New York: Routledge.

Hein, J. (1992). *States and international migrants: Incorporation of Indochinese refugees in the United States and France.* Boulder, Colo.: Westview Press.

Hing, B. O. (1993). *Making and remaking Asian America through immigration policy 1850–1990.* Stanford, Calif.: Stanford University Press.

Hing, B. O. & Lee, R. (Eds.) (1996). *State of Asian Pacific America: Reframing the immigration debate: A public policy report. Executive summary.* Los Angeles: University of California, Los Angeles, LEAP/Asian American Studies Center.

Horton, J. (1995). *The politics of diversity: Immigration, resistance and change in Monterey Park, California.* Philadelphia, Pa.: Temple University Press.

Huang, F.-Y. (1997). *Asian and Hispanic immigrant women in the workforce: Implications of the United States immigration policies since 1965.* New York: Garland Publishing.

Lee, S. & Edmonston, B. (1994). The socioeconomic status and integration of Asian immigrants. In B. Edmonston & J. S. Passel (Eds.) *Immigration and ethnicity: The integration of America's newest arrivals* (pp. 101–38). Washington, D.C.: The Urban Institute.

McClain, C. (Ed.) (1994). *Asian Indians, Filipinos, other Asian communities, and the law.* New York: Garland Publishing.

Nakanishi, D. T. (1994). Transforming Asian-Pacific America: The challenges of growth and diversity. *Asian Pacific Migration Journal, 3,* 497–509.

National Asian Pacific American Legal Consortium. (1995). *Audit of violence against Asian Pacific Americans: The consequences of intolerance in America, 1995.* Washington, D.C.: Author.

Ong, P., Bonacich, E., & Cheng, L. (Eds.) (1994). *The new Asian immigration in Los Angeles & global restructuring.* Philadelphia, Pa.: Temple University Press.

Puente, M. (1996, March 28). Study: Asian immigrants fastest-growing U.S. group. *USA Today,* p. A4.

Takaki, R. (1994). *Spacious dreams: The first wave of Asian immigration.* Broomall, N.Y.: Chelsea House.

Takaki, R. (1995). *From exiles to immigrants: The refugees from Southeast Asia.* Broomall, N.Y.: Chelsea House.

Takaki, R. (1995). *Strangers at the gates again: Asian American immigration after 1965.* Broomall, N.Y.: Chelsea House.

Tseng, Y. F. (1994). Chinese ethnic economy: San Gabriel Valley, Los Angeles County. *Journal of Urban Affairs, 16* (2), 169–89.

Wong, W. (1995, January). The California dream: Often a surreal distortion for Asian Americans. *California Journal, 26* (1), 41–42.

Caribbean Immigrants

Bouvier, L. F. & Simcox, D. (1986). *Many hands, few jobs: Population, unemploy-*

ment, and emigration in Mexico and the Caribbean. Washington, D.C.: Center for Immigration Studies.

Chierici, R. M. & Cassagnol, D. (1991). *"Making it": Migration and adaptation among Haitian boat people in the United States.* New York: AMS Press.

Diaz-Briquets, S. & Weintraub, S. (Eds.) (1991). *Determinants of emigration from Mexico, Central America and the Caribbean.* Boulder, Colo.: Westview Press.

Fusco, C. (1995). *English is broken here: Notes on cultural fusion in the Americas.* New York: The New Press.

Grasmuck, S. & Pessar, P. (1991). *Between two islands: Dominican international migration.* Berkeley, Calif.: University of California Press.

Grenier, G. & Stepick, A. (Eds.) (1992). *Miami now! Immigration, ethnicity and social change.* Gainesville, Fla.: University Press of Florida.

Guarnizo, L. (1994). Los Dominicanyork: The making of a binational society. *Annals of The American Academy of Political and Social Sciences, 533,* 70–86.

Jordan, H. (1995, November–December). Immigrant rights: A Puerto Rican issue? *NACLA: Report on the Americas, 29* (3), 35–38.

Palmer, R. W. (1995). *Pilgrims from the sun: West Indian migration to America.* New York: Twayne Publishers.

Rivera, M. L. (1991). *Decision and structure: U.S. refugee policy in the Mariel crisis.* Lanham, Md.: University Press of America.

Economics

Bean, F. D. & Cushing, R. G. (1995, August). The relationship between the Mexican economic crisis and illegal migration to the United States. *Trade Insights, 5,* 1–4.

Borjas, G. J. (1996, November). The new economics of immigration. *Atlantic Monthly, 278,* 73–80.

Borjas, G. J., Freedman, R. B., & Katz, L. F. (1996, May). Searching for the effect of immigration on the labor market. *American Economic Review, 86* (2), 246–51.

Borjas, G. J. & Tienda, M. (1993). The employment and wages of legalized immigrants. *International Migration Review, 27,* 712–47.

Briggs, V. M. & Moore, S. (1994). *Still the open door? U.S. immigration policy and the American economy.* Washington, D.C.: American University Press.

Enchautegui, M. E. (1993). *The effects of immigration on the wages and employment of Black males.* Washington, D.C.: Program for Research on Immigration Policy, Urban Institute.

Friedberg, R. & Hunt, J. (1995). The impact of immigrants on host country wages, employment and growth. *Journal of Economic Perspectives, 9* (2), 23–44.

Jackson, J. J. (1995). Competition between blacks and immigrants. *The Social Contract, 5* (4), 247–54.

Lamphere, L., Stepick, A., & Grenier, G. (Eds.) (1994). *Newcomers in the workplace: Immigrants and the restructuring of the U.S. economy.* Philadelphia, Pa.: Temple University Press.

Lidstrom, D. P. (1996). Economic opportunity in Mexico and return migration from the United States. *Demography, 33* (33), 357–74.

Martínez, R. (1994, January 30). The shock of the new. *Los Angeles Times Magazine,* pp. 10–14, 16, 39.

McDonnell, P. J. (1997, January 23). Study finds immigrants economic effect mixed. *Los Angeles Times,* p. B1.

Pachón, H. C. & DeSipio, L. (1994). *New Americans by choice: Political perspectives of Latino immigrants.* Boulder, Colo.: Westview Press.

Portes, A. (1995). *The economic sociology of immigration: Essays on networks, ethnicity, and entrepreneurship.* New York: Russell Sage Foundation.

Sassen, S. (1991). *The global city: New York, London, Tokyo.* Princeton, N.J.: Princeton University Press.

Sassen, S. (1994). *The mobility of labor and capital.* New York: Cambridge University Press.

Sassen, S. (1996). *Losing controls: Sovereignty in the age of globalization.* New York: Columbia University Press.

Waldinger, R. (1996). *Still the promised city? African-Americans and new immigrant in post-industrial New York.* Cambridge, Mass.: Harvard University Press.

Education

Delgado-Gaitan, C. & Trueba, H. T. (1991). *Crossing cultural borders: Education for immigrant families in America.* London: The Falmer Press.

Reid, G. (1995, June–July). Guardians at the bridge: Will immigrants maintain equal access? *Community College Journal, 65* (6), 14–19.

Rumbaut, R. & Cornelius, W. (1995). *California's immigrant children: Theory, research, and implications for policy.* La Jolla, Calif.: Center for U.S.-Mexican Studies.

Suárez-Orozco, C. & Suárez-Orozco, M. (1995). *Transformations: Immigration, family life, and achievement motivation among Latino adolescents.* Stanford, Calif.: Stanford University.

Suárez-Orozco, C. & Suárez-Orozco, M. (1989). *Central American refugees and U.S. high schools: A psychosocial study of motivation and achievment.* Stanford, Calif.: Stanford University.

Suárez-Orozco, M., Roos, P., & Suárez-Orozco, C. (1997). Cultural, educational and legal perspectives on immigration: Implications for school reform. In J. Heubert (Ed.) *New perspectives on school reform* (pp. 160–204). New Haven, Conn.: Yale University.

Trueba, H. T. (1993). Race and ethnicity: The role of universities in healing multicultural America. *Educational Theory, 43* (1), 51–54.

Vernez, G., et al. (1996). *How immigrants fare in U.S. education.* Santa Monica, Calif.: Rand Corporation.

Environment

Bouvier, L. F. & Grant, L. (1994). *How many Americans? Population, immigration, and the environment.* San Francisco, Calif.: Sierra Club Books.

Cone, M. (1998, April 26). Sierra Club to remain neutral on immigration. *Los Angeles Times,* pp. A1, A34.

Simon, J. L. (1990). *Population matters: People, resources, environment, and immigration.* New Brunswick, N.J.: Transaction Publishers.

General

Anderson, A. (1997). *Immigration issues: A bibliography.* Los Angeles: University of Southern California. Retrieved January 25, 1998, from the World Wide Web: http://www-lib.usc.edu/~anthonya/imm.html

Bach, R. (1993). *Changing relations: Newcomers and established residents in U.S. communities.* New York: Ford Foundation.

Beck, R. (1994). *Re-charting America's future: Responses to arguments against stabilizing U.S. population and limiting immigration.* Petoskey, Mich.: The Social Contract Press.

Beck, R. (1996). *The case against immigration: The moral, economic, social, and environment reasons for reducing U.S. immigration back to traditional levels.* New York: W. W. Norton.

Booth, W. (1998, February 22). America's racial and ethnic divides: One nation, indivisible, is it history? *Washington Post,* p. A1.

Borjas, G. (1996, November). The new economics of immigration. *Atlantic Monthly, 278,* 73–80.

Briggs, V. (1996). *Mass immigration and the national interest.* 2nd ed. Armonk, N.Y.: Sharpe.

Brimelow, P. (1995). *Alien nation: Common sense about America's immigration disaster.* New York: Random House.

Chavez, L. (1995, March). What to do about immigration. *Commentary, 99* (3), 29–35.

Chavez, L. (1997). *The new immigrant challenge.* Washington, D.C.: Center for Equal Opportunity. Retrieved January 25, 1998, from the World Wide Web: http://www.ceousa.org/strang.html

Clinton, W. J. Office of the President. (1994). *Accepting the immigrant challenge: The president's report on immigration.* Washington, D.C.: U.S. Government Printing Office.

Conniff, R. (1993, October). The war on aliens: The right calls the shots. *Progressive, 57* (10), 22–29.

Cornelius, W. A., Martin, P. L., & Hoffefield, J. F. (1994). *Controlling immigration: A global perspective.* Stanford, Calif.: Stanford University Press.

Duran, L., Gallegos, B., Mann, E., & Omatsu, G. (1994). *Immigrant rights and wrongs.* Los Angeles: Labor/Community Strategy Center.

Edmonston, B. & Passel, J. (Eds.) (1994). *Immigration and ethnicity: The integration of America's newest arrivals.* Washington, D.C.: The Urban Institute.

Espenshade, T. (1997). *Keys to successful immigration: Implications of the New Jersey experience.* Washington, D.C.: The Urban Institute.

Espenshade, T. & Hempstead, K. (1996). Contemporary American attitudes toward U.S. immigration. *International Migration Review, 30* (2), 535–70.

Freeman, G. (1994, July). Can liberal states control unwanted immigration? *Annals of the American Academy of Political and Social Science, 534,* 17–30.

Goldring, L. (1996). Blurring borders: Constructing transnational community in the process of U.S.-Mexico migration. *Research in Community Sociology, 6,* 69–104.

Hartman, C. (Ed.) (1995). *Focus on immigration.* Washington, D.C.: Poverty and Race Research Action Council. (ERIC Document Reproduction Service No. ED385403).

Immigration and Naturalization Service. (1996). *Operation gatekeeper: Two years of progress.* Washington, D.C.: U.S. Government Printing Office.

Isbister, J. (1996). *The immigrant debate: Remaking America.* West Hartford, Conn.: Komarian Press.

Johnson, H. (1993). *Immigrants in California: Findings from the 1990 census.* Sacramento, Calif.: California Research Bureau.

Jonas, S. (1996). Rethinking immigration policy and citizenship in the Americas. *Social Justice: A Journal of Crime, Conflict and World Order, 23* (3), 68–85.

Jost. K. (1995, February 3). Cracking down on immigration. *CQ Researcher, 5* (5), 97–115.

Koelin, P. H. (1991). *Refugees from revolution: U.S. policy and third world migration.* Boulder, Colo.: Westview.

Lamphere, L. (Ed.) (1992). Structuring diversity: Ethnographic perspectives on the new immigration. Chicago: University of Chicago Press.

Levinson, D. & Ember, M. (Eds.) (1997). *American immigrant cultures: Builders of the nation.* New York: Simon & Schuster.

Lustig, J. & Walker, D. (1995). *No way out: Immigrants and the new California.* Berkeley, Calif.: Coalition for Human Rights and Social Justice.

Maharidge, D. (1996). *The coming white minority: California and America's immigration debate.* New York: Times Books.

Millman, J. (1997). *The other Americans: How immigrants renew our country, our economy and our values.* New York: Viking Press.

Mills, N. (Ed.) (1994). *Arguing immigration: The debate over the changing face of America.* New York: Simon & Schuster.

Muller, T. (1993). *Immigrants and the American city.* New York: New York University Press.

Mylopoulos, C. (2000, March). Tending to the city's needs, serving newcomer immigrants: The value of community information. *Multicultural Review 9* (1), 24–27, 57–59.

Padilla, A. M. (1991*). Public library services for immigrant populations in California.* Sacramento, Calif.: California State Library Foundation.

Pessar, P. R. (1995). *A visa for a dream.* Boston: Allyn and Bacon.

Portes, A. (1996). Transnational communities: Their emergence and significance in the contemporary world-system. In R. P. Korzeniewicz and W. C. Smith (Eds.) *Latin America in the world economy* (pp. 151–68). Westport, Conn.: Greenwood Publishing Group.

Portes, A. & Rumbaut, R. (1996). *Immigrant America.* Berkeley, Calif.: University of California Press.

Purcell, L. E. (1995). *Immigration.* Phoenix, Ariz.: Oryx Press.

Reimers, D. M. (1992). *Still the golden door: The third world comes to America.* New York: Columbia University Press.

Rose, F. (1996, July 3). Some immigrant groups fare poorly after arrival in U.S., Rand study finds. *Wall Street Journal,* p. A2.

Simon, R. J. (1993). *The ambivalent welcome: Print media, public opinion and immigration.* Westport, Conn.: Greenwood Publishing Group.

Smith, J. P. & Edmonston, B. (Eds.) (1997). *The new Americans: Economic, demographic, and fiscal effects of immigration.* Washington, D.C.: National Academy Press.

Stalker, P. (1994). *The work of strangers: A survey of international labor migration.* Geneva, Switzerland: International Labour Office.

Ueda, R. (1994). *Postwar immigrant America: A social history.* Boston, Mass.: Bedford Books of St. Martin's Press.

University of California. (1997). *Migration Dialogue.* Davis, Calif. Retrieved January 25, 1998, from the World Wide Web: http://migration.ucdavis.edu

Volkan, V. D. (1993). Immigrants and refugees: A psychodynamic perspective. *Mind and Human Interaction, 4* (2), 63–69.

Weiner, T. (1993, June 13). On these shores, immigrants find a new wave of hostility. *New York Times,* p. D1.

Wiegand, W. A. (1996, Summer). The library bill of rights: Introduction. *Library*

Trends, 45 (1), 1–6.

Wilson, P. (1994, June 15). Securing our nation's borders. *Vital Speeches of the Day, 60,* 534–36.

Mexican & Latin American Immigrants

Ayala, R. & Ayala, M. (1994, June). *Report card on public library services to the Latino community: Final report.* Calexico, Calif.: Reforma, National Association to Promote Library Services to the Spanish Speaking.

Baver, S. & Haslip Viera, G., (Ed.) (1996). *Latinos in New York.* Notre Dame, Ind.: University of Notre Dame Press.

Bean, F. D., de la Garza, R., Roberts, R. et al. (1997). *At the crossroads: Mexico and U.S. immigration policy.* Lanham, Md.: Rowman and Littlefield.

Bouvier, L. F. & Simcox, D. (1986). *Many hands, few jobs: Population, unemployment, and emigration in Mexico and the Caribbean.* Washington, D.C.: Center for Immigration Studies.

Chavez, L. R. (1992). *Shadowed lives: Undocumented immigrants in American society.* Fort Worth, Tex.: Harcourt Brace College Publishers.

Chavez, L. R. & Martínez, R. G. (1996). Mexican immigration in the 1980s and beyond: Implications for Chicanas/os. In D. R. Maciel and I. D. Ortiz (Eds.) *Chicanas/Chicanos at the crossroads: Social, economic, and political change* (pp. 25–51). Tucson: University of Arizona Press.

Darder, A. & Torres, R. D. (Eds.) (1998). *The Latino studies reader: Culture, economy & society.* Oxford, U.K.: Blackwell Publishers.

DiSipio, L. (1996). Making citizens or good citizens? Naturalization as a predictor of organizational and electoral behavior among Latino immigrants. *Hispanic Journal of Behavioral Sciences, 18* (2), 194–213.

Donato, K. M. (1994). U.S. policy and Mexican migration to the United States, 1942–1992. *Social Science Quarterly, 75,* 705–29.

Flores, W. V. & Benmayor, R. (Eds.) (1997). *Latino cultural citizenship: Claiming identity, space, and rights.* Boston, Mass.: Beacon Press.

Fusco, C. (1995). *English is broken here: Notes on cultural fusion in the Americas.* New York: The New Press.

Gutierréz, D. G. (1995). *Walls and mirrors: Mexican Americans, Mexican immigrants, and the politics of ethnicity.* Berkeley, Calif.: University of California Press.

Gutierréz, D. G. (Ed.) (1996). *Between two worlds: Mexican immigrants in the United States.* Wilmington, D.E.: Scholarly Resources.

Hamamoto, D. Y. & Torres, R. D. (1997). *New American destinies: A reader in contemporary Asian and Latino immigration.* New York: Routledge.

Hayes-Bautista, D. E., Schink, W. O., & Rodríguez, G. (1994). *Latino immigrants in Los Angeles: A portrait from the 1990 census.* Los Angeles: Alta California Policy Research Center.

Healy, M. (1996, May 30). Study points to differences in Latino groups. *Los Angeles Times,* p. A12.

Huang, F.-Y. (1997). *Asian and Hispanic immigrant women in the workforce: Implications of the United States immigration policies since 1965.* New York: Garland Publishing.

Jones, P. A. (1999). *Libraries, immigrants, and the American experience.* Westport, Conn.: Greenwood Publishing Group.

Luévano-Molina, S. (2000). Ethnographic perspectives on transnational Mexican immigrant library users. In S. Güereña (Ed.) *Library services to Latinos: An anthology* (pp. 169–80). Jefferson, N.C.: McFarland.

McDonnell, P. (1997). Immigration, naturalization and dual citizenship. *Migration News, 4,* 2.

Massey, D., Alarcon, R., Gonzales, H., & Durand, J. (1987). *Return to Aztlán: The social process of international migration from western Mexico.* Berkeley, Calif.: University of California.

Massey, D., Goldring, L., & Durand, J. (1994). Continuities in transnational migration: An analysis of 19 Mexican communities. *American Journal of Sociology, 99,* 1492–1534.

Muller, T. & Espensade, T. J. (1985). *The fourth wave: California's newest immigrants.* Washington, D.C.: The Urban Institute.

Mylopoulos, C. (2000, March). Tending to the city's needs, serving newcomer immigrants: The value of community information. *Multicultural Review, 9* (1), 24–27, 57–59.

Pachon, H. & De Sipio, L. (1994). *New Americans by choice: Political perspectives of Latino immigrants.* Boulder, Colo.: Westview Press.

Repack, Terry A. (1995). *Waiting on Washington: Central American workers in the nation's capital.* Philadelphia, Pa.: Temple University Press.

Rodriguez, R. (1995, July). Go north, young man. Who is "North American"? *Mother Jones, 20* (4), 30–35.

Romero, M., Hondagneu-Sotelo, P., & Ortiz, V. (1997). *Challenging fronteras: Structuring Latina and Latino lives in the U.S.* New York: Routledge.

Salgado de Snyder, V. N., Diaz-Perez, M. D. J., & Acevedo, A. (1996). Dios y el norte: The perceptions of wives of documented and undocumented Mexican immigrants to the United States. *Hispanic Journal of Behavioral Sciences, 18,* 283–96.

Scheliga Carnesi, M. & Fiol, M. A. (2000). Queens Library's New American Programs: 23 years of services to immigrants. In S. Güereña (Ed.) *Library services to Latinos: An anthology* (pp. 133–42). Jefferson, N.C.: McFarland.

Sundell, J. (2000). Library services to Hispanic immigrants of Forsyth County, North Carolina: A community collaboration. In S. Güereña (Ed.) *Library services to Latinos: An anthology* (pp. 143–68). Jefferson, N.C.: McFarland.

Trueba, H. T. (1993). *Healing multicultural America: Mexican immigrants rise to power in rural California.* London: Falmer Press.

U.S. Census Bureau. (1996). *Population projections of the U.S. by age, sex, race, and Hispanic origin: 1995 to 2050.* Washington, D.C.: U.S. Government Printing Office.

Proposition 187

Alarcon, R. (1994). *Proposition 187: An effective measure to determine undocumented migration to California?* Sacramento, Calif.: META, Inc. (ERIC Document Reproduction Service No. ED396901).

Armbruster, R., Geron, K., & Bonacich, E. (1995). The assault on California's Latino immigrants: The politics of Proposition 187. *International Journal of Urban and Regional Research, 19* (4), 655–63.

Calavita, K. (1996, August). The new politics of immigration: Balanced-budget conservatism and the symbolism of Proposition 187. *Social Problems, 43* (3), 284–305.

Cornelius, W. A. (1995, February 20). Reactions of residents of Tlacuitapa, Mexico to

Proposition 187. *Los Angeles Times,* p. B5.

Croddy, M. (1995). *The immigration debate: Public policy, Proposition 187, and the law.* Sacramento, Calif.: Constitutional Rights Foundation. (ERIC Document Reproduction Service No. ED 393784).

Davis, M. (1995, November). The social origins of the referendum. *NACLA: Report on the Americas, 29* (3), 24–28.

Del Olmo, F. (1997, February 16). Human behavior skews best intentions. *Los Angeles Times,* p. M5.

DeSipio, L. (1995–1996). After Proposition 187, the deluge: Reforming naturalization administration while making good citizens. *Harvard Journal of Hispanic Policy, 9,* 7–24.

Diamond, S. (1996). Right-wing politics and the anti-immigration cause. *Social Justice, 23* (3), 154–68.

Espinosa, S. (1993, August 27). Backlash against Asians, Latinos. *San Francisco Chronicle,* p. A1.

Fenton, J. J., Catalano, R., & Hargreaves, W. A. (1996, Spring). Effect of Proposition 187 on mental health service use in California: A case study. *Health Affairs, 15* (1), 182–90.

Finnigan, D. (1995, December 29). Hate crimes up since Proposition 187, group says. *National Catholic Reporter, 32* (10), 6.

Flewellen, K. (1996, February). Whose America is this? *Essence, 26* (10), 154.

Gaffney, E. M., Jr. (1995, March 1). Immigrant bashing. *Christian Century, 112* (7), 228–29.

Gutierréz, L. (1995, Summer). The new assault on immigrants. *Social Policy, 25* (4), 56–63.

Hammond, B. (1994, June 15). Grass-roots movement pushes SOS initiative. *San Francisco Chronicle,* p. A21.

Hayes-Bautista, D. E. (1994, November 11). A rude awakening for Latinos. *Los Angeles Times,* p. B7.

Heller, M. A. (1994, April). Stemming the tide. *Hispanic, 7* (3), 20–27.

Hinojosa Ojeda, R. & Schey, P. A. (1995, November–December). The faulty logic of the anti-immigration rhetoric. *NACLA: Report on the Americas, 29* (3), 18–23.

Houston, P. (1996, October). For whom the bell tolls. *Phi Delta Kappan, 78* (2), 124–26.

Jackson, R. L. (1994, December 17). Rights panel voices concerns on Proposition 187. *Los Angeles Times,* p. A27.

Jost, K. (1995, February 3). Cracking down on immigration. *CQ Researcher, 5* (5), 97–115.

Kadetsky, E. (1994, October 17). Bashing illegals in California, Proposition 187, the "Save Our State" initiative. *Nation, 259* (12), 416–22.

Lively, K. (1995, February 24). Confronting "Proposition 187." *Chronicle of Higher Education, 41* (24), A29–A30.

Martin, P. (1995, Spring). Proposition 187 in California. *International Migration Review, 29* (1), 255–63.

Martinez, R. (1995, November–December). Fighting 187: The different opposition strategies. *NACLA: Report on the Americas, 29* (3), 29–33.

McCarthy, D. (1994, December). Proposition 187: One for the (law) books; why court battles loom either way. *Business Mexico, 4* (12), 39–41.

McCray, E. (1995, November–December). A school principal speaks out against 187. *NACLA: Report on the Americas, 29* (3), 33.

Navarrette, R., Jr. (1995, April 30). Is this what Proposition 187 sought? More Latino citizens? *Los Angeles Times,* p. M6.

Ocasio, L. (1995, November–December). The year of the immigrant as scapegoat. *NACLA: Report on the Americas, 29* (3), 14–17.

Perea, J. F. (Ed.) (1997). *Immigrants out!: The new nativism and the anti-immigrant impulse in the United States.* New York: New York University Press.

Pyle, A. & McDonnell, P. (1996, March 22). Proposition 187 issue moves onto national stage. *Los Angeles Times,* p. A1.

Quiroga, A. (1995, April). Copycat fever: California's Proposition 187 epidemic spreads to other states. *Hispanic, 8* (3), 18–24.

Ramos, G. (1997, March 22). A positive immigrant portrait; research: County's Salvadoreans, Guatemalans are hard working, though poor, and rely less on public aid than other groups, study finds. *Los Angeles Times,* p. B1.

Reid, G. (1995, June–July). Guardians at the bridge: Will immigrants maintain equal access? *Community College Journal, 65* (6), 14–19.

Roberts, S. V. (1994, October 3). Shutting the golden door: Economic fears, ethnic prejudice and politics as usual make the melting pot a pressure cooker. *U.S. News & World Report, 117* (13), 36–40.

Rodriguez, G. (1996, September). The browning of California Proposition 187 backfires. *The New Republic, 215* (10), 18–19.

Rose, F. (1995, April 26). Anti-immigrant measures of the past bear striking resemblance to today. *Wall Street Journal,* p. A6.

Rose, G. (1995, January 9). Drop the prop. *The Nation, 260* (2), 40–41.

Rosen, J. (1995, January 30). The war on immigrants: Why the courts can't save us. *The New Republic, 212* (5), 22–26.

Schrag, P. (1995, Jan. 30). Son of 187: Anti-affirmative action propositions. *The New Republic, 212* (5), 16.

Schuck, P. H. (1995, Spring). The meaning of 187: Facing up to illegal immigration. *American Prospect.* Retrieved January 25, 1996, from the World Wide Web: http://epn.org/prospect/21/21schu.html

Shuit, D. P. (1996, April 17). Proposition 187 fears tied to mental health woes. *Los Angeles Times,* p. A3.

Simon, L. A. (1997). *Fear and learning at Hoover Elementary.* VHS. Color. 54 min. Los Angeles: Transit Media.

Simpson, M. D. (1995, February). Immigrant backlash puts kids at risk. *NEA Today, 13* (6), 17.

Smith, M. P. & Tarallo, B. (1995). Proposition 187: Global trend or local narrative? Explaining anti-immigrant politics in California, Arizona, and Texas. *International Journal of Urban and Regional Research, 19* (4), 664–679.

State of California. Attorney General. (1994). 1994 California Voter Information. Retrieved November 2, 1994, from the World Wide Web: http://ca94.election.digital.com/e/prop/187/home.html

A sourcebook for the immigration debate. (1994, Summer). *Urban Institute Policy and Research Report, 24* (2), 20–21.

Tamayo, B. (1995, January–February). Proposition 187: Racism leads to deaths and more poverty. *Poverty & Race, 4* (1), 16.

Tolbert, C. J. & Hero, R. E. (1996, August). Race ethnicity and direct democracy: An analysis of California's illegal immigration initiative. *The Journal of Politics, 58* (3), 806.

Waldinger, R. (Ed.) (1996). *Ethnic Los Angeles.* New York: Russell Sage Foundation.

Welcome to America: The immigration backlash [Special Issue]. (1995, November). *NACLA: Report on the Americas, 29* (3), 13.

Ziv, T. A. & Lo, B. (1995, April 20). Denial of care to illegal immigrants: Proposition 187 in California. *The New England Journal of Medicine, 332* (16), 1095–98.

Zuckerman, M. B. (1994, December 12). Beyond Proposition 187. *U.S. News & World Report, 117* (23), 124–25.

Proposition 209

Asadulla, S. A. (1997, November 12). Proposition 209: Plessy vs Ferguson again. *Los Angeles Sentinel,* p. A1.

Barkan, J. (1998, Summer). Affirmative action: Second thoughts. *Dissent, 45* (3), 5–10.

Barreto, M. & Enriquez, J. (2000, February). *University of California acceptance rates continue to be low for Latinos and African Americans in wake of elimination of preferences.* Tomas Rivera Policy Institute. Pomona, Calif.: California State Polytechnic University, Pomona.

Bergmann, B. (1996). *In defense of affirmative action.* New York: Basic Books.

Bowen, W. G. & Bok, D. C. (1998). *The shape of the river: Long term consequences of considering race in college and university admissions.* New York: Princeton University Press.

Browne Miller, A. (1996). *Shameful Admissions: The losing battle to serve everyone in our universities.* San Francisco, Calif.: Jossey-Bass Publishers.

Chavez, L. (1998). *The color bind: California's battle to end affirmative action.* Berkeley, Calif.: University of California Press.

Chavez, L. (1999, March 26). Perspectives: It is time to focus on outcomes; veteran educator proposes new emphasis. *The Hispanic Outlook in Higher Education, 9* (14), 26.

Chavez, L. (1999, November–December). The preference problem. *The American Enterprise, 9* (6), 68–69.

Chin, G. J. (1998). *Affirmative action and the constitution.* New York: Garland Publishers.

Cooper, M. R. (1999, September 24). Why we still need affirmative action. *Washington Afro-American, 108* (6), A5.

Curry, G. (Ed.) (1996). *The affirmative action debate.* Reading, Mass.: Addison-Wesley.

Delgado, R. (1996). *The coming race war? And other apocalyptic tales of America after affirmative action and welfare.* New York: New York University Press.

Eastland, T. (1996). *Ending affirmative action: The case for colorblind justice.* New York: Basic Books.

Eastland, T. & William, B. (1979). *Counting by race: Equality from the founding fathers to Bakke and Weber.* New York: Basic Books.

Edley, C., Jr. (1996). *Not all black and white: Affirmative action, race, and American values.* New York: Hill and Wang.

Eisaguirre, L. (1999). *Affirmative action: A reference handbook.* Santa Barbara, Calif.: ABC-CLIO.

Ethridge, R. W. (2000, March–April). Book review of *On higher ground: Education and the case of affirmative action. The Journal of Higher Education, 71* (2), 256–57.

Feinberg, W. (1998). *On higher ground: Education and the case for affirmative action.*

New York: Teachers College Press. (ERIC Document Reproduction Service No. ED 423800)

Fields, C. D. (1997, May 1). Harvard scholars convene civil rights think tank: Experts to search for ways to curtail assault on affirmative action. *Black Issues in Higher Education, 14* (5), 8.

Flanders, L. (1999, March 8). Affirmative racism. *The Nation, 268* (9), 7.

Fox, T. (1999). *Defending access: A critique of standards in higher education.* Portsmouth, N.H.: Boynton/Cook Publishers-Heinemann.

Friedl, J. (1999, July–August) Needed: Documentation of how affirmative action benefits all students. *Change, 31* (4), 40.

Garcia, M. (Ed.) (1997). *Affirmative action's treatment of hope: Strategies for a new era.* New York: State University of New York Press.

Gladieux, L. E. & Watson, S. S. (2000, May). Beyond access. *Phi Delta Kappan, 81* (9), 688–92.

Gorman, S. (2000, April 8). After affirmative action. *National Journal, 32* (15), 1120–24.

Guerrero, M. A. J. (1997, October). Affirmative action: Race, class, gender and NOW. *The American Behavioral Scientist, 41* (2), 246–55.

Halford, J. M. (1999, April). A different mirror. *Educational Leadership, 56* (7), 8.

Healy, P. (1999, August 13). California governor rejects minority preferences. *The Chronicle of Higher Education, 45* (49) A34.

Holzer, H. J. & Neumark, D. (2000, January). What does affirmative action do? *Industrial Labor Relations Review, 53* (2), 240–71.

Hoplains, D. R. (1997, December 7). Racism then and now! *Oakland Post,* p. A1.

Kahlenberg, R. D. (1996). *The remedy: Class, race, and affirmative action.* New York: Basic Books.

Lawrence, C. (1997). *We won't go back: Making the case for affirmative action.* Boston, Mass.: Houghton-Mifflin.

Lewis, R. M. (1998, Winter–Spring). The pendulum swings: Affirmative action and recent Supreme Court decisions. *Challenge: A Journal of Research on African American Men, 9* (1), 43–62.

Locke, M. (2000, April 27). Minority enrollment is up, but that's only part of the story. *Black Issues in Higher Education, 17* (5), 14.

Malos, S. B. (2000, March). The new affirmative action. *The Journal of Applied Behavioral Science, 36* (1), 5–22.

Manzo, K. K. (2000, May 11). Sorry, wrong numbers. *Black Issues in Higher Education, 17* (6), 14.

McWhirter, D. A. (1996). *The end of affirmative action: Where do we go from here?* New York: Carol Publication Group.

Mejia, A. (1999, January). *Hispanic and black acceptance rates and enrollment drop in wake of the University of California elimination of "preferences."* Tomas Rivera Policy Institute. Pomona, Calif.: California State Polytehnic University, Pomona.

Mosley, A. G. & Capaldi, N. (1996). *Affirmative action: Social justice or unfair preference?* Lanham, Md.: Rowman & Littlefield Publishers.

Mueller, T. (1999, January 31). What's the solution? The affirmative action debate is hotter than ever— all in the name of civil rights. *Diversity Monthly, 1* (1), 23.

Munoz, C., Jr. (1999, April 23). Punto final! Educational prospects for Latinos post-affirmative action. *The Hispanic Outlook in Higher Education, 9* (16), 80.

Negative action. (1998, May). *The Progressive, 62* (5), 9–10.

Ong, P. (Ed.) (1999). *Impacts of affirmative action: Policies and consequences in California.* London: Sage Publications Ltd.

Paterson, E. & Sellstrom, O. (1999, Summer). Equal opportunity in a post-Proposition 209 world. *Human Rights, 26* (3), 9–12.

Reza, M. A. (1999). *The ups and downs of affirmative action preferences.* Westport, Conn.: Praeger.

Saito, L. T. (1998). *Race and Politics: Asian Americans, Latinos, and Whites in a Los Angeles suburb.* Urbana: University of Illinois Press.

Schneider, A. (1998, November 20). What has happened to faculty diversity in California? *The Chronicle of Higher Education, 45* (13), A10–A12.

Schumaker, P. & Kelly, M. (1999, May). Affirmative action, principles of justice, and the evolution of urban theory. *Urban Affairs Review, 34* (5), 619.

Siler, M. J. (1998, Fall). Reduction of minority public university access in California: An analysis of the long-term human rights implications. *Journal of Intergroup Relations, 25* (3), 16–33.

Skrentny, J. D. (1996). *The ironies of affirmative action: Politics, culture, and justice in America.* Chicago: University of Chicago Press.

Taylor, U. (1999, Spring). Proposition 209 and the affirmative action debate on the University of California campuses. *Feminist Studies, 25* (1), 95–103.

Tomasson, R. F., Crosby, F. J., & Herzberger, S. D. (1996). *Affirmative action: The pros and cons of policy and practice.* Washington, D.C.: American University Press.

Vincent, N. (2000, April 4). The new math on race. *The Village Voice, 45* (13), 12.

Webb, J. (2000, May 22). Taking on the status of quotas. *The Wall Street Journal,* p. A36.

Whitaker, B. (2000, April 5). Minority rolls rebound at University of California. *New York Times,* p. A16.

Wilson, J. Q. (1996, December 23). The case for ending racial preferences. *U.S. News & World Report, 121* (25), 31–32.

Wu, F. (1999, Summer). A new thinking about affirmative action. *Human Rights: Journal of the Section of Individual Rights & Responsibilities, 26* (3), 19.

Women

Donato, K. M. (1993). Current trends and patterns of female migration: Evidence from Mexico. *International Migration Review, 27,* 748–71.

Donnelly, N. D. (1994). *Changing lives of refugee Hmong women.* Seattle: University of Washington Press.

Hondagneu-Sotelo, P. (1992). Overcoming patriarchal constraints: The reconstruction of gender relations among Mexican immigrant women and men. *Gender & Society, 6,* 393–413.

Hondagneu-Sotelo, P. (1994). *Gendered transitions: Mexican experiences of immigration.* Berkeley, Calif.: University of California Press.

Huang, F.-Y. (1997). *Asian and Hispanic immigrant women in the workforce: Implications of the United States immigration policies since 1965.* New York: Garland Publishing.

National Council for Research on Women. (1995). The feminization of immigration. *Issues Quarterly, 1* (3), 1–7.

Pam, E. (1994, Summer). Needed: A feminist immigration policy. *On the Issues,* 22–25.

Romero, M. (1992). *Maid in the USA.* New York: Routledge.

Romero, M., Hondagneu-Sotelo, P., & Ortiz, V. (1997). *Challenging fronteras: Structuring Latina and Latino lives in the U.S.* New York: Routledge.

Salgado de Snyder, V. N., Diaz-Perez, M. D. J., & Acevedo, A. (1996). Dios y el norte: The perceptions of wives of documented and undocumented Mexican immigrants to the United States. *Hispanic Journal of Behavioral Sciences, 18* (3), 283–96.

Index

About the Contributors

JoAnn K. Aguirre is an Assistant Professor in the Department of Occupational Studies at California State University, Long Beach. She completed her joint doctorate in Educational Administration/Leadership Studies at the University of California, Los Angeles and Irvine. In fall 2001 Dr. Aguirre will begin an appointment to the California State University, Chancellor's Office as the Pre-Doctoral Coordinator wherein her major responsibility will be the recruitment of underrepresented students to doctoral programs and ultimately as professors in the California State University system.

Richard Chabrán is Director of the Center for Virtual Research at the University of California, Riverside. Chabrán directs the UCR Community Digital Initiative, a Computers In Our Future project that is funded by the California Wellness Foundation. He contributes to local, state, and national policy discussions concerning the digital divide. He is a founder of Chicano/LatinoNet. He is also a founder now advisor for the *Chicano Database*. Along with his brother Ráfael he is a coeditor of the *Latino Encyclopedia*. In addition, Chabrán is a lecturer at UCLA's Department of Information Studies. He was recently awarded the 21st Century Award from Syracuse, School of Information Studies.

Evelyn Escatiola is Library Chairperson, at the East Los Angeles College Library. Ms. Escatiola has also worked at the East Los Angeles Branch of the Los Angeles County Public Library. Over her eighteen year tenure with the system she served as a Children's Librarian, Chicano Resource Center Librarian, and Community Library Manager. Ms. Escatiola received her Master's of Library Science from the University of Michigan, Ann Arbor.

Ling Hwey Jeng received her Ph.D. in library Science from the University of Texas at Austin. She has taught at the University of Maryland at College Park and UCLA. Currently Jeng is an Associate Professor at the School of Library and Information Science, University of Kentucky. Dr. Jeng specializes in organization of information and database searching, and is a frequent speaker on diversity issues. She is a past president of the Chinese American Librarians Association, and past Chair of the ALA Diversity Council. The author will be the Executive Director of the Asian/Pacific American Librarians Association in 2001/2002.

Kenneth M. Knox is a reference library at the Pollak Library, California State University, Fullerton. He received his Master's of Library Science from San José State University.

Susan Luévano-Molina is the Ethnic, Women's & Multicultural Studies Librarian, California State University, Long Beach. In addition, the author has worked in California and Texas community college settings for seventeen years. She has conducted numerous community analysis studies for public libraries in Orange County, California. Ms. Luévano-Molina is a past president of Reforma, the National Association to Promote Library and Information Services to the Spanish Speaking and a graduate of the University of Oregon, School of Library Science.

Rhonda Rios-Kravitz is the Access Services Librarian, at the California State University, Sacramento, Library, in Sacramento, California. She is a past president of Reforma, the National Association to Promote Library and Information Services to the Spanish Speaking. The author co-chairs the Association of Mexican American Educators at California State University, Sacramento. She was awarded the 1997 YWCA Outstanding Women of Year Award for her commitment and work in the area of diversity and equity. Ms. Rios-Kravitz is currently completing a doctorate in Public Administration.

Marcelo M. Suárez-Orozco is a Professor and Co-Director of the Harvard Immigration Project, Harvard University, Graduate School of Education. Dr. Suárez-Orozco is the author of numerous articles and books on Latino migrants. His latest book, published by Harvard University Press, is entitled *Crossings: Mexican Immigration in Interdisciplinary Perspectives*.

Ninfa Almance Trejo is an assistant librarian and member of the Social Sciences Team at the University of Arizona, University Library, in Tucson, Arizona. She received her Master's of Library Science at San José State University. Ms. Trejo has worked at the San Diego and Santa Ana public libraries. She is a member of the Board of Directors for the Trejo Foster Foundation for Hispanic Library Education.

Xiwen Zhang is the Electronic Resources Librarian at California State University, San Bernardino. She received her Masters in Library Science from the University of California, Los Angeles and a second Master's of French Literature from the University of California, Santa Barbara. Zhang is currently the President of the Asian Faculty, Staff, and Student Association at California State University, San Bernardino.